Praise for
WAITER RANT

"The Waiter pulls you to the frontlines of a busy, high-priced New York café. War stories of Mother's Day and Valentine's Day, shady managers, and patronizing clients smack of shades of David Sedaris and Augusten Burroughs, but with a purpose: to educate foodies on the dos and don'ts of proper dining etiquette. . . . [*Waiter Rant*] will entertain readers with a taste for the sardonic and might just inspire a precious few to leave more than a 15 percent tip at the Cheesecake Factory."   —*Variety*

"Extremely funny, no-nonsense, and insightful."
—*New York Times Book Review*

"The main attraction here is [Dublanica's] acerbic, biting, and often hilarious accounts of life behind-the-scenes at the front of the house."   —*Wall Street Journal*

"I really enjoyed *Waiter Rant*. The book is engaging and funny, a story told from my polar opposite perspective. I will now do my best to act better as a chef—and I dare say I'll never be rude to a waiter again, as long as I live."
—John DeLucie, Chef at Waverly Inn and author of *The Hunger*

"Here is my unabashed recommendation: if you eat out with any regularity, read this book!"   —*Chicago Sun-Times*

"*Waiter Rant* has all the fixings for fun. . . . What Anthony Bourdain's tell-all about life in the kitchen did for hollandaise sauce, *Waiter Rant* will do for side salads."   —*Los Angeles Times*

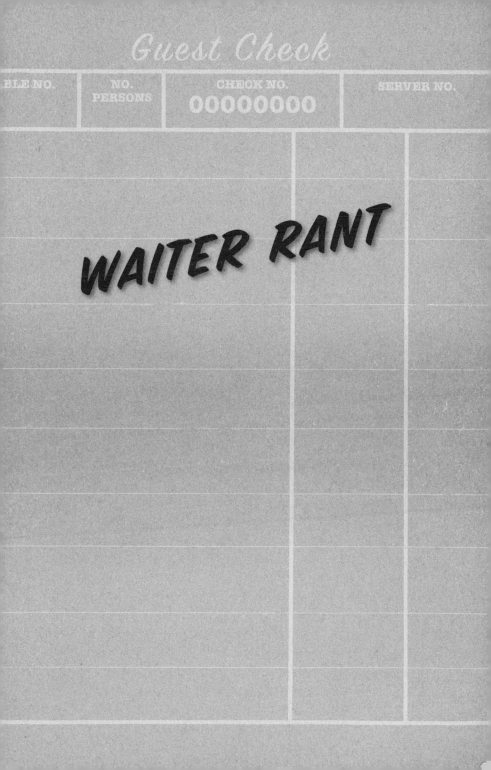

WAITER RANT

Guest Check

ABLE NO.	NO. PERSONS	CHECK NO. 00000000	SERVER NO.

WAITER RANT

THANKS FOR THE TIP— CONFESSIONS OF A CYNICAL WAITER

THE WAITER,
Steve Dublanica

AN ECCO BOOK

HARPER PERENNIAL

NEW YORK • LONDON • TORONTO • SYDNEY • NEW DELHI • AUCKLAND

HARPER ● PERENNIAL

A hardcover edition of this book was published in 2008 by Ecco, an imprint of HarperCollins Publishers.

P.S.™ is a trademark of HarperCollins Publishers.

FIRST HARPER PERENNIAL EDITION PUBLISHED 2009.

Designed by Renato Stanisic

Library of Congress Cataloging-in-Publication Data is available upon request.

ISBN 978-0-06-125669-1

09 10 11 12 13   OV/RRD   10 9 8 7 6 5 4

THIS BOOK IS DEDICATED TO MY MOTHER, MY FATHER,
AND EVERYONE WHO'S EVER WAITED TABLES.

Acknowledgments

y brother got me my first job in the restaurant business, so I guess I have to blame him for everything that came after that. Thanks, bro! I'm sorry I sucker punched you at Amici's.

I'm indebted to Farley Chase, my agent at the Waxman Literary Agency, for convincing me that this book was possible. I'm deeply grateful to Emily Takoudes for her insightful and graceful editing and to Ecco's publisher, Dan Halpern, for giving me the opportunity to bring this book to fruition. I would also like to thank Eleanor Birne at John Murray for her editorial comments and Emily's editorial assistant, Greg Mortimer, for his contributions.

Ben Hammersley and Jason Kottke merit a special note of thanks. I am also indebted to the inestimable Laurie Pietsch for her warm words of encouragement and to my tech-savvy friend Charles Prothero for patiently explaining everything I didn't know about computers. I'm also grateful to my friend Andrew Barone for his years of steadfast support.

A special thank-you goes to all the staff who ever worked with me at "The Bistro." To my customers Barry and Clarice and Bob and Linda, thanks again for all your kindnesses. (And the tips!) Thanks are also due to Christy; Jen; Launa; Tara; Patrick;

Liong; the Poker Boys; Carmen Giglio, DDS; Peter Schessler; Dr. Michael Lynn and Richard; and Tina for their years of friendship and support. Thank you, Renee! My eternal gratitude to Richard Binkowski and Harry Dawson for showing me the power of words. Thank you, "Rizzo," for showing me how to be a Waiter Jedi. Profound thanks to the late Rev. Msgr. Theodore Humanitski for all the life lessons he taught me. "One day we shall hold the star in our hand and ring in the triple hymn of the heavenly chorus!" See you there, Ted.

Finally! A gigantic thank-you to all the wonderful people who read and commented on my blog Waiter Rant over the past four years. Thanks for your support!

This book is for all of you.

Contents

Preface xi

1 | Amici's 1
2 | The Sacred and the Profane 14
3 | Fascists and Freshwater Ostrich 23
4 | Waiter Jedi 39
5 | Paupery 57
6 | The Box of Chocolates Saint 70
7 | Big Brother 81
8 | The Back Alley of Affluence 92
9 | The Tip's the Thing 105
10 | Why Be a Waiter? 119
11 | A Little Knowledge Is a Dangerous Thing 131
12 | Filth 143
13 | I Hate Mother's Day 160
14 | Vengeance Is Mine 175
15 | Snapshots 183
16 | Heaven and Hell 194

17 | Substance Abuse 204
18 | The Fourth of July 215
19 | Russell Crowe and Me 226
20 | If It Can Go Wrong, It Will 241
21 | The Demons 257
22 | Throwing in the Apron 270

Epilogue 283
Appendixes:
   A 40 Tips on How to Be a Good Customer 289
   B 50 Ways to Tell You're Working in a Bad Restaurant 297
   C Items a Waiter Should Carry
       at All Times (or Have Close By) 300

Preface

'm a waiter. I bring food to tables in exchange for tips. At first glance it seems like a simple job. Just be neat, polite, display some salesmanship, and don't forget to smile. Easy, right? What world are you living in?

Today waiters are expected to be food-allergy specialists, sommeliers, cell-phone-rule enforcers, eye candy, confessors, entertainers, mixologists, emergency medical technicians, bouncers, receptionists, joke tellers, therapists, linguists, punching bags, psychics, protocol specialists, and amateur chefs. Foodie-porn TV programming has generated a new class of entitled customers with already overblown culinary expectations and a rapidly diminishing set of social graces. Economists say that the restaurant business is a bellwether of the nation's economic health—but I think it's a bellwether of America's mental health as well. And let me tell you, 20 percent of the American dining public are socially maladjusted psychopaths. We should start putting Prozac in the Perrier.

Ordering from a waiter is one of the most-taken-for-granted human experiences in modern life. We're never more ourselves than when eating out with family and friends. While engaging in the basic rituals of breaking bread, we become a lot less guarded and a lot more primitive. Thinking that the waiter is a power-less tip slave, customers often direct that primitiveness toward the person trying to take their order. Waiting should be a simple job, but it isn't. It's not all gloom and doom, though. If you keep your eyes open, you'll see the occasional crumb of human grace fall from the table. Eighty percent of my customers are the nicest people you'd ever want to meet. But I'm concerned that the percentage of people who know how to act in a restaurant is diminishing at an exponential rate.

For the last four years I've been anonymously chronicling my restaurant exploits at a Web site called Waiter Rant. From my server station at a white-tablecloth restaurant called "The Bistro," I've written about the joys and pains of working in the food-service industry. Staying anonymous has let me freely chronicle my customers' bad behavior without fear of retribution and bad tips, but it's also allowed me to talk about people behaving beautifully, too. I've been fortunate that my writing has attracted millions of readers, won a few awards, and grabbed a little bit of that crazy stuff called quasi-fame. Despite all the attention I've received, very few people know who I am or where The Bistro is located. After three years I was confronted by a customer only *once*.

This book is a natural outgrowth of Waiter Rant. In addition to dishing about insane customers, tyrannical owners, and drugged-up servers, I also hope to give you a real "pain in your bones" sense of what it's like to be a waiter in America today. After you read this book I doubt you'll ever look at your server the same way again. And maybe you'll learn how to be a better customer in the process.

So how did I end up becoming a waiter? Why did I start writing about the restaurant industry? If I'm ranting about it all the time, why don't I just quit and get another job? Just who the hell do I think I am?

As with all good stories, let's begin at the beginning.

Guest Check

BLE NO.	NO. PERSONS	CHECK NO. 00000000	SERVER NO.

WAITER RANT

CHAPTER 1

Amici's

S o, you take it up the ass?" Benny asks me.

"What kind of question is that?" I reply.

"You're a fag," the chubby Mexican says, glancing slyly at his coworkers. "We all know you are. It's okay. You can tell us."

"Benny . . ."

"C'mon. We know you're queer."

No, I'm not being set upon by a gang of amorous inmates in a prison laundry. It's 1999, and I'm in the kitchen of Amici's, a two-hundred-seat Italian restaurant located in a hyper-affluent New York suburb. Two weeks ago I was fired from my job as marketing rep for a psychiatric health care company. Facing immediate penury, I asked my brother, a longtime waiter at Amici's, to get me a job so I could keep eating. As a thirty-one-year-old baby waiter learning the ropes, I'm quickly discovering that the hot topic of kitchen conversation is figuring out which waiter's gay and discussing the merits of inserting foreign objects into other people's rectal cavities. Ah, restaurant kitchens—they're all about tequila, buggery, and the lash.

"Why you want to know, Benny?" I ask. "You interested in me?"

"Me?" Benny says, untangling a wad of half-cooked spaghetti with his bare hands. "I'm no *maricón*."

"You're asking a guy you don't know whether or not he's gay. Doesn't that seem strange to you?"

"No," Benny says, staring at me blankly. "I just want to know if you take it up the ass."

I guess Benny's never heard of the "fear is the wish" thing.

"I don't take it up the butt," I reply, a half smile playing on my lips. "But your wife does. Tell her I said hi."

The kitchen guys start whooping with laughter.

"Oh shit!" the grill man hoots.

"He got you, yo," the dishwasher says.

"*Pendejo*," Benny says, his face reddening.

"It's not my fault you can't make you're wife happy," I say, rapidly egressing the area. Benny *does* have access to sharp knives.

"Screw you, *pendejo*!" Benny shouts after me.

"Right back at you," I shout over my shoulder. "*Bitch.*"

After reading about this exchange you might be thinking I'm some kind of misogynistic homophobe. You'd be wrong. I'm merely engaging in a legitimate act of restaurant self-defense. My brother gave me an invaluable piece of advice when I started working at Amici's: never take flak from the kitchen lying down. "You're always gonna get shit from the cooks," he warned. "But if you just sit there and take it, they'll run right over you." That's why I brought it to Benny. Most waiters would get killed if they brought it to a cook in front of his crew like I did, but I'm not worried that my exchange with Benny is going to cause any problems. He's a tough hombre who, unlike many cooks, can dish it out *and* take it. Besides, we actually have the makings of a friendship going on. Benny teaches me little kitchen tricks, like how not to cut off my fingers when I slice the cheese, and I help him with the occasional English words he doesn't understand. Of course, Benny wants to know about only the weird words. Yesterday he asked me what *pederast* meant. I never should have told him. He kept trying to use the word in a sentence all day.

But getting into a profanity pissing contest with the kitchen crew can take you only so far. If a waiter wants respect from the back of the house, he or she has to show respect in return. And the best way to do that is to understand that kitchen staff and waiters are like the Palestinians and Israelis—separate and distinct nationalities uncomfortably sharing the same volatile piece of real estate.

A big difference between waiters and cooks is the hours they work. Waiters usually work an eight- or nine-hour shift and go home. The kitchen guys, however, are often the first to show up and the last to go home. Fourteen-hour days are common. When a restaurant closes its doors for the night, you'll probably find half its servers getting blasted at a nearby bar. But you'll find the kitchen guys sharing a taxi or waiting at a bus stop for a public transportation ride home. Because most fine-dining establishments are located in neighborhoods where residential rents are high, kitchen personnel seldom can afford to live close to their place of employment. That means they often have a very long commute to and from work. One of Amici's prep cooks buses it from Queens every day. Depending on traffic, that can be a three-hour round-trip six days a week—*on top* of working a fourteen-hour shift. The waiters at Amici's (at least the ones without DUIs) have cars and shorter commutes. They have free time. This disparity in leisure hours often leads to resentment between the front and back of the house. At the end of the night the exhausted kitchen guys just want to go home to enjoy what little free time they have left.

Because they're often exhausted, I'm learning it's in my best interest not to make the cooks work any harder than they have to. That means not running into the kitchen and begging the grill man to cook me a new steak because a customer wanted a medium-rare filet mignon and I mistakenly ordered it well done. It's also good not to inflame the resentments constantly simmering between the front and back of the house by acting like an arrogant prick. While kitchen guys usually work at a single location for years, waiters tend to be a more nomadic lot. Cooks see the waiters come and go, so, in their minds, they're the stable nucleus at the core of the restaurant. Waiters consider themselves the public face of the restaurant—hustling to generate the revenue that pays everyone's salaries, including the cooks'. Many waiters view themselves as elite frontline troops while dismissing the cooks as mere logistical support. Couple this attitude with the fact that waiters usually make more money, work fewer hours, and perform less physically intensive labor, and you'll understand why the kitchen occasionally wants to run a mouthy server through the industrial-strength dishwasher.

The kitchen guys will manifest their displeasure by screwing up servers' orders, subjecting them to a stream of verbal abuse, or threatening impromptu sexual-reassignment surgery with a meat cleaver. I've met several waiters who have at least one knife-throwing-chef story in their repertoire. The servers at Amici's aren't saints either. Always shifting blame for their screw-ups onto the kitchen, they act like the cooks are dirty hoi polloi unfit to tie the servers' shoes. They respond to the kitchen staff's taunting with juicy comebacks laden with lovely adjectives like *wetback*, *sand nigger*, and *Eurotrash*.

When peaceful coexistence develops between the front and back of the house, it's because there's a good executive chef or general manager at the helm. By making everyone realize that they're in a symbiotic relationship, that cook and waiter in the long term need each other, good management can be like Jimmy Carter at Camp David, brokering a cease-fire between historical enemies.

Unfortunately, Sammy, the manager at Amici's, is a good example of how not to run a restaurant. A short fat Syrian man with the demeanor of a smug cherub, Sammy's a verbally abusive, power-mad sexual deviant—traits not uncommon in restaurant managers. Underpaid and aggravated that the waitstaff takes home more money than he does, Sammy extorts the servers into paying him bribes. Want to work on the lucrative Friday and Saturday shifts? Switch a shift? Take a vacation? Sammy's response is to hold out his hand and say, "Pay me." In addition to abusing his authority, Sammy, a married man with children, revels in making salacious comments to the female staff and spends most of his free time trying to get into their pants. He does little to encourage cooperation between the front and back of the house. In fact, I think he does his best to keep everyone fighting and off balance. "Divide and conquer" is Sammy's motto. All in all, he's a despicable little man.

Amici's head chef, Fluvio, hates Sammy's guts. Forty years old with long black hair tied into an aging hippie ponytail, Fluvio wears thick eyeglasses that are always smudged with grease, and his ample stomach seems incongruous on top of strong legs conditioned from years spent working on his feet. In addition to his native Italian, he's fluent in Spanish and speaks a good bit of Arabic and French. He runs a professional kitchen, but he's intimidated by Caesar, the manipulative and tyrannical owner who treats everyone who works for him like livestock. Caesar, an Italian raised in South America, acts like his restaurant's a nineteenth-century plantation on the Argentinean pampas. Expecting the kitchen staff to address him as *"patrón,"* he has a penchant for calling the busboys "peasants" and the hostesses "whores."

Here's a typical example of Caesar's nonsense. Not liking his grease-splattered cooks using the patrons' bathrooms and offending the customers' delicate sensibilities, Caesar insists that everyone use the tiny windowless bathroom next to the deep fryer in the kitchen. That miserable bathroom's so small it would give Harry Houdini panic attacks. Technically, the waiters are supposed to use this bathroom, but none of us ever do. Half the cooks don't either. I'm not surprised. Rizzo, Amici's headwaiter, lovingly refers to the kitchen's hot, cramped, porn-decorated bathroom as the "phone booth of sodomy." After eyeballing that miserable toilet, I'm beginning to understand why the kitchen crew is so obsessed with my sexual orientation.

Leaving Benny and his sexually conflicted comrades behind,

I enter the trattoria's main dining room. It's only five o'clock on Saturday night, and the place is already filling up with customers. Influxes of bull-market nouveau riche transformed this formerly picturesque suburb into a gigantic outdoor shopping mall. Oozing with corporate-branded hipness, the town's countless rows of boutiques, restaurants, and art galleries ruthlessly compete with one another for the well-shod discretionary incomes of the yuppies prowling its streets. Situated in the heart of the town's retail district, Amici's sucks yuppies off the sidewalk like a black hole consuming dust from a dying star. Amici's has the three things any restaurant needs to survive—location, location, location.

"So you ready to rock and roll, newbie?" Rizzo, the head-waiter, asks me.

"Ready as I'll ever be, I guess."

"You're gonna be busting your ass tonight. We're down two waiters."

"You mean there are only four of us taking care of two hundred people?"

"That's right."

"What happened?"

"Toomey and Giselle quit." Rizzo says. "They got sick of Sammy's shit."

"Four waiters have quit since I started."

"This place is a meat grinder, kid," Rizzo grunts. "You're the meat. Get used to it."

"Do you think I'll make it?"

"Probably not."

"Gee," I say. "Don't hold back. Speak your mind."

"It's nothing personal," Rizzo replies. "In the 'Nam I never bothered to learn the new guys' names. Why get close? They were gonna get killed anyway."

"How reassuring."

Rizzo stares at me. Gray-haired and rangy, with a build topping out at six feet two, the thirty years he's spent toiling in the restaurant business are carved into the lines of his weathered face. If every restaurant has to have a stereotypical grizzled veteran, Rizzo is it. Like a bacterium living in acid or a tube worm eking out an existence next to heat vents several thousand leagues under the sea, Rizzo is the kind of waiter who thrives in hostile environments that would crush most servers. With calm black eyes peering out from behind a pair of rose-colored wire-rim spectacles, he looks like a cross between John Lennon and Leon, the hit man from Luc Besson's movie *The Professional.*

"You gave Sammy money to work tonight, didn't you?" he asks me.

"Yeah. Fifty bucks."

"That was dumb. Now he's gonna hit you up all the time."

"Don't you ever give him money?"

Rizzo peers at me over the top of his glasses. "Screw that," he says. "Don't forget. I used to own a restaurant. I know every illegal thing Sammy and Caesar ever pulled in this joint."

"So you know where all the bodies are buried."

"Indeed I do, son," Rizzo says. "And unless they want the IRS raiding the joint, they'll leave me the fuck alone."

Suddenly, there's a clatter of noise by the front entrance. A crowd of hungry-looking people surging through the front door is overwhelming the skinny girl at the hostess stand.

"Oh man," Rizzo groans. "Here comes the pain."

Before long the restaurant is rocking. It doesn't help that the anorexic crackhead hostess seats me two eight tops, three deuces, and a twenty-person wedding-rehearsal dinner inside half an hour. (In waiterspeak, a deuce or two top denotes a table of two. A four top is four people, a six top is six customers, and so on.) I get the two tops squared away quickly. Rizzo taught me to always take care of deuces first. His logic is that couples at a table are probably married and sick of talking to each other, making them hypersensitive to any kind of waiting.

Of course, I get slowed down by an eight top of little kids suffering from every food allergy known to man. I am beginning to think yuppie parents lie to their offspring, telling them they're suffering from food allergies when they're actually not, hoping to con their hypercompetitive children into eating whatever trendy diet promises to help them grow into big, strong, overly self-esteemed junk bond traders.

"I want French fries!" one little brat yells in psychologically healthy protest.

"We have French fries, young man," I reply, trying to keep the smile from falling off my face.

"Dylan can't have French fries," his mother says. "He wants zucchini fries instead."

"We don't have zucchini fries, madam," I reply.

The soccer mom's surgically altered perky nose scrunches up. She looks at me like I've crawled out from under a rock.

"The waiter I had last time got them for us," she says.

I want to find "waiter I had last time" and snap his neck. This lady's eating into my precious time. I can feel the wedding party's eyes crawling up and down my back. They've been nibbling on bread and water for twenty minutes. I feel bad for them. If it was my rehearsal dinner, I'd be pissed, too. I've got to get over there.

"I'll ask the chef what we can do," I say.

"You do that," the woman snaps.

I run to the kitchen to ask Fluvio if he can make some zucchini fries.

"Get the fuck out of here!" he screams.

I return to the table. "I'm sorry, madam. The chef regrets that he cannot make zucchini fries."

"I want to speak to the manager," the woman barks.

The last person I want to deal with is Sammy. He'll probably want $5 just to talk to this lady. To humor the woman, I disappear in the back to make it seem like I'm looking for the manager. After a minute I return to the kiddie table with the bad news.

"This is outrageous," the mother sputters.

"Madam—"

"We're leaving."

"Madam, I—"

"Waiter!" I hear a voice cry out from the wedding party. "Can we have some service over here?"

"Right away, sir!" I yelp.

I disengage from the zucchini-obsessed mommy and give some attention to the twenty top. They hand me two bottles of expensive champagne. That means I've got to scrounge up twenty champagne glasses and some ice buckets pronto. I race over to the coffee station where we store them.

"Minnie," I say to the cute Iranian girl who brews all the cappuccinos and espressos. "Do you have twenty champagne glasses?"

"Not clean ones."

"Can you help me, please?" I plead. "I'm in the weeds."

Being "in the weeds" (otherwise known as being "in the shit") is waiter lingo for what happens when the demands put on a server exceed his or her ability to fulfill them. This can happen when a waiter's new, incompetent, or placed in an impossible situation. For me it's all three.

"I'll help you," Minnie says, smiling.

"Hey, Ahmed," I call out to one of the busboys, "could you get me two ice buckets for table six?"

"Fuck you *sharmout*," Ahmed snarls, using the Arabic equivalent of *maricon*. I guess a waiter's sexual orientation is the subject of speculative interest among the bus people as well as the kitchen staff.

"*Elif air ab tizak!*" I shoot back. That's a nice way of saying "A thousand dicks your ass!"

Since Ahmed is virulently homophobic, my words hit home. As I watch him turn red I'm grateful I memorized a few Arabic comebacks. I was rehearsing that one for three days. When you work in a restaurant, you can never go wrong with remarks about anal penetration.

"Fuck you!" Ahmed repeats.

"Ahmed," I reply, "if you're gonna live in America, you've got to learn to say something besides 'Fuck you.'"

"Fuck you!" Ahmed yells, storming off.

"Wow," Minnie says, as she steam cleans a glass. "You speak some Arabic?"

"Only the dirty words."

"I'm impressed."

I grab a bucket, fill it with ice and water, and drop a champagne bottle inside. Minnie runs ahead of me to put the champagne glasses on the table.

The rehearsal party's table is set up like a long rectangle with nine people on each side. The bride and groom are seated cutely next to each other at the far end of the table. As I approach, Ahmed sneaks up behind me and slams into my back. The ice bucket I'm holding slips out of my hands and crashes onto the table. The champagne bottle shoots out of the bucket like a torpedo firing out of a submarine. It smashes down the length of the table—targeting the bride-to-be's bosom.

"Oh shit!" I cry out.

The slick bottle bounces off the bride's boobs, hits the floor, and skitters off into oblivion. Everyone's dripping with ice water. The bride's expression transmutes from shock into pure rage.

"You idiot!" she screams.

Saying "I'm sorry" seems pointless, so I don't. I turn around. Ahmed's laughing smugly.

"Fuck you!" he mouths. "Fuck you!"

Sammy comes running over. Speaking rapid-fire Arabic, he orders Ahmed and the other busboys to reset the table. Before I can go looking for the champagne bottle, he grabs me by the elbow.

"You're a moron," Sammy hisses. "You better smooth things over with that table."

"I'm a new waiter, and I've got forty customers," I plead. "I need some help."

Sammy looks at me coldly. "Sink or swim, motherfucker."

I stare at Sammy in shock. I've worked for some real jerks in my time, but they've all been the smiling-on-the-outside/scumbag-on-the-inside types. Sammy's a bastard up front.

"Fine," I say, yanking my arm out of his grasp. "I'll handle it."

A few seconds later, as I'm scurrying on my hands and knees looking for the errant bottle of bubbly, the owner decides to make an appearance.

"What the hell's happening here?" Caesar huffs.

At first glance, you can tell Caesar was once a handsome and powerfully built man. While the remnants of his youthful vigor occasionally peek out from inside his black eyes, you can tell the ravages of time and alcohol are pulling down the scaffolding of his once good looks. Vain for almost seventy years of age, Caesar decided to combat his thinning hair by shaving his head completely bare. A fastidious dresser to boot, today he's sporting a white silk shirt, a red silk tie, gray slacks, tasseled Italian shoes, and a double-breasted blue blazer. If he added a monocle to his ensemble, he'd look like a dissipated version of Colonel Klink.

"I'm looking for a champagne bottle I dropped on the floor," I reply. "It rolled under the tables somewhere."

"Smooth move," Caesar says. "Real good."

"Could you help me look for it?" I ask innocently. "I'm really pressed for time."

The owner's eyes retract into his skull. "You think I'm going to help you?" he hisses. "That's your job, *peasant.*"

Behind me I hear a diner gasp. Suddenly I'm aware that I'm on my hands and knees before a man who thinks nothing of insulting the people who work for him right in front of his customers.

"Forget it, Caesar," I say. "I'll find it."

"*Stupido,*" the owner says, walking away.

I continue to search for the bottle. It's disappeared. The rehearsal dinner's freaking out. To this day I think a customer at another table stole it. I dart out of the restaurant and run to a nearby liquor store. They have the same champagne at eighty bucks a bottle. I put it on my credit card and run back inside.

The table's so touched that I bought a replacement bottle with my own money that they calm down. I get a grip on my section and bring everything under control. When the dust clears, the rehearsal party leaves me a $200 tip. They were nice people. Even after spending eighty bucks on the champagne and tipping out the bus people, I'll still make a small profit.

Finally the night ends. The other waiters and I assemble at a back table and drink cheap white wine out of pint glasses while we wait for Sammy to accept our cash-out—the money and credit card receipts we accumulated during our shift. Sammy, being a petty tyrant, won't let any of the waiters leave the restaurant until everyone's cash-out matches to the penny. At the end of every shift, Sammy always eats a dish of vanilla ice cream dripping with chocolate sauce. He won't even look at our receipts until he finishes. Deliberately lingering over his dessert to remind us of his importance, Sammy's end-of-the-night shenanigans usually tack twenty minutes onto an already long day.

"C'mon, Sammy," my brother moans. "I've been here all day, and I want to go home. Stop stuffing your face."

"Just for that, I take care of you last," Sammy says, smiling mischievously into his ice cream.

"Screw this," my brother says, tossing his paperwork next to Sammy's dish of ice cream. "I'm going outside to have a cigarette. Call me when you're done."

"Suit yourself," Sammy chuckles.

"Wait," I tell my brother, grabbing my Marlboro Lights. "I'll go with you."

"Sit down," Sammy says. "I didn't say you can leave."

"What is this, Sammy?" I reply hotly. "The military?"

"Kind of," Sammy snorts.

"What do you want?"

"Caesar was pissed you messed up that table's champagne," Sammy says, once my brother's out of earshot.

"Hey, I bought a new bottle with my own money."

"Doesn't matter," Sammy says, shaking his head. "Caesar told me to give the bride a hundred-dollar gift certificate out of your money."

"What?" I gasp. The price of the champagne combined with buying this woman a gift certificate means I'll have worked this entire hellish day practically for free.

"That's the deal," Sammy says. "It's out of my hands."

"Goddamnit."

"There's another thing," Sammy says, an avaricious glint forming in his eye.

"What?"

"Caesar wanted me to fire you. I didn't out of respect for your brother."

"Thanks."

"So give me fifty bucks."

"Are you kidding?" I ask. "You want another bribe?"

"It's not a bribe. Let's say it's a gift—for my birthday."

"No fucking way. Fire me if you want. No more bribes."

Sammy looks at me, a cautiously surprised expression on his face.

"Suit yourself, newbie," he says. "Suit yourself."

When I get home at two A.M., there's a message from Sammy on my answering machine. He's taken away all my lucrative dinner shifts and replaced them with a motley assortment of low-revenue lunch gigs. To add insult to injury, he's making me work Sunday brunch tomorrow. That means I have to be back at work in seven hours. As I toss and turn in bed, anxious because I know I'm returning to that hellhole, one question keeps looping through my mind.

How the hell did I end up becoming a waiter?

CHAPTER 2

The Sacred and the Profane

Honestly? I never thought I'd be waiter when I was in my thirties. When I was eighteen years old, I dreamed about becoming a Catholic priest. According to the life schedule I had mapped out for myself, I was to be ordained a priest at twenty-five, consecrated a bishop at thirty, inducted into the Sacred College of Cardinals at forty, and assume the Throne of Peter to universal acclaim soon after that. I even had my pontifical name picked out. I'll bet I was the only teenager in the Northeast doodling prospective versions of his papal coat of arms in his notebook to keep from falling asleep in physics class. I was a religious geek.

If the thirty-one-year-old me could travel back to 1986 and tell that pimply-faced kid that he'd be working in a restaurant asking "You want *pommes frites* with that?" instead of running the archdiocese of New York, I'm fairly certain that kid would have broken out bell, book, and candle and singlehandedly tried to cast my unclean spirit into hell. Let's just say that being a waiter wasn't in that kid's plans.

Full of theistic fervor, I began my assault on the Vatican by enrolling in a college seminary—an undergraduate program designed to prepare young men for the priesthood. Operated under the auspices of a major Catholic university, my college campus was sandwiched between an affluent suburb and a decaying, poverty-stricken city.

The seminary was an interesting place. Intellectually stimulating and emotionally gut-wrenching, it was one of the most formative experiences of my life. While the other kids on campus were getting stoned, having sex, and basically having a great time, I was absorbing the arcane language of metaphysics, learning how to comfort people in times of sorrow, and immersing myself in the life of the Church. I spent so much time praying in chapel that my seminary mates whispered that I was a mystic. There was talk that I'd be sent to Rome for theological studies. My bishop said I was destined for great things. I was an ecclesiastical up-and-comer. I was also a self-righteous little shit.

Girls were verboten, but that was okay because I was afraid of them anyway. Since I was planning to dedicate my life to God, I did my best to avoid the inconsiderately buxom sources of temptation buzzing around campus in their tight T-shirts, leg warmers, and big hair. But biology always trumps theology, and by the end of my freshman year I was madly in puppy love with a co-ed named Gwen. Since I was in the seminary and ignorant of women, the relationship flamed out quickly. I was devastated. The first time your heart is broken is always the worst. I eventually got over it.

The seminary ended up breaking my heart, too. Don't get me wrong, I've always thought the priesthood was full of good men trying to make a genuine difference in the world. I still do. But as my time in the seminary wore on, it became obvious that the institution was also a hiding place for emotionally stunted head cases. While most of the priests I met were men struggling to do the right thing within an imperfect system, I also met quite a few individuals who used the priesthood as a home base for their sexual acting out—gay or straight. When the sexual abuse scandal rocked the Church in the late 1990s, I wasn't surprised at all. Years of bad karma and church politics were simply coming home to roost. The chasm between the ideal of what I thought the priesthood should be and what it actually was ended up being too much. When I got older, I began to realize the Church doesn't have a monopoly in the hypocrisy and stupidity department. It's everywhere. But since I didn't have the experience back then to give me a sense of perspective, I got angry. That anger coupled with the realization that celibacy wasn't a viable lifestyle choice caused me to leave the seminary after I completed my fourth year of undergraduate work. Studying theology in the Eternal City wasn't in the cards for me. That's just as well. By the time I had made up my mind to leave, the whole process had transformed me into such a cynical, bitter, angry person that my leaving saved Church officials the hassle of kicking me out.

Unlike most of my divinity school comrades, I didn't major in philosophy or religious studies. Some tiny realistic part of my brain knew I'd never be a priest and influenced me to get my degree in psychology. After I graduated from college I got a job working at a psychiatric and drug-rehabilitation facility that catered to the rich, famous, addicted, and confused.

Basically I was the guy in the proverbial white coat. My biggest job was to clap rich people in restraints whenever they engaged in self-harmful or violent behaviors and give them a chance to "take a time-out." (How I'd miss that option when I became a waiter!) Often we'd discover that the soft leather restraints the hospital used were missing. An internal investigation concluded that staff members were taking them home for kinky extracurricular activities. When we got them back, we would wash them in hot water. Twice.

When I wasn't busy hog-tying patients, escorting them to electroshock therapy, or going insane with boredom on interminable suicide watches, I played Ping-Pong in the staff room, liberated food from the cafeteria, and hit on the nurses. I also became tight with a group of perpetual frat-boy staffers who lived to go to the shore, play bad golf, ski, and lose their money in weekly poker games or trips to Atlantic City. Even though they teased me about my seminary background, these fellows provided me with the "regular guy" peer socialization I missed out on in college. I actually enjoyed my job. The pay wasn't great, but I found the work stimulating. I was even making my first forays into the administrative side of health care. Then the whole thing collapsed.

The hospital and its corporate parent were accused of running a criminal operation. Allegations of insurance fraud, keeping patients against their will, and administrative callousness that resulted in the suicide of a former patient prompted Diane Sawyer to expose the whole can of worms on national television. Law enforcement got involved. Soon after *Prime Time Live* aired, I arrived at work to discover FBI agents carting boxes of paperwork out of the administrative offices and conducting interviews with the staff. The patients and their families saw this, and, within weeks, the patient census dropped from 270 to 70. The facility rapidly became a shell of its former self. Arrests were made, indictments handed down, lawsuits filed, and, of course, the layoffs began. I was among the first people to lose their job.

I found the whole experience very unsettling. It was like thinking you worked for the Peace Corps only to discover that you were actually an unwitting goon in the health care version of the Mob. After the seminary I had hoped to find a healthy and stable environment where I could figure out what I wanted to be when I grew up. No such luck. It was the second time in my life that dysfunctional and corrupt people pulled the rug out from under me. First the disappointment of the seminary and now this.

I was twenty-four when the hospital laid me off. Afterward I floated from job to job; I ran group homes for the mentally retarded and residential programs for traumatically brain injured adults. Eventually I became the office manager for a small outpatient psychiatric clinic. During this time I took the test to become a Secret Service agent, thought of becoming a stockbroker, toyed with the idea of going to medical school, interviewed to be a cop, and flirted with plans to get my master's degree in psychology. Of course, none of this amounted to anything. Nothing could hold my interest or ambition.

Then a pretty college senior named Regan walked into my psychiatric clinic to perform her summer internship. I fell head over heels for her. The sun rose and set with this girl. When Regan completed her internship and went back to school three states away, I racked up major mileage to see her on the weekends. When I wasn't with her, I paced inside my small apartment waiting for her to phone. To me, her voice was a form of sustenance. I was crazy about her.

We had a lot of fun, but, as Regan began nearing graduation, the mood between us began to sour and we started fighting more often. When she got accepted into a top-flight school for social work, I think she realized that I was a twenty-eight-year-old man in a dead-end job who still didn't know what he wanted to be when he grew up. I think that scared her. Not because she was looking for some rich guy to provide for her, but because she wanted a strong, confident guy to share her life with. That was not me.

So the relationship began falling apart. As it entered its death throes my good friend Kevin, a member of my weekly hospital frat-boy poker group, was diagnosed with terminal pancreatic cancer. At the same time the psychiatric outfit I was working for was in negotiations to be bought out by a health care concern headquartered in another part of the country. By March, the irresolvable issues between Regan and me came to a head, and I decided to end it. It was a definitive moment in my life. I learned that love is only one ingredient among many in a relationship.

I picked March 27 as breakup day. Regan was coming home for Easter, so I told her I'd meet her that night at a local T.G.I. Friday's for beers (I know, I was such a class act). At lunchtime that day, however, I got a phone call. Kevin, who was home under hospice care, had just died. Numb, I told my boss what happened and got into my car and left. I'll never forget the drive to Kevin's house. It was a beautiful spring day. Shawn Colvin's song "Sunny

Came Home" was a big hit and playing over every radio station. Today, of all days, the lyrics were particularly haunting:

> *I close my eyes and fly out of my mind . . .*
> *The world is burning down*

I must've heard that song play three times during the drive to Kevin's house. When I pulled up to the curb, the undertakers were carrying my friend's plastic-shrouded body toward a waiting hearse. When the black-suited men pushing the gurney saw me approach, they stopped. I reached out and placed my hand on the blue plastic covering Kevin's corpse. I couldn't tell if I was touching his arm or his chest. The cancer had whittled him away to nothing. I couldn't believe he was dead. Not my friend. Not the guy I played poker with. Not the fun-loving guy who tried to hook me up at parties. It couldn't be. But what I felt under the shroud didn't move. Frightened, I pulled my hand away. The funeral guys continued on their way and slid what was once Kevin into the hearse. Inside the house I could hear Kevin's wife wailing. It was one day after their first wedding anniversary. As I watched the hearse drive away I remembered that Kevin had requested to be cremated. Those somber men were going to put my friend into a fire.

I went inside the house and gave my condolences to the widow in a haze. Her screams are something I'll never forget. A few hours later, against the advice of all my friends, I drove to the restaurant to break up with Regan. In retrospect, that was a truly stupid thing to do. I must've been in some sort of state of emotional shock. To make things worse, my ham-fisted attempts at breaking up caused Regan to run into the bathroom and throw up her beer. By the time it was all over, I drove home and got stinking drunk. I had lost my buddy and my girlfriend on the same day.

Kevin's memorial service was the following Monday. On Tuesday I showed up at work early, eager to bury the pain I was feeling under the mountain of paperwork stacked on my desk. As I walked through the hallways I noticed everyone was looking at me funny. I didn't think anything of it at first. It was a small office, and news traveled fast. I figured they all knew I was having a rough time and were keeping a respectful distance. The real reason for the awkward stares soon became apparent, though. Before I could even get a cup of coffee my boss walked into my office and broke the news that our clinic had been bought out by that other company. My position had become redundant. I was being laid off.

Professional gunmen have a little maneuver they call the "Mozambique Drill." That's when they put two rounds into some poor slob's chest and then, just to make sure he's dead, shoot him in the head. Well, my boss had just delivered the third shot. I could handle losing my girlfriend. I could handle losing Kevin. I could handle losing my job. But I couldn't handle losing all three things at the same time. I was down for the count. I walked out of the office feeling abandoned and lost. I felt like that song was coming to life. *"I close my eyes and fly out of my mind / The world is burning down."*

And I almost did fly out of my mind. I had a mini–nervous breakdown, saw a shrink, and started popping Zoloft like M&M's. I also spent six fruitless months looking for a new job. Just before my unemployment benefits were due to run out I was offered the position of marketing director for a geriatric outpatient clinic opening up in an inner-city hospital. I didn't know squat about being a marketing rep or opening a clinic, but the job paid well, so I jumped all over it. It was hard work, but within a few months the clinical director and I had the place up and running. The staff we hired was top notch, and the senior citizens we treated got excellent care. The only problem? There were never *enough* patients.

The hospital that housed our clinic was in a bad neighborhood. Latin King gang members stabbed a kid to death outside our ER in broad daylight. A low-rent go-go bar was visible from my office. Trying to convince nervous grandmas to come to the ghetto for treatment was a tough sell. Several other hospitals in the area had similar programs, so competition for the shrinking Medicare pie was cutthroat and fraud was rampant. Unscrupulous marketing reps trolled nursing homes in order to stuff their programs with Alzheimer's patients and bill bingo games as group therapy. I didn't want to play that game. Neither did my therapists. We were honest.

The reward for our righteousness was a low patient census. When you're a health care marketer, you live and die by the census. Some days we'd have twenty patients, and other days we'd have two. I spent hours languishing in waiting rooms trying to persuade doctors to choose my clinic over others and suffered through countless sales lunches with power-mad nursing home administrators who wanted only to gobble up expense-account-subsidized food. Eventually the low census drove my corporate overlords crazy. By the middle of my second year the powers that be were calling for my head.

The outfit I worked for operated a swath of psychiatric clinics throughout the region. Like every American company in 1999 with more than five employees, they were dreaming about going public. Drunk on New Economy Kool-Aid, the higher-ups droned catchphrases such as "best practices" and "due diligence" like cultic mantras and were so busy dreaming about stock options and yacht clubs that they forgot to attend to small details like ethics. The last straw came when one of the regional VPs started insisting we admit mentally retarded people into our program, technically a violation of Medicare law. Just like at the seminary and in my previous job, I once again found myself surrounded by well-educated people who looked good, said the right things, and behaved dishonestly. The therapists and I refused to cave in to their demands. The company decided to get rid of me.

Because the company was scared of lawsuits, they didn't fire me right away. Instead, they took their sweet time, drafting warning letters for my personnel file and waging a rather cynical campaign to prove that I was incompetent. At that point I probably was incompetent. I had tried being a good corporate soldier, but the office politics wore down my enthusiasm. Like my old seminary overlords I think everyone was hoping I'd have the good grace to leave on my own.

That meant I had plenty of time to jump ship and look for another job. But instead of hitting the bricks, I hid out in a small park for two months, smoking cigars, reading books, feeding the ducks, and trying to figure out what do to with my life. I was like a Wall Street guy who'd been downsized but was afraid to tell his wife he's been fired. The only difference was I wasted time smoking in a park instead of pantomiming a daily commute. I knew I was going to be canned, so I figured I might as well get paid for goofing off right up until the last minute. Bleed the suckers dry. That was my motto.

But I had bills to pay, and I didn't want to languish in unemployment hell again while looking for another job. Some part of me understood that if I didn't get a job and keep moving, I'd get depressed again. But what could I do? I couldn't get a health care job. Everyone in my close-knit industry knew I was a screwup.

My brother was working at a busy restaurant while going to school part time. When I told him how bad things were at my job, he said he could get me a brief gig at his place until I got back on my feet. When he initially proposed the idea, I laughed at him. Me? A waiter? I always thought that was a gig for bad actors, cokeheads, and teenagers.

But I had to face a hard, cold reality. I was a college-educated thirty-year-old with no real marketable skills. I'd never had a job lasting longer than two years. I knew nothing about working in a restaurant. But it was better than nothing, and what did I have to lose? So I called my brother and asked him if the job offer was still good. It was.

And that, my friends, is how the whole waiter thing started.

CHAPTER 3

Fascists and
Freshwater Ostrich

Since Sammy screwed me over by calling me in for an unscheduled brunch shift, I've got to haul myself in early and prep Amici's dining room for the Sunday morning crowd. Brunch is, without a doubt, the worst shift a waiter can work. The after-church crowds are the worst tippers. Sometimes they like giving the servers religious tracts in lieu of a tip. Often the pamphlets are full of descriptions of eternal hellfire. Trust me, on Sunday morning, most waiters are hungover and wiped out from doing the things that are supposed to get you into hell in the first place. Giving a waiter a religious tract is like giving Mephistopheles a parking ticket. We just rip it up and throw it in the street.

On very little sleep, I start dragging the large Pellegrino shade umbrellas out of the storage room and onto the outdoor patio. As I'm struggling to unfurl one of the rusty umbrellas, I notice a tired-looking man smoking a cigarette by the front door. He doesn't look like he wants to come in and eat.

"Can I help you, sir?" I ask.

"I'm looking for job," the man replies. He has a thick Russian accent.

I look at the man. He looks like a laborer. His hands are calloused, and his shoes are caked with grime. He smells like fish.

"The owner will be here soon," I reply. "You can ask him if he's hiring."

"Thanks."

The man cups his cigarette inside his palm to protect it from the wind. I've seen my Eastern European relatives do the same thing a thousand times.

"You want some coffee?" I ask.

The Russian man looks surprised. "Yes," he murmurs. "Thank you."

"Come inside. I'll get you a cup."

The Russian guy takes a seat near the entrance. I bring him a cup of coffee, sugar, and cream. I even put a piece of biscotti on the plate.

"Thanks," the man says.

"No problem," I say. "Caesar'll be here in a minute."

The Russian man settles into his seat and sips his coffee. A sad smile plays out on his face. I feel bad for the man. I can tell he's hurting for money.

I go back to setting up my station. Caesar walks in, nattily dressed as always, holding an Italian newspaper under his arm.

"Who's that?" he asks me, pointing to the Russian man.

"Some guy looking for a job."

Caesar puts down his paper and walks up to the man.

"Are you a Jew?" Caesar asks.

"Huh?" the Russian replies.

"Are you a Jew?"

The Russian man puts down his coffee. He looks confused. "I looking for job," he says.

"I knew it," Caesar says. "I can hear it in your voice. You're a Jew. A filthy fucking Russian Jew."

I stand rooted to the floor in shock.

"Get out of my restaurant!" Caesar yells. "Get out before I call the cops and tell them you're stealing."

The Russian man makes a quick exit. Caesar watches him go, then walks up to me.

"Who gave that guy a cup of coffee?" he demands.

"I did," I reply.

"Why'd you let him in here?"

"He was looking for a job, Caesar."

"I DECIDE WHO WORKS HERE!" Caesar screams. "NOT YOU! YOU FUCKING LOSER!"

"R-relax, Caesar," I stammer. "You're gonna give yourself a coronary."

"YOU THINK YOU'RE FUNNY?" Caesar shouts. "I'LL FIRE YOU *AND* YOUR BROTHER."

It's then I realize the gleam in his eyes isn't the remnants of youthful vigor—it's hatred. My brother's in school and needs this job. He can't afford my telling Caesar to shove it. Come to think of it, I can't afford it either.

"Sorry, Caesar," I mumble.

"Fucking Jews," Caesar growls, storming off.

I stare at the floor. Why am I taking shit from a guy like Caesar? *Because I need money, that's why.* I wonder how many people are like me, trapped in jobs they don't like, afraid to risk their paycheck by confronting a depraved boss.

When Rizzo comes in, I tell him about the entire exchange.

"Good old Caesar," Rizzo sighs. "He won't be B'nai B'rith's Man of the Year anytime soon."

"How can he run a restaurant and be like that?"

"Oh, Caesar's all smiles taking your money. Jew, black, gay, he doesn't care, just as long as your money's green."

"Jesus," I mutter.

"Haven't you noticed there're no black or gay waiters here?" Rizzo says. "And if you're Jewish, don't advertise."

"Why is he like that?"

"Caesar was born in Italy, but he grew up in Paraguay after

the war," Rizzo says. "I think his dad was probably some kind of Mussolini dude."

"No way."

"Didn't you see *The Boys from Brazil*?" Rizzo snorts. "A lot of those fascist shits moved down there."

"If you're right," I say, "that'd explain a lot."

"Welcome to the restaurant business."

Somehow I survive working that crazy sleep-deprived day. As the week progresses another waiter refusing to be shook down by Sammy quits in disgust. I catch a lucky break. The pool of available labor has tightened up. Sammy has no choice but to put me back on the primo dinner shifts. Since I have a good work ethic and show up on time, Sammy has to depend on me now. That keeps his predatory instincts at bay—for a while.

My first weeks as a waiter go by slowly. Physically and mentally I manage to tough it out. It's amazing how the threat of poverty helps you acclimate to anything. My feet stop hurting, and I graduate out of the special-ed section Rizzo had me training in. By my sixth Saturday night I beat Rizzo in tips.

I'm proud of myself. I'm already working Saturday night shifts, and, to my amazement, I'm making more money than I earned at the hospital. Not having medical or vacation is incidental; I dove into a new job and made it work for me. That makes me feel good. As the weeks turn into months my anxiety level dissipates.

I credit Rizzo for keeping me sane as I learned the waiter ropes. He's a very strange man who's led a very interesting life, and I quickly learn he's never set foot in Vietnam. "The 'Nam?" he confessed to me. "Dude, I smoked so much pot that I don't remember Nixon's first term. I was never in the army. I just say that shit to scare the kiddies."

While Rizzo avoided battling the Vietcong, he couldn't avoid the long arm of the Internal Revenue Service. Back in the 1970s Rizzo owned a high-end restaurant in Manhattan. "The place was so popular," he told me, "that high-class models—*Vogue* types, you know?—they would eat lunch there every day. The waiters'd be sniffing the seats when they left." With unfettered access to drugs, discothèques, and women, Rizzo claimed he bedded more conquests than Wilt Chamberlain. "I had so many girlfriends that I redecorated my apartment more times then Neiman Marcus!" was a favorite saying of his. (No, I don't know what that means either.)

Rizzo, however, was not fond of paying taxes. I don't know the whole story, but at some point he sold his Manhattan eatery and skipped town owing the IRS a huge tax bill. Spiritually desolated, he fled to a remote corner of Montana, bought a .357 Magnum, and began a Ted Kaczynski existence living inside an abandoned railroad car. Growing his own food and hunting his own game, he became interested in Buddhism. After attending a few retreats at a nearby Buddhist monastery Rizzo became a semi-vegetarian, got a dog, and started learning everything he could about karma. He kept the Magnum, though. After a while his mother fell ill, and Rizzo, now sick of his eremitical existence, decided to move back east to care for her. On his day off he would travel into Manhattan and do his mom's shopping, prepare all her meals for the week, and keep her company. While many people taking care of aging parents might consider that level of effort a burden, Rizzo did it with gladness in his heart. Some of the Buddha must have rubbed off on him.

Because he knew I had studied to be a priest, Rizzo and I had some interesting discussions about religion. For my part, I didn't know much about karma. I always thought it was about the bad things you did in life coming back to bite you on the ass. The more I talked to Rizzo, however, the more I learned that karma's not about retribution, it simply deals with what *is*. To grossly simplify the concept, the effects of all our deeds impact all our past, present, and future experiences. We are, in the end, responsible for all our actions and the pain and joy it brings to others. The older I get, the more sense that belief system makes to me.

Rizzo was a pistol-packing Buddhist, mind you, so he was attracted to the stranger and contradictory stories about his faith.

He loved telling me the story about the two Tibetan lamas who were such bitter enemies that, when they died, they tried using their considerable powers to kill each other in the womb as they attempted to reincarnate into new bodies. "Baby ninja karmic assassins!" was how Rizzo described them.

While one part of Rizzo was very spiritual, another part of him was tough as nails. Rizzo didn't take shit from anyone, and he didn't suffer fools lightly. He'd verbally pimp slap chefs, owners, customers, and especially other waiters. The best example of this was how he brought it to Wahdi, the worst waiter I ever had the displeasure to work with.

Wahdi, a hulking, sweaty brute from Syria who was in the country on a student visa, got hired by Sammy a few months after I started at Amici's. Devoid of social skills, knowledge of American culture, or patience, Wahdi was ill suited for the job of waiting tables. Worst of all, he was a greedy son of a bitch. New waiters normally start off with the worst shifts and lowest-earning sections. Not Wahdi. Because he was tight with Sammy, he thought he was entitled to the best sections and yelled at the hostess whenever he fell behind in the customer count. If he discovered that he made a dollar less than any other server, he started shouting that we were discriminating against him because he was from the Middle East. After being a pain in the ass for several weeks, Wahdi decided to start a turf war with Rizzo. Big mistake.

"Hey, Rizzo," Wahdi says at the start of a Friday night, "I'm working your section tonight."

"The hell you are," Rizzo replies.

"I talk to Sammy," Wahdi continues. "I tell him it not fair you always have the best section. He agreed and give it to me."

Rizzo looks over the top of his glasses and gives Wahdi a look that zips right through his eyeballs, punches a hole out the back of his skull, and continues traveling through windows, masonry, pedestrians, and several parked cars before its energy dissipates somewhere over the Hudson River. I've seen Rizzo reduce customers to quivering lumps of gelatin with that look before. Rizzo calls it his "thousand-yard waiter stare." It's devastatingly effective. I've got to develop my own one day.

"If you fuck with me, Wahdi," Rizzo growls, "I am going to call the Syrian consulate in New York and tell them you're a Mossad agent."

We all hear Wahdi's sphincter pop. The Syrian intelligence services are not known for their subtlety. After Wahdi cries in Arabic to the manager, Sammy sticks him in Rizzo's section just to shut him up.

Chagrined, Rizzo turns to me and says, "Time to dance a little jihad on Wahdi's head."

Rizzo runs off to the kitchen. He returns with Fluvio in tow, ostensibly to tell us the evening's specials. After reviewing the night's offerings the chef tells us he's prepared a special dish.

"Tonight we have freshwater ostrich in a Dijon mustard sauce," Fluvio says. "Make sure you tell the customers it's freshwater ostrich—not saltwater—the taste is entirely different."

All the waiters stare at their dupe pads and pretend like they've heard nothing out of the ordinary. Wahdi writes down the specials furiously.

"You got that, Wahdi?" Fluvio asks. "*Freshwater ostrich.*"

"Yes, I got it," Wahdi says.

Rizzo and the chef smile at each other. This is going to be fun.

The restaurant fills up immediately, and Wahdi's in trouble from the start. Greedy for sales, he pitches freshwater ostrich to his tables and can't understand why everyone's laughing at him. Embarrassed, but not knowing why, Wahdi's social ineptitude takes over, and he starts arguing with the customers. "Of course ostrich is a fish!" he yells. As he gets angrier and angrier he moves slower and slower. His tables wait half an hour just to get sodas.

Finally a customer walks up to Sammy and starts complaining. "That waiter is a complete asshole," he yelps. "I want another one. He thinks ostrich is a fish!"

Sammy knows what's up. He pulls Wahdi off to one side and tries to calm him down. Before long the two of them are screaming at each other in Arabic. Seeing this, Rizzo and I swoop in to snap up the unattended tables and, before you can say *baba ganoush*, Wahdi loses his section.

Sammy's pissed, but there is nothing he can do. Wahdi's temper has gotten the better of him. One of the Egyptian busboys starts taunting Wahdi mercilessly. "Freshwater ostrich? You asshole! Go back to Syria!"

Wahdi, in turn, starts screaming at the busboy. In the background I can hear Rizzo crowing, "Hello? Damascus information? Could I have the number for the secret police?"

Realizing he's been set up, Wahdi runs up to Rizzo, screaming. "YOU HAVE DONE THIS TO ME!"

Rizzo smiles and yells back. "WELCOME TO AMERICA, MOTHERFUCKER!"

Wahdi breaks down, crying in rage.

He was fired several weeks later.

A short time after Wahdi's departure Caesar decided to have a massive heart attack. I know, you're not surprised, but let me tell you the story anyway. Earlier that fateful day the industrial-strength dishwasher went on the fritz. That's stressful for any restaurant owner since the dishwasher is one of the most expensive and complex machines in the kitchen. Ironically, it's always run by the lowest-paid guy in the place. Because the machines are so expensive, most establishments lease the machine and/or have service contracts.

Ralph, the rep from the company that leases the machine to us, comes over to examine the washer's innards. After he finishes his examination he informs Caesar that a $500 part will have to be ordered to get the thing up and running. Caesar's response is to start screaming profanities in the middle of the lunch rush and chase Ralph out of the restaurant. Horrified, several customers flee the restaurant without paying their bills. Later that day, Caesar is rushed to the hospital suffering chest pains. Go figure.

The morning after the myocardial event Sammy held an emergency staff meeting to tell us the news.

"Caesar's in the hospital," Sammy says, close to weeping. "I want all of us to remember him in our prayers."

It soon becomes obvious the waiters aren't besieging heaven with requests to speed up Caesar's recovery. In fact, they're probably asking the Almighty for the exact opposite. Rizzo's biting his hand to keep from laughing. Most of the waiters are openly smiling.

"You guys think this is funny?" Sammy says, his voice rising.

"No, of course not," Rizzo says, his laughter starting to get away from him.

"You're a bastard, Rizzo."

Rizzo's laughter's contagious. I find myself smiling, too. I remember the Russian Jew. I remember how Caesar called me a peasant. Fuck Caesar.

"It couldn't have happened to a nicer guy," I say.

Sammy looks at me in shock. "What'd you say?"

"You heard me."

Sammy storms off, furious. Caesar's the source of his power. Without Caesar, Sammy's just a tubby, impotent leech.

"Oh man," Rizzo giggles.

"Like no one saw that heart attack coming," I mutter.

"You think Caesar's blowout with Ralph had something to do with it?"

"A piece of arterial plaque or something must've dislodged when he was screaming his head off," I say. "It floated around for a while, then—whammo!"

"It wasn't arterial plaque," Rizzo says.

"What was it?"

"It was karma, man," Rizzo says, shaking his head. "It was motherfucking karma."

While the Dali Lama might disagree with Rizzo's theological interpretation of events, karma or no, Caesar survived his heart attack and came back to work several weeks later. During this time, unbeknownst to us, Fluvio had been sneaking around trying to open up his own restaurant. He was being covert because Caesar—with his Wagnerian, *Godfather*-esque notions of loyalty—would view Fluvio's desire to have something for himself as a betrayal deserving of death. If Caesar couldn't control you, he hated you. Then again, he hated everyone.

But Fluvio made the mistake of advertising for waitstaff in the Help Wanted section three months before his restaurant was scheduled to open. My brother, who never liked Fluvio, answered the ad, discovered what he was up to, and ratted him out. Caesar fired Fluvio soon afterward.

Now, a restaurant without a chef is a problem. Fluvio was experienced, and his services didn't come cheap. Being a tightwad, Caesar decided now would be a good time to increase his profit margin by going with a less-expensive and less-experienced chef.

The first guy Caesar hired, Ray, was a disaster. His management style was to let the kitchen guys do whatever they wanted—so they had no respect for him. Sammy even caught Ray on the phone asking his mother how to make risotto. Ray was a dead chef walking. Caesar took away his spatula after two weeks.

After Ray an assortment of con artists and criminals pretending to be chefs waltzed in and out of the kitchen. Considering what Caesar was probably paying them, the substandard applicants were no surprise. Without a firm leader in the kitchen, things started to go awry. The health department issued Amici's a summons for unsanitary conditions. When Caesar didn't remediate the problems quickly enough, the health inspector quickly publicized that we were a dirty restaurant. Business took a nosedive.

Caesar finally hired a no-nonsense guy named Jeff. He wasn't going to win any culinary awards, but he was a good manager. The kitchen got cleaned up, and the health department got off our backs. Business started to pick up. But Caesar wanted Jeff to be a world-class cook for less than world-class wages. That would be my undoing at Amici's.

The end comes on a beautiful June day. I'm enjoying my only day off when the phone rings. It's Sammy.

"Two of my waiters called out," Sammy says, panic rising in his voice. "I only have one server on for lunch."

I consider suggesting that Sammy's problems retaining wait-staff might be symptomatic of a broader systemic problem. Amici's is dysfunctional because the owner is dysfunctional. A well-run restaurant putting out a good product usually attracts good staff. But dysfunctional restaurants tend to retain staff with less-developed professional skills. A few months earlier I'd had the chance to dine at Gramercy Tavern. I was dumbfounded by how *polished* the waiters were. As I watched the restaurant's elegant servers gracefully navigate the crowded dining room floor, I felt like a bush-league player watching the Yankees take the field. Compared to Gramercy, Amici's seems like a hot-dog stand. Why the difference? Simple—quality flows from the top down. Gramercy's owner, Danny Meyer, is a driven, classy guy who, unlike Caesar, treats his employees with respect. Sure, he has problems like every other business owner, but he deals with them professionally. Meyer and his staff's attention to detail and customer service is tremendous, and that's a large reason for their success. And the reason Meyer's staff can stay so focused is because they're basically happy and secure in their jobs—most of the time.

But in a restaurant where the manager's shaking down waiters and the owner's pining for the glory days of the Third Reich, you shouldn't be surprised if the service and the food are below par. Not only does all that negative energy result in horrible staff, it attracts crazy customers like a moth to a flame. The customers at Amici's are awful. Granted, you may get evil customers at Gramercy, too, but you get more déclassé (that's French for "trailer trash") customers at a place like Amici's. Since the owner and manager treat the staff like slaves, it's no surprise that many of the customers display similar attitudes toward the hired help. *A restaurant gets the customers it deserves.* I feel like telling

Sammy all this but decide against it. He wouldn't understand what I was talking about.

"So you want me to come in on my day off?" I reply. "I have plans tonight."

"But I just need you for lunch," Sammy whines.

"I know you, Sammy. You'll make me stay for dinner, too."

"I swear on my children that you'll leave at three o'clock."

I sigh deeply. As much as I don't like Sammy, I was raised with a good work ethic.

"I'll be there in a few minutes."

"Thanks," Sammy says. "I owe you one."

"Don't forget it."

I hang up and drive into work. When I get there, it's a madhouse. As I race around taking orders I notice Caesar is sitting at his customary table, sucking down red wine, oblivious to the fact that he should be helping to keep *his* restaurant going.

"Come over here," Caesar barks, waving me over to his table.

"What's up, Caesar?" I say impatiently. "I've got fifteen tables to take care of."

"Tell the chef I want the fish special for lunch."

"Okay, no problem."

"But don't tell him it's for me," Caesar whispers.

"Why?"

"I don't want him to know it's for me!" Caesar snaps imperiously. "Don't question me!"

"Okay, Caesar," I reply, rolling my eyes.

"Don't be a smart ass."

I put Caesar's order into the POS computer. Then I go into the kitchen and tell Jeff it's for the boss. The reason I'm disobeying the owner's instructions is because I'm following a cardinal rule for waitstaff—always stay on the chef's good side. A chef can make or break a waiter. He or she can make sure everyone gets their food but you. If the kitchen staff turns on you, it's all over.

Jeff thanks me for the heads-up. After a while the owner's top-secret striped bass gets plated. I drop it off at Caesar's table.

"Jeff doesn't know this is for me?" Caesar asks, his breath reeking of onions and red wine.

"He doesn't know a thing," I lie.

"Good."

I dive back into the lunchtime fray. Things are so bad Sammy's taking tables. I run up to a couple eating with small children, apologize for taking so long, and get their order. As I'm punching the kiddie meals into the POS a hand grabs my upper arm and almost yanks me off my feet.

"YOU COCKSUCKER!" Caesar screams, his face an inch from mine. "You lying piece of shit!"

"Wha—" I reply, stunned.

"YOU'RE FIRED!"

"Why?"

"I told you I didn't want the chef to know the food was for me!" Caesar screams.

I look over at the kitchen. Jeff's standing in the doorway. He shrugs innocently and walks back into the kitchen.

"Caesar—"

"Get the fuck out!" Caesar screams. "GET THE FUCK OUT!"

"Do you mind?" the father at my table says. "There are children here!"

Ignoring the man, Caesar grabs my shirt with both hands. "Get the fuck out, you cocksucker!" he shrieks, shaking me.

Caesar's hot spittle sprays onto my cheek and lips. I raise my hand to wipe it away. Caesar knocks it down.

Sammy comes running over. "Caesar," he yelps, "let go of him."

"You want to get fired, too?" Caesar yells, the veins popping out of his neck. "I'll fire you next, Sammy!"

Sammy slinks off with his tail between his legs. Caesar's pulling on my shirt. My vision starts to tunnel. My hands ball into fists. A red haze starts to surround me. I'm seriously considering picking up where Caesar's heart attack left off.

But years of working with psychiatric patients kicks in. I realize I'm thinking about pummeling an alcoholic septuagenarian. Caesar's not worth going to jail over. I disentangle myself from his grasp and head for the door.

"GET OUT!" Caesar yells, chasing me. "GET OUT!"

I race onto the sidewalk. Caesar follows me, screaming. I don't want to leave because I have some of the restaurant's money in my pocket. If I take off, I could be arrested for stealing. I'm not giving Caesar that opportunity.

"Caesar," I warn ominously, "if you take another step closer, there's going to be trouble."

A reptilian wariness creeps into Caesar's eyes. He backs up, sputtering obscenities. After a few tense seconds he heads back inside. Sammy pokes his head cautiously out the door. When he realizes the coast is clear, he comes out to talk to me.

"Thanks for not killing him," Sammy says, genuinely shocked.

"Something's seriously wrong with that guy," I reply, handing over the restaurant's money. "I come in on my day off, and he treats me like that?"

"I'm so sorry."

"I'm outta here."

"I'll talk to Caesar," Sammy says. "Maybe I can get you your job back."

"Tell him to shove it up his ass."

I walk to the back of the restaurant to get my car. My hands are shaking. As I round the corner I see Jeff standing on the back staircase having a cigarette.

"Jeff, man," I say, "what happened?"

"Caesar asked me if you told me the fish was for him," Jeff says. "You did, so I told him."

"Dude," I reply, flabbergasted. "I was trying to help you. Why'd you rat me out?"

"I'm taking care of number one, man," Jeff says, taking a drag off his smoke. "And I don't give a shit what you think."

For the second time in two minutes I think about strangling someone with my bare hands. That walls-are-closing-in-around-me sensation starts pressing in on me again. A cold sweat trickles down my back. My heartbeat and respiration go into overdrive. I feel like I'm having an anxiety attack. I forgo throttling Jeff. In my current mental state discretion is the better part of valor. I get in my car and drive home.

Later that evening my brother calls. "What the hell happened?" he asks.

I tell him.

"Caesar's crazy," my brother replies, a weariness creeping into his voice.

"Thanks for getting me into Amici's," I say. "But you need that job there more than I do. I'll just go quietly."

"Maybe Sammy can work something out for you. He's grateful you didn't punch Caesar out."

"Believe me, I felt like it."

"Let me see what I can do on my end."

"Okay."

"Later, bro."

Sammy calls me a few hours later. He tells me he can get my job back for a hundred bucks. After a few choice words I hang up on him. He forgot his gratitude real quick.

The next day I'm out looking for another job. When applying for these gigs, applicants should always show up in person and never pester management during service. That just screams you're inexperienced. Hopeful waiters should apply before lunch or during the lull before dinner, preferably with an appointment. As I'm driving to my next interview my cell phone rings.

"Hello?"

"Ah yes, hello, is that you?" a vaguely familiar voice says.

"Who is this?" I ask.

"This is Fluvio."

"Fluvio," I say, "how are you? How's the new restaurant?"

"It's okay," he says. "But my manager disappeared."

"Disappeared?"

"He do drugs, you know?" Fluvio says, his voice pushing through the cellular static. "He don't come to work for three days. I have no idea where he is."

"That sucks."

"So you got fired, eh?" Fluvio asks.

"News travels fast." The restaurant grapevine is faster than Reuters.

"Sammy's a piece of shit," Fluvio says. "Listen, come up by my new place. We'll talk."

"You need a waiter?"

"I need a manager," Fluvio says. "I don't know you well, but from what I've seen I think I can trust you."

"Even though my brother got you fired?" I ask incredulously.

"Don't you worry," Fluvio says. "Why don't you come see me tomorrow and we talk."

"How about two o'clock?"

"See you then."

I hang up the phone. A smile creeps across my face. I know Fluvio will hire me. I chuckle softly to myself. I've been a waiter for only eight months, and I've already ended up with an offer to manage a place. I'll work at Fluvio's bistro for a couple of months, a year tops, and then move on to something else. I crumple up my list of restaurants and throw it into the garbage.

CHAPTER 4

Waiter Jedi

aiter!" my customer, an expensively dressed Wall Street type, whines. "Why can't I have the Pollo Cardinale tonight? I have it here all the time."

"Because it's New Year's Eve, sir," I reply patiently. "We have a special menu tonight."

"So I can't have anything off the regular menu?"

In a few hours it will be 2006. I've been working at Fluvio's restaurant, The Bistro, for six years. No longer that Padawan waiter from Amici's, I've developed into a full-fledged Waiter Jedi. Along the way I even started a popular Web site, called Waiter Rant, to share my restaurant war stories. To millions of people I'm the anonymous Internet writer known only as "The Waiter." The experience I've gleaned over the years tells me to answer this customer carefully. When people go out to eat, they don't want to hear the word *no*.

"Pollo Cardinale's usually served in autumn, sir," I explain. "To celebrate New Year's, the chef's offering the traditional winter foods he grew up with as a child in Tuscany."

"Oh," the man says, his face brightening, "that sounds wonderful."

My explanation is complete and utter bullshit. Pollo Cardinale, a chicken dish made with roasted peppers, mozzarella cheese, and mushrooms, doesn't have a seasonal niche. I lied.

I lied because if I had to explain to every customer that the owner limited his holiday offerings to a small selection of items guaranteed to deliver a high profit, the unpleasant smack of cold, hard reality would start exerting a downward pressure on my tips. Since I couched my reply in foodiespeak, however, the gastronomically seductive language of Big Food Media, the guy bought my line of bullshit hook, line, and sinker. My tip is secure.

"The wild boar is very good tonight, sir," I continue. "This evening we're offering it in either a porcini mushroom truffle sauce or a preparation of white beans, goose confit, and rabbit sausage."

The man stares at me, his mouth slackening with desire. A good server can make a customer order anything he or she feels like selling. It's an old Jedi—I mean, waiter—mind trick.

"Oh my God," the man breathes. "I think I'll have that."

"I recommend you have it medium rare, sir."

"I'll take your advice, waiter. You seem to know your stuff."

"Yes, sir. Thank you, sir. Will that be with the mushroom sauce or the goose confit and sausage?"

"With the goose stuff."

"Very good, sir."

My next table orders a $300 bottle of Brunello. I fetch it from the wine cellar and present it to the host. After he examines the label I take out my expensive black horn Laguiole wine opener, flick open the blade, make a quick vertical incision in the foil, score it below the bottle's neck, and remove the cap in one fluid motion. Folding the blade, I open the corkscrew one-handed, place the stainless steel spiral into the center of the cork, and screw it in, careful not go in to far and push bits of cork into the wine. I brace the lever on the lip of the bottle's mouth, pull the handle upward, and slide the cork out without a pop.

As I'm executing this maneuver I'm not paying attention to what I'm doing. I don't have to. I've done it twenty thousand times. It's all muscle memory by now. Instead, I'm listening to the young couple at the table behind me. They're talking about having a baby.

I pour out an ounce of the wine, gently twisting the bottle so I don't spill a drop. The host samples it. He likes it, so I pour out some more. I wipe the lip of the bottle with a napkin and start answering questions about the holiday menu. The rehearsed adjectives tumble out of my mouth with practiced ease. Fooled by my mask of feigned interest, the customers think my attention is riveted on them. It isn't. I'm still listening to the couple behind me. The girl's afraid to have children. She's afraid she'll abandon them like her mother abandoned her. Her husband tells her not to worry: She's not her mother. She's a different person. She'll be a wonderful mother. They'll be happy.

My four top's host thanks me. His wife compliments my memory. How can you remember so much stuff? I respond with a witty stock answer. They all laugh. I tell them I'll give them time to consider their choices. I turn and look at the table behind me. The girl has tears in her eyes. The boy's holding her hand. For the thousandth time I marvel how much people reveal about themselves inside a restaurant. I shouldn't be surprised. When people are stuffing their faces, they often let their guard down. Eating is a primal activity that triggers an array of emotional responses. Think of all the arguments that erupt around family dinner tables. Food and the human condition are inextricably linked. Because of this, waiters often get to see the unpleasant sides of people. Yet, amid all the petulance, anger, and entitlement, the occasional crumb of human grace falls from the table. I look at the boy and girl. They need their privacy. This is an important moment. Do not disturb. I walk way.

The Bistro's a small fifty-seat restaurant nestled in an artsy neighborhood somewhere in the New York area. A long rectangle tucked inside an old building, its walls are painted off-white, and the high ceilings and exposed ductwork are terra-cotta red. The kitchen occupies most of The Bistro's left-hand side, pushing the tables running parallel to it against the restaurant's right wall, forming a narrow aisle connecting the tables clustered near the front window with the three semicircular banquettes in the back. Impressionistic Italian landscapes hang on the walls while large wooden ceiling fans gently stir the air overhead. Votive candles flickering in the center of the linen-covered tables provide a warm counterpoint to the subdued lighting, allowing shifting patterns of light and shadow to play against the walls and polished hardwood floors. The Bistro's cuisine is northern Italian—Tuscan to be precise—lots of game, wild boar, fowl, fish, dried legumes, and the ever present porcini mushroom. Zagat rated and *New York Times* reviewed, the restaurant enjoys an excellent reputation and is patronized by many of the famous celebrities who live nearby. When you combine supersized incomes with high menu prices and an expensive wine list, it doesn't take long to realize that, for a waiter, The Bistro's a goldmine.

As my fingers glide along the POS computer's touch screen inputting an order, I look at how the other waiters are faring on the floor. Toward the front door I spot Inez, our Peruvian waitress with the expired student visa, struggling to keep pace with the other waiters. Tall, blond, and built like an athlete, Inez is a disaster as a server; she's slow, argumentative, and always trying to scam out of work early. Yet Inez and I are the type of people who hate each other on the job but get along after work. When Inez sheds her mannish waitress uniform of dress shirt, black pants, and badly knotted tie, it's like she transforms into a different woman—pretty, exuberant, and a delight to be around. Right now, however, I want to throttle her.

"Louis," I ask the waiter waiting for me to finish with the computer, "how many customers has Inez had tonight?"

"Not many," Louis grunts. "I can't believe we're gonna divvy up our tips with her."

I understand Louis's feelings. For most waiters New Year's Eve is the biggest money night of the year. Last year I made most of my month's rent in ten hours. Because of the amounts of money involved, Fluvio makes us combine our tips into a "pool" and divides the money evenly among the servers at the end of the night. Normally waiters at The Bistro are lone operators, keeping only the tips they earn from tables they personally work. New Year's Eve, Valentine's Day, and Mother's Day are the few times a year when we abandon the independent-contractor model and act as a "pool house." Pooling tips is okay—as long as everyone pulls his or her own weight. Inez's slowness, however, makes it certain that she'll make the same amount of money as the rest of us but serve only half the customers.

"Goddamnit," I say, "I'm already up to four hundred in tips."

"I'll bet she hasn't even cracked a hundred yet," Louis mutters.

Standing over six feet tall, Louis is one of the most experienced waiters ever to work at The Bistro. Having worked everything from diners to exclusive French restaurants, if every restaurant has to have at least one gay waiter, then Louis is gay enough for two. Alternating between the polar extremes of being flamboyantly gay and staunch Republican, Louis is a schmoozer and a favorite with the customers.

"Look on the bright side," I say. "She's moving upstate in a couple of months."

"Going back to school?"

"That's what she tells me," I say. "She said she's gonna get a restaurant job up there."

"They'll kill her the first day."

I log off the POS computer and let Louis in.

"How you doing?" I ask, patting him on the back.

"Hanging in there, brother."

"Only five more hours to go."

"The moment I get home," Louis says, grinning, "I'm gonna smoke a major bowl."

"Whatever works for you," I chuckle.

Marijuana seems to be the waiter's drug of choice. Tonight, stressed-out servers worldwide will smoke up 20 percent of the global supply. Me? I'm more of a vodka man myself.

New Year's Eve shouldn't be a stressful holiday. Because customers are restricted to ordering a small number of holiday entrées, taking orders is a snap. There are no complicated menus to navigate or impossibly long lists of specials to memorize. Since The Bistro offers only three seatings on New Year's Eve—5:30, 7:30, and the last and most expensive at 10:00 P.M.—we're able to hustle the patrons along in a nice orderly fashion. What makes New Year's stressful is that customers are spending large amounts of money and expecting a superb restaurant experience in return. I don't blame them. But any waiter will tell you holidays are the worst time to eat in a restaurant. The sheer volume of customers guarantees that most kitchens will be pushed beyond their ability to produce a high-quality product. Think about all the orders of rubber chicken Francese you've eaten at two-hundred-person wedding receptions. Combine this phenomenon with harried waiters and owners cutting corners to milk profits, and you're looking at a very expensive and disappointing night out. Since shit rolls downhill, customers, in turn, usually vent their displeasure on the waiters.

Of course, every restaurant is different. The Bistro's kitchen is crazy busy, but food quality hasn't suffered—portion size has. When I delivered the plates to my first table of the evening, I noticed the salads had shrunk by half and the rack of lamb was missing a few pieces. The regular customers noticed and weren't afraid to bitch about it. I felt like telling them. "What did you expect? It's the same story all over the world tonight." Savvy customers avoid eating out on busy restaurant days, namely holidays and Saturday nights. Hey, the greatest meals I've ever had in a restaurant were on a quiet Tuesday or Wednesday evening.

Suddenly I feel a finger tap my shoulder. It's Saroya.

"There's a problem," she says.

Saroya is the longest-serving waiter at The Bistro after me. A curvy twenty-seven-year-old Nicaraguan woman with a winning smile and a pile of lustrous black hair, Saroya is mother to a very smart and friendly seven-year-old girl. In a bit of romantic restaurant drama, Saroya recently moved in with Armando, the Bistro's sous-chef. Since Armando is the owner's cousin, Saroya's acting like she's gotten some kind of promotion. These inter-restaurant romances are always problematic. I like Saroya, but I've always been aware that her sweet, smiling exterior hides a tough-as-nails personality. I guess you have to be tough to travel to America at nine months pregnant so your daughter can be born a U.S. citizen. I give her credit. She's taken excellent care of herself and raised a well-adjusted kid. I'm almost forty, and I've never come close to having a kid myself.

"What's up?" I ask.

"There's a man and a woman in the ladies' room," Saroya whispers, her Central American accent barely noticeable, "and they've been in there a *long* time."

"Lovely."

"Ladies are getting pissed they can't use the bathroom."

The Bistro has two small bathrooms that each can accommodate only one customer at a time. Occasionally a drunken couple let horniness get the better of them and try doing the wild thing in the restroom, often using the sink as a less-than-sturdy platform for their coital maneuvering. (I know a restaurant where a couple's amorous thrusting snapped the bathroom sink right off the wall.) Since the ladies' room is slightly bigger and nicer than the men's room, most customers have their alcohol-fueled trysts in there.

"I'll take care of it," I sigh. When did making people stop having sex become part of my job? I thought I had quit the seminary.

I walk over to the ladies' room and find several women anxiously waiting for their turn to get inside.

"They still in there?" I ask one of the women.

"Yes," she says unhappily.

I lean in close to the bathroom door. I don't hear the sounds one normally associates with sexual congress. Maybe they're finished. I knock on the door authoritatively.

"Is everything all right in there?" I ask through the door.

"We're fine," a tremulous female voice answers. In the background I swear I can hear a zipper being pulled up.

"We have several people who need to use the bathroom," I say, letting my words hang in the air.

"I'm coming," the woman replies. I'm sure no pun's intended.

A few seconds later the door opens and a man and woman stumble out. The lady's face is flushed, and her cocktail dress is rumpled. The boyfriend's pupils are red pinpricks floating on top of the whites of his eyes. He's high as a kite. The couple bow their heads, mutter embarrassed apologies, and take the walk of shame back to their table. Before I permit access to the ladies' room I take a quick peek to make sure everything's in order. Sometimes people forget to clean up after themselves. Noting with satisfaction that the bathroom sink's still attached to the wall, I reopen the commode to the female dining public.

"Can you believe that?" Saroya asks.

"I believe it," I reply.

"What happened?" Louis asks, joining the conversation.

"People having sex in the bathroom again," I say.

"Those two?" Louis snorts. "I saw them in the bathroom together earlier."

"You think they went two rounds in a restaurant bathroom?"

"Nah," Louis says. "I think they were snorting coke the first time around."

"Classy."

I look at my watch. My customer's entrées should be ready. I look back at the young couple's table. They're still holding hands. The girl's stopped crying. Two people sharing an ordinary moment in an ordinary restaurant. Sometimes everyday little moments become chances for people to start over. That young couple is having such a moment. A light's shining in the girl's eyes. Maybe she's gonna have that baby after all. Generational redemption's happening inside a busy restaurant, and I'm the only one seeing it.

When you work in a restaurant, there's never a shortage of interesting stories. Anyone can learn about people by watching them eat, but I think I'm especially attuned to what's going on around me. You see, I've always had a need to know people's *stories*. Part of that need developed early in life. Knowing what made people tick helped me to protect myself from them. I became adept at gauging other people's moods and emotions. To this day I often know what people are feeling before they know what they're feeling themselves. As a child I learned to pay attention to the timbre of people's voices, note the words they used, and watch how their faces and bodies moved as they talked. I developed a talent for spotting liars and forecasting emotional storms. My rector in the seminary told me I was adept at quickly reading horizons. But sometimes I misread those horizons and got into trouble. Sometimes I acted without possessing all the facts. Time on the analytical couch eventually stopped me from doing stupid things, but like military training from a long-ago war, my ear for dialogue and antenna for human emotions never went away. I still needed to know people's *stories*. And at The Bistro these stories can go from the sublime to the ridiculous in ten seconds flat. It's amazing what you see when you keep your eyes open.

Heading back toward the kitchen, I jink and dodge busboys carrying heavy trays of dirty dishes and roll under the beckoning stares searchlighting out of the customers' eyes. Pushing aside the thin curtains that separate the kitchen from the dining room, I plunge into a different world. Inside the kitchen's cramped confines tempers flare, Spanish music plays, aprons twirl, loud strong men yell, water splashes, and dishes clatter like oversize dimes on metal countertops. It's controlled bedlam.

"Where's my food?" I shout over the din.

"Fuck you," Armando yells from his post near the roaring-hot convection ovens. "Can't you see I'm busy?"

Armando is a good-looking, powerfully built man. Blessed with a handsome Roman nose and lean and narrow face, his lips are usually graced with a humorous smile. Even though he slaves sixty hours a week in the kitchen, Armando somehow manages to hit the gym almost every morning. Thanks to his exercise regimen, he can easily bench four hundred pounds. Luckily for me, in a world where the media lionize foul-mouthed and abusive chefs, Armando's blessed with a fairly pleasant disposition and a strong sense of professionalism. In all the years we've worked together I've seen him flip out only once. Trust me, that's miraculous for a chef.

"I fired the food twenty minutes ago!" I yell back.

Armando looks at the ticket, realizes I'm right, and flips me the bird.

"You're right this time," he yells.

"Don't give up your day job," I shout back.

"Whatever."

"Move it," yells Dawn, a young blond waitress tugging on my shirtsleeve.

I step back. Dawn, impatient as usual, angrily tries to wedge past me. At that moment a bus person slams into my back. I fall forward. Dawn reaches out to steady me, and we end up in one of those accidental embraces. For a moment I feel the fullness of her breasts rise and fall against my chest. Dawn, ever the flirt, tosses me a seductive flash through her blue eyes. Suddenly I want to kiss her. I wonder if she wants to kiss me. Then the thinking part of my brain reminds me that Dawn was wearing diapers when I was a junior in high school.

"You wanna dance or something?" Dawn asks, giving me the up-from-under look.

"My bad," I say hoarsely. The moment passes. Like two boxers in a clinch, we break.

Dawn grabs her stuff and runs out. Armando's still working on my entrées, so I decide to give myself a mental cold shower and grab a cup of coffee. As I sip thin brew out of a chipped porcelain cup I watch Fluvio as he maneuvers eight pans across a six-burner stove.

"Glad to see you remember how to cook, boss," I yell. "I thought you forgot how."

His face a mask of concentration, Fluvio doesn't display any indication that he hears me. Fluvio seldom does any of the cooking in his own restaurant. Since tonight's crazy he's been forced to strap on his apron and wade into the fight. After working his way up from the sadistic environment in which chefs are forged, Fluvio would much rather leave the heavy lifting in the kitchen to others. This is not unusual in the restaurant world. Have you ever wondered why the smocks of so many executive chefs are pristine white? Because they spend most of their time in the dining room hobnobbing with customers and lapping up the praise like honey. Several years after the publication of *Kitchen Confidential*, Anthony Bourdain's iconic exposé of what really goes on in restaurant kitchens, people are still shocked to discover that it's usually an illegal immigrant named Ramon who's doing all the cooking.

Fluvio's an interesting guy. Before he ever got near a cooking school he served in the Italian navy, did a stint as a bodyguard, worked in a pharmacy, and even tried his hand at club promoting. Along the way he blundered into a bad marriage, had two kids, and ended up getting divorced. After leaving Italy with his chef's diploma he cooked in exotic locations like Saudi Arabia, India, New York, and New Jersey. While he was working at Amici's, he met Bridget, a respiratory therapist from Long Island. Within eighteen months they decided to get married, open a restaurant, buy a house, and have a baby. Compressing all those life changes into such a short time frame would crush most people, but not Fluvio. Now, after six years at this location, he's getting restless. Just a couple of weeks ago he told me that he's thinking about opening another restaurant. I wouldn't put it past him.

Suddenly the pickup bell rings. My food's up. I balance the hot platters on my hands and arms and set out across the restaurant to deliver the entrées to my table. Halfway to my destination I realize I misjudged the temperature of the plates. I can feel the platter balanced on my forearm radiating intense heat through the sleeve of my shirt. As the pain begins to set my teeth on edge, I remember how the Shaolin students in the TV series *Kung Fu* would grip a burning-hot iron cauldron with their bare forearms and brand themselves with the raised relief of a tiger and a dragon as a final test before becoming full-fledged monks. If they can do it, I can do it.

"Be one with the pain, Grasshopper," I silently chant to myself. "Be one with the pain."

By the time I get to the table the nerve endings in my arm are screaming at me to let the plate crash to the floor. Since that would be a disaster, I let the pain wash over me and try not to let anyone see the agony crawling up my limb toward my face.

"Your entrées, ladies and gentlemen," I announce.

I gingerly place the dishes in front of the customers—ladies first, then the men. Of course the platter that's reverse branding the words MADE IN CHINA into my flesh belongs to the last person to be served. As I lift the plate off my arm I swear I hear something peel loose. My epidermis probably got fused to the polyester fabric of my uniform shirt.

After I make the appropriate polite noises I race to the beverage station and stick my arm into a wine bucket filled with ice water. After a minute I pull out my arm and roll back the dripping shirtsleeve to survey the damage. A nice red welt is forming on the top layers of my skin, similar to the burn you get when you're careless in handling a red-hot clothes iron. I know from experience that the burn will be visible on my arm for several days—my own Shaolin waiter mark. It's inevitable that anyone working in the restaurant business will pick up at least a couple of burns and scars along the way. I've got a bunch of them.

The second seating clears out, and the third seating piles in. This is the heavy-spending crowd. This is the seating that will make or break our evening. Of course, one of my two tops is a drunk regular squiring a hooker clad in a skimpy outfit that has no back and barely covers her breasts.

"Good evening, sir," I say. "Nice to see you again."

"Gimme a bottle of Dom Pérignon," the man says. He's a wealthy bond trader. He can afford it.

"Yes, sir."

"What's Don Perpignoooan?" the man's delightful companion replies.

"It's champagne, baby," the man says.

"Huh?" the woman says. Poor dear. She's out of her depth.

"It's like ginger ale with a kick," I explain.

"Oh good," the hooker says. "I like ginger ale."

I fetch the expensive bubbly from the walk-in fridge and pour it out. The man has obviously premedicated at home. Reeking of gin, he's already swaying in his chair as he fades in and out of consciousness. My God, I think to myself, this is straight out of the movie *Arthur*. I must be playing John Gielgud's part.

The hooker is stone-cold sober. As she looks at the New Year's menu her face knits itself into a scowl of incomprehension. "I don't know what any of this stuff is," she says, vulnerability leeching into her tough voice.

I look at the woman. She's younger than me by at least ten years, but the heavy makeup and overdone eyeliner make her look far older. All waiters who work in high-end restaurants deal with prostitutes from time to time. Usually they're expensive call girls who blend in with their high-society environs. This woman looks like she got picked up off the street. The bond trader could afford a less shopworn sex worker, but something tells me this guy likes them sad and desperate. I feel bad for this girl.

"Miss," I whisper, "what do you like to eat?"

"I like spaghetti and meatballs."

"We don't have meatballs, madam," I reply. "But we have whole wheat spaghetti with mushrooms and sausage." It's the rabbit sausage we're using for the wild boar special, but she doesn't need to know that.

"Is that with red gravy?" the hooker asks.

"Of course, madam." The dish is made with a white sauce, but switching to red will be no problem.

"Thank you," the hooker says. "I like sausage."

I'm sure no pun was intended here either.

The man and his date eat their dinner. I can tell the hooker's really enjoying her food. Good. At least she'll get something positive out of this whole sordid transaction. Her date, however, has drunk the entire bottle of Dom and is valiantly attempting to polish off a $700 bottle of wine. If I dug up a corpse and fed it to him he'd never know the difference.

I encounter many rich and successful people in my line of work. It never ceases to amaze me how people can be completely capable in one part of their lives but total fuckups in most of the others. This guy's a super-smart financial type—but he's also a desperate alcoholic who picks up whores. And believe me, I feel sorry for the whores. This guy's a pig.

Before you know it the clocks are striking midnight. The customers toot their paper horns, crank their noisemakers, and scream "Happy New Year" at the top of their lungs. I go around to wish all my tables a happy and healthy 2006. The woman with the fake pearls at table 26 just glares at me. That's odd. She's been smiling at me the whole time she's been here. Before I can think about it any further Louis liberates a bottle of champagne and starts passing it around.

"Happy New Year's, man," Louis says, offering me a swig.

"Happy New Year's, Louis," I say, taking the bottle out of his hands.

"How's our bond trader?"

"His blood alcohol must be, like, twenty-five percent." I say, taking a pull from the bottle. Ugh. Cheap domestic. I prefer Veuve Clicquot.

"He's not driving home, is he?"

"No," I say. "He always goes home in a cab."

"You think he'll be able to get that tiny pecker of his up when he gets home?"

"Probably not," I chuckle. For the hooker's sake, I'm happy.

By one-thirty the customers start going home. Of course, the bond trader and the hooker are the last to leave. I drop the man's $1,500 check. Half an hour later he still hasn't looked at it, preferring to babble profanities at his paid companion instead. I decide to move him along.

"May I take care of that for you, sir?" I ask, gesturing toward the check. (That's waiterspeak for "get out.")

"Uh, no," the drunk trader says. After a few clumsy seconds, he produces an American Express Black Card from his wallet.

"Bet you've never seen one of these before," he says, handing me the credit card. A Black Amex card feels like a piece of ceramic tile. They say you can use it to buy a yacht. I see at least one every week.

"No, sir," I gush. "I don't. They're very exclusive."

"Damn straight," the trader says, releasing a profane belch.

"I'll be right back, sir."

I run the man's Amex. It goes through. A $1,500 check is child's play for this guy. When I return to the table, the trader grabs the check holder out of my hand, inks in a tip, signs it with a flourish, and hands it back to me.

"Howdya like the tip I left ya?" he asks, eyeballing me strangely.

I open the check holder. On $1,500 the man's left me $250. Roughly a 17 percent tip. Of course, $250 is nothing to sneeze at, but this guy's been a consummate pain in the ass all year long. I want *more*.

I look into the man's drunken eyes and unleash my thousand-yard waiter stare. Over the years I've improved on Rizzo's version. Already a Bistro legend, my gaze has been known to frighten kitchen staff, scare waiters, silence screaming children, and cause movie stars to stutter. This guy has no chance.

"No," I say. "I don't like it."

The man stares at me openmouthed. After a few seconds he asks for the check holder, crosses out the old tip, and writes in a new one.

"Here ya go," he says.

"Thank you, sir," I reply.

"You're welcome, kid."

"Madam," I say, turning to the hooker, "have a happy and healthy New Year."

"Thanks, sweetie," the prostitute says.

"Yeah," the trader blurts. "Happy New Year's."

I walk to the back and open the check holder. The new tip? $500.

"Look at this," I say, showing the check to Louis.

"Holy shit," he exclaims. "How'd you do that?"

I smile cannily. "I'm not above rolling the occasional drunk."

"You're bad."

"The guy's a pain in the ass all year. Maybe it's his way of making up for it."

"You might be right."

"Now I've got to divvy up my tips with Inez," I sigh. "I've made, like, twelve hundred dollars. What's she at?"

"About five hundred," Louis says.

"Bitch."

Finally, The Bistro's empty. Because I earned the most tips I sit on my ass and drink champagne while watching the other servers do the postshift cleanup. I see to it that Inez works extra hard. By the time everyone finishes and gets his or her tips from Fluvio, I'm half in the bag. Despite the drag Inez put on my earning potential, I still made a ton of money. After Fluvio locks up we head over to a nearby nightclub to continue the New Year's festivities. Inez and I, forgetting our earlier rancor, cha-cha on the nightclub's afterthought of a dance floor. That's the nice thing about being a waiter—what happens at work usually stays at work. Too bad I can't dance for shit.

"So what you gonna do this new year?" Inez asks me as we flop down at the bar for another martini.

"I have no idea," I reply.

"What about your Web site?" she asks. "How's that going?"

"Waiter Rant?"

"Yeah."

"I enjoy writing it," I reply. "It's cheaper than psychotherapy."

Inez laughs. "Every waiter should have their head examined."

"Tell me about it."

"So," Inez asks, "you think the Web site will lead to something else?"

"Something else?"

Inez leans in close to me, her body suddenly resonating seriousness.

"I've read your stuff," she says. "You're a good writer."

"Thanks."

"Maybe you should think about writing as a career. It could be your ticket out of here."

"Maybe," I reply quietly.

Inez squeezes my arm. "Stop waiting tables! You've got to do something else with that big brain of yours."

"Well," I reply, trying to change the subject, "all this big brain wants to do now is get drunk."

"Promise me you'll try," Inez says. "Stop working for Fluvio; he doesn't appreciate you."

"C'mon. Fluvio's not that bad."

"Promise me you'll write a book one day."

"I will."

The bartender sets drinks down in front of us.

"*Salud,*" Inez says. "To my friend, the writer."

"Here's looking at you, kid."

The night drags on. I drink myself stupid. By the time I stumble home it's almost morning. As I creep through my sleeping building the rattling of my key in the lock echoes through the empty hallway like the tattling cry of a small child. As I step inside my apartment the only sound that greets me is the whistle of steam escaping from the release valve of an ancient radiator. The apartment is empty. My ex-girlfriend Allie lived here until she left me two years ago. We still share joint custody of our dog, Buster. He's not here tonight either. Trudging through the silence, I go into the kitchen and wash down two prophylactic aspirins with a bottle of water. The Bistro's open on New Year's Day, and I have to be at work in eight hours. The last thing I need is waking up dehydrated and hungover.

As I drink my water I look out my kitchen window. The sun is already coloring the gray edges of the cold eastern sky. I wonder if I'll be waiting tables this time next year. The thought troubles me. Waiting tables was supposed to be a temporary solution until I figured out what I wanted to do with my life. Now I'm entering my seventh year in the restaurant industry. I guess I'm still struggling to figure out what I'm going to be when I grow up.

I finish my water and go into my bedroom. I peel off my garlic- and grease-permeated clothes and toss them into a corner. I should take a shower, but I'm too tired. Smelling slightly like truffle oil, I slip under the covers and lay my head on the pillow. Just before my conscious mind crosses over into oblivion, I remember I forgot to bring the lady at table 26 her third cosmopolitan.

No wonder she stopped smiling at me.

CHAPTER 5

Paupery

It's an early afternoon two weeks later. The lunch crowd, what there was of it, has come and gone. I'm sitting at a back table reading the newspaper when I notice Beth, the lunch waitress, staring glumly into her $3 double caramel mocha latte.

"What's the matter?" I ask her. "Lunch tips that bad?"

"I've got a lot on my mind," Beth replies sullenly.

"Anything serious?"

"Bills," she says.

"Oh."

"It's almost the end of the month, and I'm broke as usual."

I nod sympathetically. Been there, done that.

"I'm so pissed at myself," Beth mutters angrily. "I'm always short because I spend my money on stupid shit."

For a brief second I think about telling Beth how I blew $500 at a strip club in under fifty minutes. I wisely reconsider. What happens in Atlantic City stays in Atlantic City.

"We've all done stupid things with our money," I say instead.

"Yeah?" Beth says. "How's this for stupid? I bought a three-hundred-dollar bottle of Grey Goose at Butter last night."

"Three hundred for a bottle of vodka?" I say. "You can buy Goose for forty bucks in a liquor store."

"My friends wanted to sit at a table," Beth says. "And if you want a table at Butter, you have to buy a bottle. You just can't order drinks."

"That's insane."

"That's New York City," Beth says. "And now I don't have enough money to pay my cell phone bill."

I look at the cell phone holstered on Beth's hip. It's a sophisticated slab of plastic sporting a 2.0 megapixel camera, pullout keyboard, Internet access, MP3 player, and an oversize color screen. The gizmo even lets you download TV shows off the Web. It's a very cool and very expensive toy. I used to have a cell phone, but I got rid of it after paying one too many usurious wireless bills. My friends, dismayed they actually have to talk to me instead of communicating by text message, snipe that I'm some kind of Luddite al-Qaeda yearning for a return to the letter-writing days of the nineteenth century. I used to dismiss them as technology junkies until I realized that proclaiming you don't have a cell phone is like saying you watch only public television. While I'm smugly proud of my disconnection from the modern communications grid, I don't want to sound like some Birkenstock-shod intellectual telling everyone how "evolved" he is. Now I just keep my mouth shut and save money. $2.50 for a ringtone? You're smoking crack.

"Can't you just use your regular telephone?" I ask. "I haven't had a cell phone for years, and I've survived."

"I only have this phone," Beth says, running her fingers over it protectively. "I've never had a landline."

"Oh."

"God," Beth sighs. "I hate being broke all the time."

Even though Beth's in a bad mood, I still enjoy being near her. That's probably because she's one of the most beautiful girls I've ever met. A twenty-three-year-old brunette with piercing black eyes and a slender, graceful body, Beth's at that stage in her life when she's navigating the bumpy transition from immaturity to adulthood. Although she has a wild and impulsive side that gets her into trouble, Beth also possesses a level of wisdom and insight uncommon in people her age. When she was nineteen, her best friend, Alice, was killed in a car wreck. The grieving parents, figuring Beth would know their daughter's tastes, asked her to pick out Alice's burial clothes. Beth went one step further and did Alice's makeup at the funeral home. There aren't too many people, at any age, who are capable of that much courage and tenderness. When Beth told me about what she did for her friend, I was instantly captivated by her. Here, I thought, was someone beautiful on the inside and out. Obviously I took an immediate liking to Beth. She's the first girl I ever met who made me wish I was ten years younger.

But I'm not surprised Beth's behind the financial eight ball. When you factor in her $3 cups of coffee and $300 bottles of grain alcohol, it doesn't take an accountant to figure out why Beth's strapped—she's living beyond her means.

"Whenever money's tight, I try economizing," I gently suggest. "Renting movies at the library, cooking at home, stuff like that."

"Yeah," Beth murmurs. "I should try that."

"Drink the coffee here," I say, nodding at her caffeinated chemistry experiment. "Treat yourself to Starbucks once or twice a week. Think of all the money you'll save."

Beth looks at me in horror. "I can't give up my double caramel mocha lattes!"

"Listen," I say, shrugging. "I used to buy cocktails at Café American after every shift. Then one day I realized I was spending a hundred dollars a week on vodka. Like your lattes, it adds up."

"That's four hundred dollars a month!" Beth squeaks. "That's more than my car payment!"

"That's right," I answer. "But how much are you spending on coffee and nightclubs?"

"Too much," Beth says. "When I woke up this morning, I realized I had worked two days to buy one bottle of vodka."

"Messed up, ain't it?"

"Yeah."

"Now I only treat myself to a nice bar once a week. I enjoy it more and save money."

"So how do you reward yourself at the end of the day?" Beth asks.

"I have a little bar at home."

Beth laughs. "Really?"

"It's cheaper to buy the stuff in a liquor store," I say. "Unless you're an alcoholic, it's the more economical choice."

"Do you make yourself dirty martinis?"

"With blue cheese–stuffed olives and everything."

"You're so weird," Beth says.

"Just try economizing."

"Are you gonna start giving waiters financial advice on your Web site now?" Beth asks, half seriously.

"I should," I reply. "Waiters tend to be irresponsible, broke asses."

Beth giggles, but only because it's true. Waiters, for the most part, are terrible with money. I know that sounds like a terrible overgeneralization, but, tell me, how many hedge fund managers and financial planners do you see waiting tables? Let's be real, if waiters were super-financial types, they wouldn't be waiters. I include myself in that generalization.

"So why *are* waiters so bad with money?" Beth asks. "Have you written about that on your Web site?"

"Not yet," I reply. "But I have a theory I'm working on."

"Let's hear it."

"Waiting tables is like gambling," I announce dramatically.

"It is not!"

"Hear me out," I reply. "Have you ever played slot machines?"

"Sure."

"Enjoy it?"

"Not really," Beth says. "I never could see the point."

"But I bet you saw hundreds of little old ladies dumping bucketfuls of quarters into those machines."

"Oh my God," Beth says. "Those one-armed bandits acted like they were in a trance or something."

"Have you ever wondered why slot machines are so successful?"

"No. Why are they?"

"Because slot machines operate on the principle of intermittent rewards," I explain. "When you pull the handle on a slot machine, the odds are good that you're going to lose. But occasionally you win back a few coins. When you get a reward, you feel good, so you pour more money into the machine in order to enjoy that winning feeling again. Psychologists have proven that this combination of losing coupled with an occasional, random win has a powerful reinforcing influence on behavior. Gamblers get swept up in the drama and start thinking that the *next* roll of the dice, the *next* turn of the card, or the *next* pull of the slot's going to be the big winner. Casinos love that shit."

"So what does this have to do with waiting tables?" Beth asks.

"Let me answer that question with a question," I reply. "As a waiter, do you make money on a predictable schedule?"

"Almost never."

"Me neither," I reply. "That's because too many factors influence how much money you can make in one night. The weather might turn bad and scare away the customers. You could get a run of lousy tippers, have several reservations fail to show up, or have some idiot manager schedule too many waiters on the floor. There are evenings when you don't even make the bus fare to go home."

"I've had many nights like that," Beth admits.

"But you've also had nights where you've made a killing," I say.

"That's true."

"And can you predict when you're gonna make the big money?"

"Never."

"Now, I've seen servers make ten dollars on a Saturday night and three hundred on a Wednesday lunch. So have you."

"You're right."

"So you see," I explain. "Waiters are exposed to intermittent rewards just like the one-arm bandits. While it's not exactly gambling, waiting tables can be like playing slot machines. You never know what you're going to win when you pull the handle. Sometimes you make zilch; sometimes you hit the jackpot."

"That's true," Beth murmurs.

"And waiters can get hooked on that dynamic just like a guy playing the ponies," I say. "How many times have you heard someone say, 'I'd like to quit the restaurant business, but I'm addicted to the money'?"

"I hear that all the time."

"I don't think servers get addicted to the money," I say. "The money can be good, but it's not *that* good. But we can get addicted to *how* we make the money. You can have several shitty nights in a row, start sweating the bills, and then, at the last moment, you can make all the money you need in a single shift. We can start getting caught up in the drama of it all. Just like a gambler, we start thinking that the *next* shift or the *next* table will be the big payday."

"I'm beginning to see what you mean," Beth says.

"I knew a guy who was a degenerate gambler," I say. "Whenever he won at the track, he'd forget all about his earlier losses, about the wife who was leaving him or the unsavory people he borrowed money from. Whenever he won, he always thought his life was on the upswing. When he won, he thought everything was going to get better."

"Did it?" Beth asks.

"No," I reply. "He kept losing money and one day he just 'disappeared.'"

"Do you think he's dead?"

"Maybe."

"Wow."

"But that's not my point," I continue. "How many times have you had a dozen bad-tipping customers in a row but then forget all about them because some crazy rich guy slipped you a five-hundred-dollar tip?"

"I've experienced that," Beth says, smiling knowingly.

"We all have," I continue. "We forget the cheap customers and focus on the big score. Waiters bitch about being waiters when they're not making money but sing the job's praises when they're flush. So what if I don't have health care? So what if I only made fifty dollars in three days? I just made five hundred bucks! Throw in a propensity for substance abuse and loving the nightlife, and you can see why some waiters get sucked into the lifestyle."

"I think your theory has some merit," Beth admits.

"I'm still working out the kinks," I say. "But think of all the servers you've met who want to stop waiting tables but still do it, year after year."

"Oh my God," Beth says. "I hope I don't end up like that."

"Just as long as you don't end up like Double Dip Dan," I say.

"Who?"

"You never heard of Double Dip Dan?"

"Is he the guy who ate off the customers' plates?"

"The very same," I reply.

"Gross."

"I actually saw him pull a half-eaten lamb shank out of a bus tub and start gnawing on it."

"Ew!" Beth says, shuddering. "That's so disgusting."

"Hey, when you're broke and hungry . . ."

"Didn't Dan make decent money here?"

"He did," I reply. "But he spent it on drugs and whores. Eventually he ended up sleeping in a friend's garage and washing his work uniform in the prep-kitchen sink."

"Now *that's* broke ass," Beth says.

"Tell me about it."

"At least I'm not that bad."

"Keep buying three-hundred-dollar bottles of vodka at Butter, and you will be."

"Don't be such an asshole," Beth says.

"That brings up the other part of my theory," I say. "Waiters like to think they're on the same economic level as their clientele."

"Oh no," Beth groans. "I feel another lecture coming on."

"Think about it, Beth," I say. "We spend a great deal of our lives around fine food and wine. It's normal that we develop a taste for it ourselves. An occupational hazard of waiting tables is that we develop foie gras tastes but operate on liverwurst budgets."

"Sometimes we can't even afford the liverwurst," Beth snorts.

"That's because working in high-end restaurants sometimes numbs us to the reality of how expensive these places actually are. It's like working at the U.S. Mint and thinking you can just take some of the green stuff lying around home with you."

"True."

"Can you afford to eat here?" I ask.

"Not often."

"I've only eaten here as a customer two times in six years. But doesn't it grate on you to watch people wolf down five hundred dollars' worth of food like it's ten-dollar pizza?"

"All the time."

"It's like watching a rich kid throw away a toy you desperately want but your parents can't afford to buy. I think waiters try protecting their egos by refusing to acknowledge some things are out of their grasp monetarily. I mean, how many times have you seen servers bitch about buying a new pair of work shoes but brag how they spent three hundred dollars at a restaurant?"

Beth picks up her foot and shows me the hole in her left shoe. "I guess I'm one of those people," she chuckles.

"Don't feel bad," I say. "The pants I'm wearing have a hole in the crotch."

"Good thing you're wearing an apron."

"Amen."

"You don't go to nightclubs," Beth asks. "Where do you waste money?"

"Well, after seeing foo-foo cuisine all night," I reply, "all I want is a blue-cheese burger and a beer at a diner."

"You're such a Jersey boy," Beth says.

"Hey," I reply. "Whether it's from Per Se or Mel's, what you eat ends up in the same place twenty-four hours later."

Beth laughs. "Thanks for the visual."

"No problem."

"Say," Beth says, looking around the empty restaurant. "The place is dead. Is it all right if I leave now? I'd like to be home before my boyfriend gets back from work."

"You two gonna go out and blow three hundred bucks on vodka?" I ask.

"No," Beth laughs. "We'll try being fiscally prudent."

"Good girl."

Beth gives me her cash-out. As I rifle through it, I think about how the system that pays waiters sometimes contributes to their poverty. Most servers take home all their earnings in cash at the end of their shift. For example, if you make $50 in cash tips and $100 in credit card gratuities, after taking care of the support staff (tipping bus people, bartender, food runner, and paying bribes to the hostess) you get to keep about $120. That money goes directly into your pocket at the end of the night. Because it's in your pocket, it's easy to spend it before you get home. It sickens me to think how many times I've blown my hard-earned money on fancy cocktails and late-night snacks. Ugh.

A good waiter trick is to consolidate all your take-home money into fifty- and hundred-dollar bills. I've often noticed that I'll spend a pocketful of twenties faster than I will a hundred-dollar bill. Something about Benjamin Franklin staring back at you provides a moment of fiscal pause. Another tactic is to remove $20 from the night's take for fun money or gas, and then earmark the rest for deposit in the bank. I used to be such a regular cash depositor at my local bank office that, after months of depositing small bills, my usual teller began to suspect I worked as an exotic dancer. When she asked what club I danced in, I laughed and told her to get a new eyeglass prescription. I never was or ever will be Chippendale material.

Luckily for me, Fluvio changed the system for paying his waiters a couple of years ago. After doing it the old-fashioned way he changed over to a system that lets us take home our cash tips at night, but pays our credit card tips by check at the end of the week. Getting the bulk of our compensation in a large weekly check reduced the chances that Fluvio's waiters would blow their money on pharmaceuticals, grain alcohol, and stupidity.

At first we all bitched about the change. After Fluvio explained the benefits of his system, however, we realized it was superior. You see, there's a big tax problem with how waiters get paid. Remember the tip-out? The money waiters pay out to support staff? If I make a $100 in tips and tip out $20, I'm actually making $80, right? Many establishments make me pay taxes on the entire $100! That's right. I pay taxes on a huge percentage of money I don't get to keep. I'm paying the bus people's payroll taxes! It's unfair, but that's how it's done in many places. Restaurant finances are notoriously shady. With Fluvio's new system we paid taxes only on what we actually took home. If I made $100 and tipped out $20, I was taxed on only $80. That's a tremendous difference. Fluvio also instituted a very transparent payroll system, at least as far as the servers were concerned. After every shift a waiter writes down his or her tips in a ledger that's accessible to all the staff. Everyone, including the bus people, can see how much money everyone's making. The bus people know they aren't being cheated, and the staff can double-check their weekly paycheck against the ledger. There's a system of checks and balances. If you've ever suffered under the Byzantine payroll system of a dishonest restaurateur, you know what I'm talking about is very cool. The other benefit of Fluvio's system is that I have to go to the bank less often. This may disappoint my nearsighted male-stripper-loving teller, but that's okay—I'll let her keep her fantasy.

As always, Beth's cash-out is in order, and I let her go home.

Louis and Saroya show up for work, but by eight o'clock it becomes obvious the evening's going to be a bust. The Bistro's almost empty, and the reservations have already eaten and left. Business is bad. Louis and Saroya beg me to send them home. If there's one thing these two hate, it's standing idle in an empty restaurant.

Since I have to stay and lock up I send them home. Half an hour later a party of fifteen people walks in the door. Ordering premium cocktails, fine wine, and expensive food, these polite, well-mannered people turn out to be dream customers. Their bill is massive, and so is their tip—almost $500. After tipping out the bus I make $400 on the table.

The bus people and I, happy with our good fortune, clean up the restaurant and call it a night. As I'm locking up I realize I made a nice chunk of change today. I can't wait to tell Louis and Saroya what they missed. They'll be squirming with jealousy. It's a restaurant truism that the waiter who stays late always leaves with the most cash. Tonight I was that late waiter, and the table gods smiled on me. I experience a pulse of waiter "good-money high." Maybe I should play the lottery tomorrow. When you're hot, you're hot.

As I start heading home I toy with the idea of calling in sick tomorrow but dismiss it. That's another curious waiter dynamic. After they score a big payday many waiters feel compelled to take an extra day off. Instead of saving their lucky money, they use it to fund a mental health day. I can understand. This job doesn't offer paid vacation. Waiters have to make do on their own.

I know from experience, however, that my little waiter high isn't going to last. I know I'm going to be back here tomorrow, doing the exact same thing I've been doing for seven years, and probably making shit money to boot. Servers almost never make killer money two days in a row. The table gods are fickle bitches.

I shake my head. How pathetic is it to have a theological system based on a pantheon of imaginary restaurant gods? Maybe my waiter truisms are defense mechanisms to stave off my anxiety about being in a dead-end job. I'm pushing forty. Very few people have the talent to make professional waiting a career. At some point even the best waiter moves into management or takes an ownership stake in a place of his or her own. If I'm honest, I can't imagine doing anything in the restaurant business ever again. I need to be funding a retirement plan and be happy with what I'm doing. I need to get out. But doing what?

For a while I dreamed of opening up a coffee shop. Not a Starbucks knockoff, mind you, but a classy, homey place, with a real fireplace, overstuffed chairs, cool jazz, and coffee made by human beings, not machines. I investigated business loans, scouted locations, and watched several java entrepreneurs, noting their successes and failures. The failures got to me. I saw several shops, places where the owners put their hearts and souls into the endeavor, fail. It was painful to go into their empty shops and watch them stare out the windows, praying for customers. I tried putting myself in their shoes, imagining I was the one with business loans and the friends rooting for me, only to watch my dreams collapse.

For many reasons, I'm terribly afraid of failure. Having so many jobs yanked out from under me hasn't helped either. I've become fearful that I'll never succeed at anything. The Bistro has been the most stable job I've ever had. What started out as a safe place to hide until I figured out what to do with my life has become a career. Somewhere along the line I lost the will to try to do something else. That's where I give guys like Fluvio credit. At least he has the *cojones* to put it out there and try making something for himself. My mom and dad seem to think that my blog may be an opportunity. They think I have what it takes to be a writer. Maybe that's true, but the publishing world isn't exactly beating a path to my door. When the site got popular, I tried hustling T-shirts and coffee mugs through an online store like every other blogger out there. The idea tanked. If I'm honest with myself, I'm worried my blog and my writing's just another thing in my life that won't work out.

My good-money mood evaporates, just as I expected. Suddenly I feel very lonely. Aggravated, I think about going to the bar down the street for a cocktail. I decide against it. I need something more distracting than a drink. Half an hour later I walk into a loud bar, the kind of place where the bartenders wear short shorts and the entertainment's provided by scantily clad girls twirling themselves around a pole.

By the time I finish my first overpriced martini, the nearly nude sharks are already circling around me. One of the sharks starts rubbing my neck. Next thing I know she's sitting in my lap and I'm buying her a drink.

"Wanna go in the back?" she whispers into my ear. Glitter sparkles on her cheeks.

I look over at the "Champagne Lounge," the place where girls pretend to like you for twenty bucks and the length of a song.

"And what happens in the back?" I ask, looking all innocent.

"I do a little dance for you," the girl says. Her accent's Eastern European.

"You any good?"

The girl laughs, her dyed red curls tumbling around her face. "I'm the best, baby."

The girl's very pretty. When I think about it, she lives on tips just like me. I idly think about inquiring into her money-management practices but decide against it. She manages her money by tucking it inside a G-string.

"Let's go then," I say, beyond caring at this point.

The girl leads me by the hand into the back. I told you I spent my money on stupid shit.

CHAPTER 6

The Box of Chocolates Saint

Since we're already talking about spending money on stupid shit that won't get you laid, let's talk about Valentine's Day.

If you ask me, Valentine's Day is one of the biggest scams going. Guys still paying off the baubles they bought wives and girlfriends at Christmas and Hanukkah are frightened by Madison Avenue into believing their sweethearts will transform into frigid harpies if they don't shell out for some jewelry and round-trip tickets to an exotic island. Smelling blood in the water, restaurants replace their regular menus with "special" menus that give price gouging a good name. The foods many kitchens prepare on that holiday are often items they make only a couple of times a year. If your chef hasn't had the practice of making the same dish day in and day out, your entrée's probably going to taste like rubber osso buco. If you've ever had a crappy meal on Saint Valentine's Day, you know I'm right.

Just like New Year's, many restaurants get hit with the unscrupulous stick every February 14. They hyperinflate their profit margins by shrinking portions, using cheaper ingredients, and masking inferior cuts of meat and fish with creamy or oversalted sauces. If everything you eat tastes like it's been soaked in black truffle oil, then someone's pulling shit somewhere.

And don't get me started about the pain-in-the-ass seating arrangements. Normally restaurants have several tables designated as two tops. On Valentine's Day *every* table is a two top. Restaurant floor plans are not laid out to accommodate an onslaught of romantic couples comfortably. Imagine your dining room. Pretend you have a table that seats eight people. Chop up that table up into four smaller ones and then try cramming four couples into them. Now imagine waiters, customers, bus people, and chefs tramping their grease-sodden shoes all over your carpet. Your dining room just got awfully crowded, didn't it? Ah, Grasshopper, you're beginning to glimpse the magnitude of the problem.

Then there's the never-ending drama to get the best table in the house. There are only a few best tables in any restaurant—especially on Valentine's Day. A smart option would be to remove several tables from the floor plan. Sure, you reduce the number of paying customers, but at least the kissy-faced couples will have room to breathe. Try suggesting this to a restaurant owner, however, and he'll look at you like you're smoking dope. If anything, he's trying to jam in *more* tables. Every year Fluvio drags several tables out of storage and tries wedging them into places they really shouldn't go. Every year I ask him if he's going to put a table in the ladies' room.

On Valentine's Day you're going to be sitting check by jowl with the couple next to you. Deal with it. And don't bitch about where you're sitting. You're probably lucky to get a table in the first place. The primo spots have been reserved for big spenders, big tippers, or people who've planned *way* in advance. Most Valentine's Day reservations, surprisingly, are made at the last minute. If you have a suboptimal table and try bullying me into giving you a window seat, the hostess has got the cell phone numbers of eight desperate guys who'll be happy to grab your chair before the heat from your ass has had a chance to dissipate. Go ahead—make my Valentine's Day.

It's sad, really, when you think about it. Valentine's Day used to be a much simpler, low-pressure affair. Two thousand years ago it started out as a feast day to honor the Christian martyr Valentine. It seems the pagan Roman emperor asked Valentine, a priest, to renounce his faith. Showing an appalling lack of survival skills, Valentine refused. The emperor, who I suspect was a bad tipper, rewarded Valentine's intransigence by having him beaten senseless with clubs and beheaded. While poor Valentine's bones moldered in the catacombs, he somehow ended up becoming the patron saint of engaged couples and happy marriages. If you've ever planned a wedding, you know Valentine caught a tough gig.

Time marched on, and, like many Catholic traditions, Valentine's feast got hacked by preexisting Roman mythology. Somehow the tradition of Cupid got folded into the whole mess, and the greeting-card industry, knowing a good idea when it saw one, revved up the papyrus. I know that the real history of Valentine's Day is a bit more complicated than that, but you've got to feel sorry for its progenitor. Valentine got the shit beat out of him, his head cut off, and what was his reward? Becoming the "box of chocolates" saint? That blows.

Wasn't Valentine's Day easier thirty years ago? When I was a kid, Valentine's Day meant giving Mom a box of Russell Stover candy and bringing homemade cards to all the kids in my first-grade class. Now Valentine's Day is an important profit center smack dab in the middle of winter. Candy companies, restaurants, and florists depend on this holiday to help keep them in the black. A few weeks before V-Day the department stores start revving up the commercials, and men everywhere start believing they have the ability to pick out tasteful lingerie for their wives. (You don't. Just give a gift certificate.) Restaurants start running ads reminding procrastinating men to make their reservations before it's too late.

And that's just fine with me. While I bemoan the commercialization of poor Valentine's untimely demise, I've got a living to make. Remember, I'm a waiter. Don't be fooled by my occasional bursts of sentimentality. I can be one mercenary bastard. The period between February and April is slow, and my bank account's hurting. Be warned, I'm going to do my damnedest to separate you lovebirds from your money.

When the fateful day arrives, I show up to The Bistro a few hours early. Fortified with two cups of Starbucks and a Red Bull, I'm raring to go. I want to get a head start on my prep work and review the seating plan with the hostess. Before I can even take off my coat the house phone rings.

"Where's the hostess?" I shout. I don't want to pick up the phone.

"She's not here yet," yells Imelda, one of the bus girls.

"She was supposed to be here at noon!"

Imelda just shrugs. The phone keeps ringing. I know what the caller wants already. I take a deep breath, sigh, and pick up the receiver.

"The Bistro," I answer, "how may I help you?"

"I need a reservation for tonight," a desperate male voice rasps over a cell phone.

I look at the computer, where we track our reservations. "I have an opening at five-thirty, sir," I say. "And another at ten."

"That's it?" the man answers incredulously. "I want something around seven."

"I'm sorry, sir," I reply. "That's all I have open. If you'd give me your phone—"

"Listen," the man says, "you need to squeeze me in at seven."

"I'm sorry—"

"This is Mr. Green," the man barks. "You remember me? I'm a friend of Fluvio's."

"Oh yes, Mr. Green," I lie. "I remember you. Please hang on one moment."

I put Mr. Green on hold and call up his name on the Open Table reservation terminal. The computer's database enables us to keep track of patrons' birthdays, anniversaries, favorite waiters, and a never-ending list of special requests and behavioral oddities. There's even a section euphemistically titled "customer notes." This is where the waitstaff get a chance to leave feedback/warnings about the customers. Sometimes the notes describe patrons as great tippers or contain useful information about food allergies or table preferences. Occasionally the notes read "cheap tipper," "takes forever to eat," or, less professionally, "customer's an asshole."

Despite the juvenile pranks, the reservation terminal's a serious piece of equipment. There's enough sensitive information locked inside its digital memory to give an identity thief a raging hard-on. Because The Bistro maintains mailing lists and reward programs, our computer system is a treasure trove of personal data—right down to the customers' home addresses and credit card numbers. It isn't just my restaurant doing this. Reservation and computer systems are prevalent throughout the industry. Can you imagine your Amex number being guarded by a nineteen-year-old hostess? If I ever have to flee to a country that doesn't have an extradition treaty with the United States, I'll have no problem creating a new identity.

Now the computer's telling me Mr. Green's record is pretty shabby. The notes describe him as a "difficult customer" who's sent his food back several times and refused to pay for it. Even more damning, he hasn't shown up for half the reservations he's made. Now he wants a table at the last minute on Valentine's Day? No way, pal. For every action there's an equal and opposite reaction.

"I'm *so* sorry, Mr. Green," I say. "I have nothing available."

"What?" Mr. Green sputters. "But I need reservation!"

"I'm sorry."

"Let me speak to Fluvio!"

"It's Valentine's Day, sir," I reply calmly. "As you can imagine, Fluvio's very busy."

"So you're not gonna give me a reservation?"

"I'm afraid I cannot."

"My wife's gonna kill me."

"I'm sorry, sir," I repeat for the umpteenth time.

Mr. Green unceremoniously hangs up. I smile to myself. Restaurant karma strikes again.

Mr. Green's your typical yuppie food Nazi living inside a cocoon of self-entitlement. He probably thinks that shortchanging waiters and insulting chefs is a divine right. I was never a big fan of divine right philosophy. Today Mr. Green is shit out of luck. I actually have a table free at seven, but I'm saving that for a good customer. Unfortunately, Mr. Green's never going to learn how his past behaviors cost him the table. It's not a good idea to let patrons know they're on the receiving end of vindictive waiter thunderbolts; they tend to get all indignant. I prefer to think about a blue-balling Mr. Green sleeping on his couch and wondering why he couldn't get a reservation. Customers seldom make the connection between bad behaviors and not getting the service to which they think they're entitled. Here's a dining out tip: if you *never* get the table you want at your favorite restaurant, or if reservations on a special day are *always* hard to come by, someone at that restaurant doesn't like *you*. Think about it. Review your history as a customer. Do you leave good tips? Are you a polite person? Are you an obnoxious drunk? Believe it or not, people often refuse to do business with people they don't like. Just because you have money doesn't mean you get to ride the ride. I know that's irrational and no way to run a business, but economics tells us that business isn't always about numbers. Businesses are run by people, and sometimes people are just plain crazy. Think about your workplace and the unprofessional shenanigans that occur there. Not everything that happens at work is dictated by the bottom line. So don't be surprised that chronically bad customers end up getting bad service. It may not happen right away, but it will happen eventually.

Two hours after Mr. Green's call The Bistro starts filling up with customers. I look at my watch and groan. It's only five o'clock. The realization that I'm going to spend eight busy hours on my feet hits me full force, and suddenly I'm glad I bought that new pair of shoes. I go to the kitchen and pour myself another espresso. I'm drinking way too much coffee. As I sip my demitasse I remember the time I started having heart palpitations and ended up in the ER. The doc told me I was fine—just lay off the caffeine. That doctor probably never waited tables.

Celine, the blond hostess who always reminds me of a 1940s movie starlet, pokes her head into the kitchen. "Table twenty-six just got seated," she says. "Can you get them out in an hour fifteen?"

"My dear," I reply, "I'm the king of turning and burning."

"I hope so," Celine says, walking away. "We're overbooked."

"Hey," Armando, the chef, calls out. "Don't forget to push the dessert special tonight."

Armando whipped up a special dessert for V-Day—a heart-shaped raspberry-filled chocolate ganache cake for two. It's covered in tacky red icing.

"Hey, Armando," I shoot back. "Why didn't you make an anatomically correct cake this year?"

"Huh."

"You know, Armando," I said, pointing at the cake. "Make it look like the Sacred Heart."

"You're sick," Armando replies.

"Blood dripping from it. The works."

"You're gonna burn in hell."

"You know," I continue, "the official symbol of Valentine's Day shouldn't be a heart."

"What should it be?"

"How about a pair of testicles in a jar?"

"I don't think I can make a dessert that looks like that," Armando says.

"Aw, c'mon," I reply. "You're a talented guy."

"Maybe something with chocolate-covered cherries . . ." Armando muses aloud.

As I head over to my new table I run through the day's specials in my head. Fluvio, to his credit, doesn't replace The Bistro's regular menu with some kind of Valentine's Day scam. Sure, we have some nice specials—lamb shank osso buco, wild boar in a mushroom sauce, and potato-encrusted halibut, but, unlike New Year's, customers can get away with ordering a cheap bowl of spaghetti Pomodoro if they want to.

My new arrivals at table 26 are intently studying their menus. As I draw closer I notice they don't look like The Bistro's usual clientele. The man's wearing a baseball cap and what looks like his best denim work shirt. His eyes threaten to pop out of his head as he looks at the prices. His companion's a very pretty lady, but she looks like she's wearing a reincarnated bridesmaid's gown. Her overdone makeup gives her face a startled expression. As the couple whisper back and forth about how expensive everything is, I groan again. It's not an uncommon occurrence for people to get up and leave at this point. I remember my parents yanking my brother and me out of a restaurant because it was too expensive. It was years ago; my parents were young and struggling, and money was tight. I remember feeling embarrassed. Don't get me wrong, I didn't grow up destitute, but I was at the age when you start realizing your parents aren't all-powerful. My young brain was beginning to comprehend that money was very important and that my family didn't have as much of it as other people did. I never forgot that moment. To this day, I always empathize with diners who, for whatever reason, realize they're out of their depth.

"Good evening," I say, "and welcome to The Bistro."

"Hi," the man says. His date looks up at me nervously.

"May I get something for you and your lovely companion to drink?" I ask.

"Uh," the man says, "we're not sure if we're gonna eat here."

"It's a little expensive," his girlfriend says.

"I completely understand, madam," I say, dropping my voice to a conspiratorial whisper. "I can't even afford to eat here."

The man and woman laugh.

"But if you decide to stay," I continue, "I'm sure I can help you pick out some nice entrées."

The man and woman look at each other across the table. A quiet decision's made. They're staying.

"What kind of beers you got?" the man asks. I tell him what we have.

"No Budweiser?"

"Try a Moretti, sir," I say. "That's an excellent Italian beer. I drink it at home."

"I'll have one of those, then."

"And you, madam?" I say, turning to the wife.

"Do you have piña coladas?" she asks shyly.

"We don't, madam," I reply. "But we should. I like them, too."

"They are good," the wife says.

"How about a Lemon Drop martini?" I suggest.

"What's in that?"

"Lemon vodka, orange liquor, and sugar."

"Mmmm," the lady says. "I'll try one.

"Very good," I reply. "Let me get your drinks."

I go to the back and make the couple's drinks. Okay, so I'm not quite the mercenary waiter I make myself out to be. I'm very protective toward customers for whom eating at The Bistro's a monetary stretch. Sure, I don't make a lot of money off them, but it's a rare chance to make someone's evening special. Every day I deal with entitled snobs who spend $100 on dinner the way a blue-collar couple might spend $10 at McDonald's. For many wealthy people, eating out isn't a big deal. When you work for a living like me, spending a hundred bucks on dinner's a very big deal. What's an average meal for some is an indulgent feast for others.

I make the lady's martini. On The Bistro's cocktail menu a Lemon Drop's considered a premium beverage. I ring it in as a glass of cheap Chardonnay. Oops, an honest mistake. I slip the man's beer into an ice bucket and bring the drinks to the table. My wheels are turning, trying to figure out how my couple can have a nice Valentine's Day dinner and not go into the poorhouse. I've got to do it right. If I treat the couple like charity cases, they'll get even more embarrassed. I've got to guide them toward inexpensive choices but make them feel they're just like any other customer.

I give the couple their drinks and tell them the specials. The man's ear perks up when he hears about the rack of wild boar.

"How much is that?" he asks.

"Thirty-two dollars."

"Wow."

"But it's a very large portion, sir," I say. "You could easily share it."

"How about that, honey?" the man asks.

"The wild boar sounds delicious," the woman agrees.

"It is," I say. "We're famous for it."

"Okay, then," the man says. "We'll have that."

"Very good, sir," I reply. "Can I get you both an appetizer?"

"I'm saving room for dessert," the lady says.

"You're very wise, madam. Tonight we have a nice raspberry chocolate cake for two."

"Oh my God!" the lady exclaims. "We have to have that."

I smile. Suddenly I'm glad Armando didn't make a candied version of pickled gonads.

"I'll reserve one for you, madam."

"Thank you," the lady replies.

I go to the POS computer and ring in their order. I punch in two house salads, which are free, and one wild boar. I stick my head into the kitchen and ask Moises, the salad guy, to make the complimentary salads a little grander.

"No problem, papi," Moises says, giving me the thumbs-up.

Normally I don't tell people about splitting entrées or order them free salads. Customers' eyes are usually bigger than their stomachs. People often order without thinking things through. As a waiter I encourage this phenomenon. Ordering multiple appetizers and entrées drives up check totals and leads to higher tips. That makes me happy. Even though I know customers won't eat half of what they order, I encourage overconsumption so I can make a buck. But I've taken this Valentine's Day couple under my wing. Maybe they remind me of my parents. Maybe I want to do something nice.

Or maybe Saint Valentine is really on the job after all.

My couple eat their dinner, share their special heart-shaped dessert, and pay the bill in cash. They leave a nice tip. While the lady's fixing her makeup in the bathroom, the man comes up to me and shakes my hand.

"Thanks for everything," he says.

"You're very welcome," I reply. "Please join us again soon."

I watch as the couple walk hand in hand into the cold night air. Outside the woman looks up at her man starry-eyed and gives him a "thanks for dinner" kiss. Somehow I know watching that kiss will be my best tip of the evening.

The couple who take their place, however, are the usual rude yuppie breeders who fell out of love the moment the ink on their prenup dried. I steer them toward the most expensive items on the menu and cheerily rob them blind.

I told you I could be a mercenary bastard.

CHAPTER 7

Big Brother

After the great Valentine's Day shakedown, business at many restaurants takes a nosedive until the spring. Sadly The Bistro is no exception. It's a quiet March afternoon, and I'm at my lunchtime post by the hostess stand surveying an empty restaurant. When customer traffic dries up, you'll usually find me engaging in my favorite pastime—reading. A restaurant devoid of customers can be extremely boring, so I always make sure to have some reading material lying around. If business is slow and I don't have access to a newspaper or book, I can get antsier than Popeye Doyle going through heroin withdrawal in a Marseille slum. To prevent this from happening, I always keep several magazines and paperback books stashed in secret caches around The Bistro. It drives Fluvio nuts when he sees me reading a book or a newspaper during my shift. He thinks I should be dusting off wine bottles or something.

Right now I'm reading Raymond Chandler's *The Simple Art of Murder*. It's a collection of pulp magazine stories the author wrote before his first novel, *The Big Sleep*, was published in 1939. I've always had a soft spot for Chandler. Married to a woman many years his senior, Chandler, a heavy combat veteran from World War I, was fired from his job as a California oil executive for alcoholism and womanizing. Middle-aged, out of work, and barely getting by on charity provided by wealthy friends, Chandler supported himself during the Great Depression by writing pulp fiction at a penny a word for magazines like *Black Mask* and *Dime Detective*. As you read his earliest works you see how Chandler, basically a self-taught writer, developed his hard-boiled literary style of wisecracks, metaphors, and sharp lyrical similes while sketching out the character of what would become his most famous creation—the world-weary but idealistic private eye, Philip Marlowe.

I've read these stories a dozen times, but today I'm looking at them with a new eye. My Web site's popularity has attracted the attention of a literary agent. After a few weeks of discussions I signed with his agency. Now we're putting together a book proposal for prospective publishers to consider.

Ever since Waiter Rant became popular I've toyed with the idea of becoming a writer. Despite my earlier promise to Inez, however, I haven't exactly been trying to make it happen. Now, out of the blue, I'm presented with a chance to do something many people only dream about. It's a great opportunity, but I'm frightened. Can I actually write a book? Will I fall flat on my face? Despite my excitement I feel the shadow of failure wrapping itself around me.

But reading Chandler's work gives me hope. I'm not comparing myself, but if Chandler's writing apprenticeship was in the pulps, maybe mine was on the Internet. We're both self-taught writers, and damnit, if success could happen to a forty-five-year-old man desperate to change his life, why can't it happen to a thirty-eight-year-old waiter trying to change his? For the first time in years I feel like I'm taking concrete steps toward changing my life.

Just as I'm starting to imagine my face on the back of a book cover the house phone rings.

"The Bistro," I answer. "How can I help you?"

"Do I pay you to work, or do I pay you to read?" Fluvio asks, his voice angrily pushing through the cellular static.

"Are you spying on me again?"

"Of course I am."

I look at the video camera staring down at me from the ceiling. Two years ago Fluvio had a video surveillance system installed in The Bistro. Although he claims he installed the cameras for security, I know better.

"What are you reading?"

"A book about murder."

"Planning to kill someone?"

"Don't give me any ideas, boss," I mutter. "What's up?"

"I want to fire Beth."

"Why?" I groan. Fluvio's always huffing and puffing that he's going to fire someone.

"She's switched shifts tonight with Saroya and didn't tell me."

"She told me, boss."

"This is my place," Fluvio sputters. "I'm in charge, not you. She has to call me."

"She's one of the best waitresses we have."

"Why you always acting like the staff's lawyer?" Fluvio snaps. "You work for me."

"She's a good worker, Fluvio. Leave her alone."

"Listen, you . . ." Fluvio says, his anger starting to rev up.

"Whatever, Fluvio," I reply casually. "Say, did you hear about Café Foo Foo?"

"No what?" Fluvio says, perking up. He loves gossip.

"The owner says you're imitating his menu."

"That's bullshit," Fluvio growls. "He imitate me."

"I know that. You know that. But that's not what he's saying."

"That asshole. I fix him good one day."

I hold the phone away from my ear as Fluvio vomits up invective about Café Foo Foo's owner. My job here is done. I've redirected Fluvio's nervous energy to a place where it can do no harm. Within seconds Fluvio forgets all about firing Beth, and I spend the rest of the phone call reassuring him that our food is much better than Foo Foo's. I know I'm being manipulative, but hey, you go with what works.

Fluvio's quip about my being the staff's attorney isn't far off the mark. I'm always intervening on the staff's behalf. When Fluvio hired me six years ago, he explained that I was going to be a player manager, a glorified headwaiter earning an hourly supervisory wage when he wasn't on the premises. In a sense it was a smart move. Restaurant managers often make less money than the waiters they're supervising. The last thing Fluvio wanted was another bribe-hustling manger like Sammy. But being thrust between Fluvio and the waiters meant I was forced to be a mediator from day one. That's not easy. The gap between management and staff can make the Gaza Strip look like a resort town. And Fluvio? He can be the culinary version of Yasir Arafat.

The Fluvio who owns The Bistro is not the same person I met at Amici's. The stress of opening a new restaurant exposed an unseen side of his personality—an anxious and angry side. To say Fluvio yells would be an understatement. His wife would later tell me that she never saw the choleric side of her husband until after they opened the restaurant. Many chefs yell and scream, so, in that sense, Fluvio is no exception. But in the heat of his rages he can say some truly awful things. Initially, I worried Fluvio would turn out to be another Caesar, but I quickly discovered that his emotional outbursts were like summer storms, vanishing as quickly as they started. You can have a blowup with Fluvio one minute, and he'll be buying you a drink the next. But his episodes are so sudden and cataclysmic that he often says and does things he regrets later. He once made a particularly crude comment about a woman I was dating. After I threatened to break his nose he promptly apologized and kissed up to me for weeks afterward. That's Fluvio's modus operandi; he'll blow up but then try to be your best friend. Emotionally, it's very confusing, like being in a relationship in which your partner's hitting you one moment and buying you flowers the next. I always joke that you aren't officially part of The Bistro's staff until Fluvio makes you cry at least once. When orienting new hires, I try prepping them for the inevitable verbal onslaught by giving them the "Fluvio Talk." Despite my best efforts, however, many of them quit after the first few weeks. Veteran staff members aren't immune, either. Just last week a woman who worked the lunch shift for several years threw down her apron and stormed out the front door. When Fluvio ran after her to apologize, she yelled, "You're an awful man. Leave me alone!"

Over the years I've come to realize that Fluvio's anger and anxiety stem from his fear of losing everything that he's worked so hard to create. As I mentioned earlier, Fluvio's no stranger to failure. He flunked out of a dozen jobs before finding success as a chef. He also has a strained relationship with his ex-wife and children back in Italy. Now, at forty-six, he has a new wife, a new son, and a robust business. Fluvio's got a second shot at happiness. He doesn't want anything to mess that up, but I worry his anxiety will destroy the very thing he wants to protect.

Fluvio's worrying has turned him into a jumpy, irritable, and angry man. Like a solider just home from war, his eyes are always scanning the horizon for threats. Constantly fidgeting, he tenses up and moves away if you place your hand on his shoulder. This anxiety hurts him in social settings. Because thoughts are banging around the inside of his head like electrons colliding inside a particle accelerator, his attention span can be measured in nanoseconds. You can be having a conversation with him when suddenly, and for no reason, he'll stop talking to you and walk away. He does this to vendors, staff, and even his customers. While Fluvio has the capacity to be a very charming, nice, and considerate person, he's usually on his best behavior only when dealing with people who have something he wants. Fluvio doesn't have the energy or inclination to be nice to people he perceives as beneath him. Believe me, if you work for Fluvio, he thinks you're beneath him.

Like many depressed and anxious people, Fluvio is unkempt and sloppy. His glasses are always smudged, and he often forgets to shave. His clothes are rumpled, and his shirt's never tucked in.

His physical disorganization is reflected in his personal spaces as well. His car is a mess, and his office makes a pigsty look like the interior of the Vatican. Fluvio's idea of filing something is to throw it on top of his desk. Not surprisingly, he can never find *anything*.

Fluvio's anxiety drives me up the wall. For example, if you're talking to him and the phone rings, he'll leap out of his seat and *run* to answer it. If you have the misfortune to be standing next to the house phone, he'll bark "Get out of my way" and even physically *push* you aside if you don't move fast enough. When Fluvio answers the phone, it's a violent act. Like a deadbeat sweating the creditors, Fluvio thinks that every phone call is a portent of impending disaster. The sound of a ringing phone fills him with dread. If he misses a phone call, he'll desperately scroll through the caller ID and try ringing the caller back. Fluvio can't stand not knowing what every call's about. That's because, like all overly anxious people, he always assumes the worst. To make sure he never misses a phone call, he always carries at least two cell phones, a BlackBerry, and a wireless-enabled PDA. He always has to be plugged in. Most people use pills or booze to narcotize their inner demons. Fluvio uses technology. The best example of this is The Bistro's video camera system.

Many restaurants employ video cameras to allow the kitchen to view a diner's progress or to help management keep on eye on the cash register. I think the general dining public would be shocked to know how often Big Brother is watching them as they eat and drink. But Fluvio didn't hook up any monitors in the kitchen to help Armando track a table's progress—the only monitors are in the office downstairs. The cameras are there for Fluvio to watch the staff. As far as internal security is concerned, the staff at The Bistro are incredibly honest. Missing inventory has never been much of a problem. Fluvio somehow got by without a video system for years, but as his anxiety and fear morphed into paranoia, he turned into a control freak.

On some level, most restaurant owners are control freaks. If they aren't, then they hire someone who is. But Fluvio's control-ling behavior is less about quality control and more about fear. He's always on the lookout for people trying to rip him off. When he first installed the cameras, I was furious. I knew something about the effects of larceny and corruption while working for the Church and in the business world. I take a strange pride in the fact that the restaurant workers I have known have a better-developed sense of ethics and honor than many of my former colleagues. I told Fluvio I'd understand the cameras if we had a security problem, but since we didn't, I felt like the surveillance was a slap in the face to the people who had given him long and honest service. His response was a simplistic, "Why you worried? You stealing from me? You got something to hide? You do noth-ing wrong, then you have nothing to worry about."

That hurt. I had processed millions of dollars' worth of Flu-vio's cash and inventory. I'm not claiming any kind of moral superiority. You're not supposed to steal. But it hurts to think Fluvio needed to videotape my integrity. If I had wanted to steal from him, I could have robbed him blind and he never would've known about it. Eventually, I realized that, even if The Bistro was staffed by a convent of nuns, Fluvio would still want to act like Big Brother. Why? Like every anxious paranoid, Fluvio assumes the worst about every situation and person.

That's why Fluvio freaked when Beth changed the schedule without telling him. He's not upset that she switched shifts; he's upset because he didn't know about it. When he doesn't know something, he assumes people are trying to get one over on him. So instead of indicating to Beth his desire to be kept in the loop, Fluvio immediately launched into Code Red.

Fluvio drives me insane, but I have a very soft spot for him, too. Despite his many shortcomings he can be a likable and kind man. When business is slow, he always makes sure everyone has enough hours to work and never lays anybody off. He's made health insurance available when few small business owners are doing so. He's lent money to people (including me) when they're broke. He was also quite nice to my family, cutting my brother and me a major price break when we held a surprise party for Mom at The Bistro. He takes good care of all his children and his aging father. But, despite all his good qualities, you never know when Fluvio will slip into Mussolini mode. This forces you to keep your guard up continuously. That constant expenditure of energy makes him an exhausting man to work for. Fluvio makes things a lot harder than they have to be.

I learned early, because of his personality, that I had to be the buffer between Fluvio and the staff. Whenever he screams at the staff, I calm him down. Whenever he gets hot under the collar about firing someone, I make his eternal preoccupation work for me and distract him. I've smoothed things over with aggravated customers, vendors, and staff. I've apologized many times for his rudeness. There are many people in the neighborhood who don't like Fluvio. My normal response to their trash-talking is to say, "Yeah, he can be difficult, but he's a good man at heart." So as the years have passed, I've done my best to protect Fluvio from Fluvio. I remind him to shave, tuck in his shirt, and zip up his fly.

The hours pass by. Soon it's dinnertime. The Bistro has only a few patrons sitting in the window. Saroya and I are sitting in the back keeping an eye on things. Fluvio, however, is also keeping an eye on us.

The house phone rings. I pick up the cordless handset. "The Bistro," I say cheerfully. "How may I help you?"

"What are you doing sitting down?" Fluvio says.

I look up at the video camera. "Fluvio?" I say. "Where are you?"

"Never mind where I am," Fluvio yells. "Why are you sitting down?"

"It's slow here."

"I don't like you sitting down."

I press my ear to the receiver. I can hear traffic noises in the background. "Fluvio," I say, "are you in the car?"

"I'm on my way to the airport."

"You're looking at us on your laptop while you're driving?" I shriek. "And talking on your cell phone?"

"It's a traffic jam."

"But still."

"Listen," Fluvio says. "You work for me. I do what I want."

"Well, it's not *your* highway," I snap. "Keep your eyes on the road before you kill someone."

"Goddamnit. You're—"

"Hey, Fluvio," I say, winking at Saroya. "Is your son with you?"

"Yes, he is."

"So, you're driving a car with your son in the back while talking on a cell phone and looking at a computer screen? Tell me I'm missing something."

"Hey."

"Buddy," I say. "The state troopers will execute you on the side of the road if they catch you doing that shit."

"I don't get caught."

"One in the head, buddy. *Kapow!*"

"You think you so funny."

"GET OFF THE PHONE!" I yell. "OR I TELL THE WIFE!"

Fluvio hangs up, quickly.

"He's watching us while he's driving?" Saroya asks. "Can he do that?"

"He's got one of those broadband wireless cards for his laptop," I reply. "He can watch us from wherever."

"He likes calling people out of the blue. It's happened to me a few times," Saroya says. "He tells me, 'I see what you doing.' It creeps me out."

"Makes you wonder if he keeps a jar of Vaseline nearby."

"Oh," Saroya says, shivering. "That's too creepy for words."

Saroya and I do not get up. Fluvio doesn't call back. Things are so slow I go back to reading Raymond Chandler. I flip to my favorite part of the book—the introduction Chandler wrote years after he became famous. Oddly enough, his reflection on what makes Philip Marlowe a hero became one of the most famous pieces he ever wrote.

> But down these mean streets a man must go who
> is not himself mean, who is neither tarnished nor
> afraid. . . . . He is the hero, he is everything. He must
> be a complete man and a common man and yet an
> unusual man. He must be, to use a rather weathered
> phrase, a man of honor, by instinct, by inevitability,
> without thought of it, and certainly without saying
> it. He must be the best man in his world and a good
> enough man for any world.

One of the kitchen guys interrupts my reading and asks, since it's so slow, if he can go home early.

"No problem, papi," I say. "Just be sure to clock out."

A few minutes later the worker emerges from the basement, out of his kitchen checks and wearing his civvies. He punches out on the computer. The printer spits out a receipt. The cook examines it, makes a face, and comes up to me.

"Can you fix this, papi?" he asks me.

I already know what the cook wants. I examine his printout. It says he worked fifty-one hours and fifty-five minutes. Fluvio hasn't paid employees for partial hours in years. He'll pay this guy for only fifty-one hours—and no overtime. Where does the fifty-five minutes go? Into the ether, of course. Fluvio ends up leeching a free week's worth of work out of his employees every year. This kind of bookkeeping is common in the restaurant business.

I reopen the cook's time sheet and add ten minutes. I reprint the time sheet and hand it back to him.

"If he still shorts you," I say, "let me know." Yet again I'm the buffer zone. This time I'm keeping the staff from revolting.

"*Gracias,*" the cook says. "I don't want to give him a free hour."

"I don't blame you."

"Good night, *jefe*."

"Good night."

Fluvio's a bag of contradictory impulses. He'll pay people's medical bills in a pinch, but he'll also nickel-and-dime his hardworking employees out of a couple of bucks. The restaurant world is a tough world. I'm sure Fluvio thinks he's doing the best he can by his employees, but I wonder if he truly understands how he's pushing everyone away from him. After almost seven years his nonsense is starting to wear me down.

I exit out of the time-sheet program, look up at the cold implacable eye of the video camera, and cheerily flip it the bird.

CHAPTER 8

The Back Alley of Affluence

few days later a late winter snowstorm's slamming into the East Coast. The Bistro, yet again, has almost no customers for lunch. With temperatures hovering in the single digits, I figure most of the office drones ordered in today. It's a shame we don't deliver.

I rub a hole in the condensation gauzing The Bistro's front door and peek outside. Granules of bone-dry snow pushed by the wind skittle and scrape against cars and buildings, scouring them like an Arctic sandstorm. I watch as the delivery boy from the King of Siam restaurant carefully pedals his bicycle down the treacherous street, the wire basket perched over his front tire laden with grease-stained brown-bagged orders of Pad Thai. He looks miserably cold. As I watch him pedal I have a macabre vision of his bones piled outside the entrance of a faceless office building, a skeletal middle finger stripped clean by the icy pumice thrust heavenward, protesting a lousy tip even in death. Maybe it's a good thing we don't deliver after all.

Safe and warm inside The Bistro, I feel my stomach growl. I look at my watch. It's time for lunch. Hunger pushes the delivery boy's plight out of my mind. I head into the kitchen to ask what's cooking.

"Yo, Ernesto!" I shout.

"What, *cabrón*?" replies Ernesto, one of the sous-chefs, not looking up from the sauce he's stirring.

"Tengo hambre, papi," I whine. "Feed me."

"Whatchu want to eat?" Ernesto asks.

One of the nice things about being the manager is that I can order anything I want off the menu—within reason. That's nice, but after a while you get sick of Italian food. Experience has taught me to see what Spanish grub the kitchen guys are rustling up first.

"What are you making for the troops?" I ask.

Ernesto stops and scratches the top of his crew cut. Short and powerfully built, Ernesto always reminds me of a larger version of Hervé Villechaize. Whenever I see him standing on his tiptoes trying to shove something into the oven, I have to bite my tongue not to call him Nick Nack, Scaramanga's diminutive henchman from *The Man with the Golden Gun*.

"I don't know yet," Ernesto replies, breaking away from the stove and opening the fridge. After surveying the food-stuffs he says, "Give me a minute. I'll make something nice for everybody."

"Tacos?" I ask hopefully.

"Maybe."

"You make tacos, and I'll love you."

"You only love me when I feed you."

"And you only love me when I close early."

"That's right, *cabrón*," Ernesto says, his face breaking out into a smile. "You get it now."

"It only took six years."

"Puta!" Ernesto says without rancor. "Get out of here."

Playful banter over, I exit the kitchen. The bus girls, Imelda and Lourdes, are busy leafing through the Spanish version of *People*. Unlike other restaurant managers, who'd bark at them for not doing anything, I leave them alone. If these girls are sitting down, they've finished their work. The back-of-the-house crew at The Bistro have the best work ethic I've ever seen. Besides, it's dead. I sit down next to them and start leafing though a newspaper another waiter left behind.

"Anything interesting in the paper?" Imelda asks.

"Same shit, I'm afraid," I reply.

"Does the paper say anything about the immigration thing?" Imelda asks.

"What immigration thing?" I ask.

"That law that says you can't hire illegal aliens."

Imelda's referring to bills under consideration that would force employers to be more vigorous when verifying a prospective worker's immigration status. Currently, all Fluvio is required to do is ask for documentation (Social Security card, driver's license, etc.) to verify a worker's eligibility. He does not have to validate the authenticity of those documents. Many immigrants looking for work use fake Social Security cards, fraudulent tax ID numbers, or counterfeit green cards to secure employment. They know the documentation's fake, we know it's fake, but we and countless other businesses hire them anyway. If you were to suggest to Fluvio that an applicant's papers might be counterfeit, "I don't work for Homeland Security" would be his standard response. The new law under consideration, however, would use the threat of heavy fines to force employers to use electronic means to verify eligibility. The idea is to cross-check IDs via the Internet against some kind of national database. That means thousands of illegal immigrants would be unable to get jobs anywhere in the United States. It should come as no surprise that the National Restaurant Association lobbies against these efforts. Without illegal immigrants the restaurant business in this country would come to a shuddering halt.

Some people want all immigrants stopped at the border and sent home. Others think we should accept every one of the "huddled masses, yearning to be free" who manages to jump the fence. I don't know what the solution to America's immigration dilemma is. I do know that illegal immigrants are a big part of our economy. Most domestic servants, restaurant employees, fruit pickers, landscapers, and janitors *se habla español*. Restaurants, especially operations like The Bistro, have thin profit margins. Unable to hire illegal aliens, restaurateurs will have to hire "legal employees" for higher wages. Increased wages will get passed along as higher food prices, and dining out will become even more expensive. In fact, getting rid of our illegal alien labor pool would drive up prices for many consumer goods. We enjoy cheap chicken because poultry pluckers work for low wages in factories where the owners skimp on annoying details like paying for safe equipment and health care. We enjoy cheap prices at big-box stores because corporate bean counters keep overhead low by using undocumented aliens as janitorial staff. If we could magically send every undocumented worker home, life in the United States would suddenly get more expensive. Americans might bemoan their porous borders or decry the desperate plight of immigrants, but we love paying $30 for DVD players. America is addicted to cheap labor—whether it's from China or Mexico.

"I don't think anything will come of it, Imelda," I answer.

"Why not?"

"If we sent you all home, the Anglos would have to pay more money to get their lawns mowed," I reply. "That ain't happening."

"It's not fair," Lourdes says, joining the conversation. "I work hard. I pay all my taxes and I'll never see Social Security. These people want to make me into a criminal."

"That's true," I say. "And look at the hypocrisy. Thousands of Americans try scamming their way out of paying taxes every year."

"That's right!" Lourdes says.

"But do you remember that illegal waitress we had from Colombia?" I ask. "The one with the little boy?"

"*Sí*"

"She claimed six dependents on her W-2 when she should have claimed only one. She paid almost no payroll taxes while I paid a bundle. Her child got free health care through my tax dollars, but I have to pay four hundred dollars a month to insure myself. Is that fair?"

"No," Lourdes admits.

"Anglos game the system; immigrants game the system," I continue. "People get exploited. It's a mess."

"It's a big problem," Imelda says, shaking her head.

All this heavy talk suddenly makes me want to have a cigarette. I excuse myself from the table, grab my black wool coat off the rack, and head down a small flight of stairs into the basement. The bowels of the Civil War–era building are a rabbit warren of passageways and small rooms. Tables, equipment, and boxes of food are crammed into every conceivable niche of space. It's like being on a submarine before a long patrol. The heat radiating off the walk-in freezer's condensers keeps the basement warm in the winter and oppressively hot in the summer. Come to think of it, the cramped quarters down here remind me of a World War II submarine I toured when I was a kid.

"*Hola, amigos,*" I say to the guys working in the prep kitchen.

"*Hola,*" Moises replies as he peels a red pepper. Looking at my warm jacket, he asks, "Still snowing out?"

"Yeah," I reply. "I'm going into that shit to smoke."

"Not good, man," Moises says, shaking his head. "Not good."

Moises gave up smoking a year ago. The patriarch of a large El Salvadoran family, he has a tribe of children and a mouthful of gold fillings. He's been our salad man almost as long as I've worked at The Bistro. Over the years Moises saved his pennies and now owns a house in the suburbs. When I try figuring how I can make more money than our salad man and still live in a small apartment, I remind myself that Moises has a little something called discipline.

"Think of all the money you save by not smoking," I reply.

"I need it for my house," Moises says.

"How's that going?"

"Something always needs fixing."

"*Siempre trabaja?*"

"Sí."

"Ah," I say, winking. "The joys of home ownership."

I walk through a series of doors and enter a long passageway that connects to the stairs to the back alley. The light fixture in the hallway is busted. The only illumination is provided by the red glow of the EXIT sign. As I head down the passage I see Felipe, the dishwasher, carrying an empty trash can over his shoulder. Bathed in red light we look like crewmen from my childhood submarine. I can almost hear the Klaxon sounding general quarters. I resist the urge to shout, "Dive! Dive! Dive!"

"Still cold out?" I ask Felipe.

"Muy frío, jefe," he says, his voice quaking with cold. *"Muy frío."*

I move to one side and let Felipe pass. Outside I can hear the wind shrieking. Going out in this weather to smoke is nuts. You know you're an addict when you seek to indulge a habit in environments reasonable people avoid. No matter. As I climb the stairs to the alley I pull up the collar of my coat and pretend I'm a German sub commander ascending the conning tower of his U-boat. As I indulge my *Das Boot* fantasy I imagine I'm scouring the stormy North Atlantic for Food Network cruise ships to sink.

The brutal blast of cold air that greets my face dispels my daydream. I scamper over to the side of the alley that affords some protection from the wind and spark up a Marlboro Light. Even though it's freezing out, I inhale slowly, forcing myself to relax. If I suck down my cigarette in a mad rush, I'll get dizzy and throw up.

As I watch the white smoke reluctantly struggle out of my cigarette, the door from the basement crashes open and Eduardo, one of the prep cooks, tumbles out. Clad in kitchen checks, he's not wearing a coat.

"Smoke? *Por favor?*" he asks, using the index and middle finger of his right hand to mimic smoking a cigarette, the universal sign language of nicotine addicts everywhere.

"Sure," I reply. With a practiced motion I jiggle a cigarette halfway out of my soft pack and offer it to him. After he takes it, I return the pack to my pocket, produce a Zippo, and spark up the flame. The harsh smell of lighter fluid hits my nose. In the cold air the warmth from the lighter feels good in my hand. Eduardo cups his hands around flame, leans in, and lights up, completing the cigarette liturgy.

"*Gracias,*" Eduardo says.

"*De nada.*"

Hopping up and down in the cold, Eduardo puffs on his cigarette. "Ay!" he says, smiling. "*Está frío.*"

"Yeah, man," I reply. "Where's your coat?"

"Don't need it," he says quickly.

As I watch Eduardo smoke I silently wonder if he even has a winter coat. Every day I see his countrymen huddled on street corners as they wait for contractors to hire them for a day's work. Many of them are wearing only sweatshirts to protect them from the cold. I make a mental note to make sure Eduardo has a coat. If he doesn't, the staff will all chip in to buy him one. They're good that way.

"You working all day?" I ask.

"*Como?*" Eduardo replies. He's been in the country only a few months and his English isn't great—but he's learning quickly.

"*Trabaja todo al día?*"

"*Sí. Todo al día.*"

"Ouch," I exclaim. Eduardo's going to work a fourteen-hour day.

I like Eduardo. Eighteen years old, he hails from the Iztapalapa section of Mexico City. As I watch him smoke I smile inwardly. This kid is crazy about Shakira, the Colombian hottie who sings "Hips Don't Lie." Every morning he pops his Shakira CD into the boom box, plays it all day, and cleans it lovingly with Windex before returning it to its jewel case. He treats that CD the way some people treat the Scriptures.

"Hey, Eduardo," I say. "Aren't Moises and the guys sick of listening to Shakira yet?"

Eduardo doesn't understand what I'm saying, but he recognizes the word *Shakira.*

"Shakira! Shakira!" he shouts, pumpingh his fist in the air.

"*Te gusta* Shakira?"

"*Sí, sí.*"

I chuckle softly. When I was his age, I thought Kelly LeBrock was the hottest thing going. Come to think of it, watching *Weird Science* still does it for me.

"Shakira's *muy bonita,*" I concur.

Eduardo shakes his head in the affirmative, takes a last drag of his cigarette, and flicks it into the street. "*Está frío,*" he yelps, racing back downstairs.

Alone again, I stand in the cold and savor my cigarette. I give Eduardo a lot of credit. Born when I graduated from high school, he's a stranger in a strange land trying to make a better life for himself. When I was his age, I was in the seminary, ensconced inside academia and guaranteed three square meals a day. I never worried about having a coat when it got cold out. Eduardo's a lot tougher than I was at his age. Heck, he's a lot tougher than most people in general. When you're an immigrant, you have to be.

Of course, no one brings it to immigrants like other immigrants. Caesar, who hailed from Paraguay himself, was so fearful that his undocumented peons were stealing from him that he paid one of his workers extra money to spy on everybody. At Amici's the role of undercover operative was played by Rodolfo, our socially maladjusted salad man. Bribed with the allure of covert authority and a smidgen of extra money, Rodolfo transformed into an outsize version of Bobby Brady's fascist hall monitor overnight. Of course this little shit surveilled the waiters as well, faithfully noting everyone who showed up late and recording every overheard criticism about management. Rodolfo was always solemnly whispering exaggerated tales of waiter mistakes and misbehavior into Caesar's ear. Okay, so we did misbehave and make mistakes, but I always thought it was pathetic that Rodolfo sold his soul to a scumbag like Caesar for a couple of bucks an hour. Rizzo had a special disdain for Rodolfo. You see, Rizzo drank a bottle of wine every shift. Rodolfo always reported Rizzo's drinking on the job to Caesar. But since Caesar was afraid of Rizzo, no action was ever taken. That the headwaiter was immune to his exercise of power drove Rodolfo up the wall. Rizzo loved calling attention to Rodolfo's impotence by calling him a "salad-tossing Uncle Tom house Negro motherfucker."

The use of "Uncle Toms," however, isn't limited to Amici's. Fluvio has his own control issues, so he has his own spies. And he has spies spying on the spies! For example, he'll call me and ask how things are going at the restaurant. After I tell him he'll call Max, the head busboy, and ask him what *I'm* doing. When he gets off the phone with Max, Fluvio will call Armando and ask what we are *both* doing. There are times when working at The Bistro feels like living in Stasi-saturated East Germany. At this point everyone's so sick of Fluvio's distrustfulness that I'm able to run Fluvio's "Uncle Toms" like double agents and stay informed of his machinations and plans. That Fluvio fancies himself a shrewd operator and master manipulator plays right into my hands. He's neither, but I let him think he is. Fluvio telegraphs his intentions the way a poor fighter telegraphs a punch. You can see him coming from a mile away.

I take a long drag off my cigarette. I haven't thought about Rodolfo in years. Caesar eventually fired him, of course, but I'm sure he's whoring himself out at some other restaurant. I should feel sorry for him, but I don't. The craving for recognition and respect can tempt people who don't have much to look for dignity in all the wrong places. It's the reason why criminals romanticize their stupid brutishness into codes of honor and respect. The early Mafia rationalized preying on Italian immigrants by pretending they were protecting them. Omertà, my ass.

I look around the alley I'm standing in. It's a part of the restaurant customers never see. Literally the mouth and anus of the restaurant, it's where deliveries come in and garbage goes out. It's also a place where tired guys try catching a break before returning to their never-ending routine. Some restaurants instruct their staff to use the service door when entering and exiting the building. God forbid people should see the servants.

Years ago I saw a painting of Catherine the Great, the czarina of Russia, touring the wintry Crimean countryside in her
imperial sleigh. In the painting clusters of well-fed villagers stand
in front of prosperous-looking buildings and cheerfully wave to
their passing sovereign. In another part of the painting it's re-
vealed that the buildings are actually cheap facades erected to
fool the czarina into thinking her subjects are happy. Hidden
behind the plywood theatrics are the actual villagers, starving,
dressed in rags, and freezing to death in the cruel Russian winter.
Legend has it General Potemkin, the military governor of the
Crimea, had these fake settlements built to curry favor with the
czarina—hence their name—Potemkin villages.

As I look around the dirty alley I'm reminded that restaurants are culinary versions of Potemkin villages—manufactured
glitz facades hiding a hot and turbulent reality that customers
never want to see. Behind every restaurant's jewel-box exterior
there's an overflowing Dumpster in the back. Patrons don't want
to know that illegal immigrants are cooking their meals or busing
their tables. They don't want to know that the staff's working
for an amoral ogre. They don't care that the bus girls might not
have enough money for food or that their waiter's sweating the
rent. Most customers care about only one thing—getting what
they want when they want it. They watch celebrity chefs on the
Food Network and think that restaurants are magical places designed to jerk off their taste buds. They don't realize restaurants
are places where people struggle to make a living. I've found
that most people are cravenly indifferent to what happens in the
back alleys of affluence—whether it's behind a restaurant or a
Wal-Mart.

I drop my cigarette to the ground and grind it under my heel.
Maybe I shouldn't be so hard on people. I still have a healthy core
of outraged self-righteousness left over from my seminary days.
When I go out to eat, I just want to forget my problems, too. But
then again I don't act like a complete shit.

As I head back inside, the shock of warm air cues my frozen

earlobes to start throbbing with pain. If I had stayed outside another minute, I'd be suffering from frostbite. For the thousandth time I curse the hold nicotine has on me. Years ago, trapped in my apartment by a blizzard and out of smokes, I walked three blocks in waist-high snow to buy a pack at a nearby gas station. It was a hellish, out-of-breath, forty-five-minute round-trip. At one point I feared being overcome with exhaustion and dying in the snow, my corpse hidden until the spring thaw. Like I said—it's a stupid habit.

Once upstairs I head into the kitchen. As I help myself to a small bowl of soup I notice ground meat browning on the stove and Ernesto chopping up cheese and tomatoes on a cutting board.

"Tacos?" I ask.

Ernesto gives me a thumbs-up.

"You the man, Ernesto," I say, carrying my soup into the dining room.

I eat my soup and continue reading the newspaper. Outside the wind howls. After a while Ernesto emerges from the kitchen with a platter laden with tacos. Finally. I'm starving.

"Mucho gusto tacos!" I yelp.

Ernesto gives me a look. "How long you work here?" he asks.

"Six years."

"And your Spanish still sucks."

"True," I say, grabbing a taco off the platter. "But if I was a busboy in Mexico City, I'd learn fast."

"I'd love to see you in Mexico City," Imelda says, laughing. "You'd get your ass kicked."

Ernesto shouts downstairs to the prep kitchen that lunch is ready. Bedlam breaks loose as Eduardo, Felipe, and the other kitchen guys run upstairs. Soon everyone's running around—grabbing sodas, Tabasco sauce, knives, forks, and napkins—then settling into their chairs to devour lunch. Everyone's famished.

A few minutes later The Bistro's alive with the pleasant noise of people enjoying good food and good company. Of course, the front door chimes. A man and a woman walk in off the street, trudging slush on the newly polished floor.

"Are you open?" the woman calls out.

I get up and walk to the front of the restaurant.

"Yes, we are," I reply pleasantly. "Two for lunch?"

"Yeah," the man barks. "We want to sit in the back."

The staff's eating in the back. If I pop a customer in the back, they'll get uncomfortable and rush to finish.

"I'm sorry, sir," I reply. "The back's closed. I have a lovely table in the window, though."

"We need to sit in the back," the woman says, looking around uncomfortably. Call me cynical, but over the years I've noticed that people who cheat on their spouses patronize restaurants at odd hours. Maybe that's the case here.

"Well," I say, "if you don't mind sitting with the staff. They're having their lunch."

"When will they be done?" the man asks.

Now I'm angry. The staff deserves to eat like human beings.

"When they're finished."

The man shrugs like I've said something stupid. "So when will that be?"

"Probably not soon enough for you," I snap, activating my thousand-yard waiter stare.

The couple turn around without saying a word and walk out into the windy frigid air. Watching the staff eat might mean peeking behind the facade of the Potemkin village. That might be too much reality for a pair of yuppies to handle. Or maybe I'm right about the cheating thing.

"What happened?" Imelda asks as I sit back down.

I look around the table. Moises is telling a joke. Pilar, another bus girl, is showing Lourdes pictures of her newborn baby. Felipe looks tired, and Eduardo's stuffing his teenage gut with as many tacos as he can. These guys have been doing weekend food prep nonstop all day. They deserve to sit down and enjoy their food. They are men and women—not peons. This isn't a yuppie plantation.

I think about the struggles some of my coworkers have endured to live in this country. Ernesto had to pay a human smuggler—a mule—$10,000 to get his son up from El Salvador. Moises flew his family in one at a time, while Lourdes and Imelda bounced all over the country looking for work until they settled here. When you're a native of this country, you sometimes get blasé about what this country stands for. It's like living in New York City and never going to the top of the Empire State Building. The United States has a lot of problems, sure, but when you work in a restaurant, you realize there are millions of people willing to risk everything to chase the American dream.

"Nothing happened, Imelda," I answer. "Nothing at all."

I finish my lunch. Eduardo gets up to take his plate to the dishwasher. He grabs my plate, too.

"Thanks, man," I say.

"*No problema.*"

Once Eduardo walks out of earshot, I whisper to Imelda. "Hey, does Eduardo have a winter coat?"

"Yes, he does," Imelda replies.

I look at the snow billowing outside the front window. I think about the delivery guy from the Thai restaurant, the day laborers huddled on their street corners, and the Russian villagers shivering behind their Potemkin villages. My teeth almost start chattering in the imaginary cold.

"Good," I say. "He's gonna need it."

CHAPTER 9

The Tip's the Thing

t's the first Saturday in April. The middle-aged couple at table 23 polish off $200 worth of food and wine and ask for the check.

"Here you are," I say, placing the bill in the politically correct center of the table.

"Thank you!" the woman purrs. "That was a fantastic meal."

"Yes, it was," the woman's husband says. "Please send our compliments to the chef."

"I will, sir."

"And you!" the woman exclaims. "You're a great waiter."

"Thank you, madam," I reply, executing a slight bow.

"It's been years since I've had such good service," the woman continues raving. "Isn't that right, Andy?"

"Yes, dear," the husband replies. "He's the best waiter we've had in a long time."

A sudden feeling of unease settles over me. It's not that I'm uncomfortable with praise—far from it; it's just that experience has shown me that customers who heap verbal tribute upon their servers often do so at the expense of financial tribute. Operating under the gravely mistaken assumption that my landlord will accept utterances of "Good job" or "You're the best" in lieu of government-backed currencies, these customers assign a monetary value to their laudations and deduct it from my financial compensation. We waiters call this "the verbal tip."

"Here," the man says, handing me a credit card. "And thank you again."

"I'll be right back, sir," I say. I go to the register and run the credit card. After the receipt prints up I return to the table.

"You're all set," I say, handing back the check holder. "Have a lovely weekend, and please come again soon."

"Oh, we will," the woman gushes. "And we only want *you* to be our waiter."

"Thank you, madam."

"Thanks again," the man says. "Great job. Excellent service."

The couple get up and head for the door. On their way out I overhear them tell Fluvio what a great waiter I am. After six years working together, Fluvio and I bicker and disagree on many things, but the receipts don't lie. I'm the best waiter he has. It kills him when customers remind him of that fact.

The couple give me one last wave good-bye. Smiling my best fake waiter smile, I wave back. The moment the couple goes out the door Fluvio and I race toward the table. Fluvio gets there first and scoops the check off the table.

"The tip's going to be shit," he says, grinning.

"Probably."

Fluvio opens the check and giggles. "It's shit."

"The verbal tip strikes again."

"They left you less than eight percent."

"Jesus," I mutter, "worse than I thought."

Chuckling, Fluvio hands me the check. The couple left me $15. Verbal tippers are the fucking bane of my existence.

"Assholes," I grumble.

"Great waiter, my ass," Fluvio crows.

I look at the check, shrug, and put it in my pocket. While I'm annoyed, it's not the worst fate that could have befallen me. They could have been impolite customers and left a bad tip. That would have been a lose-lose scenario. At least this couple didn't take a toll on my psychological well-being.

In seven years I've developed my own ideas about how and why customers tip. It's gotten to the point where I can tell how much money I'm going to make off a customer within ten seconds of meeting them. It's like I can see the tip percentage floating over their heads.

Tipping's origins are somewhat lost to history. Some believe that the practice developed in the tavern houses of Europe, when men would throw the bar wench a few coins to ensure the ale kept flowing. (Even back then it was hard to get a bartender's attention.) Many people erroneously believe that the word *tips* had its start as an acronym for the phase "to insure prompt service." If we hewed to a literal interpretation of that ideal, then customers should be tipping the waiter *before* the meal is served. That certainly wouldn't fly with today's dining public, and I'll bet it didn't fly in the 1600s either. Besides, the notion that *tips* is an acronym for "to insure prompt service" is just as patently absurd as the belief that *fuck* is an acronym for "forbidden unclean carnal knowledge." It sounds good, the facts kind of fit, but it isn't true. It's an etymological urban legend. According to the dictionary, the word *tip* is derived from English thieves' slang word *tip*, meaning "to pass from one to another." The notion of a *stock tip* or *racing tip* descends from the same slang word. At some point the word acquired the definition it has today, a customer giving a service provider a gratuity. In the United States, after some initial opposition, tipping for service became an established practice sometime after the Civil War. Despite all the confusion about tipping's origins, one thing's always been true—waiters often get *fucked* on the *tip*.

When you stiff servers on the tip, you're really screwing them over. Waiters in the United States, with few exceptions, are *not* paid a salary. We don't even make minimum wage. In the state of New York, tipped workers are paid $4.60 an hour. That's below the state's minimum wage of $7.15 per hour. The expectation is

that our tips, coupled with our small hourly wage, will raise our
compensation to the state minimum-wage level. Some rare states
like Oregon allow waiters to collect the full state minimum wage
of $7.80 *plus* their tips (I want to move there). If you're working
in a Nebraska diner, however, you're only getting $2.13 per hour.
The laws vary from state to state, but, suffice to say, waiters need
tips to survive. Ever wonder why waiters get pissed when cheapskates stiff them on the tip? If your boss arbitrarily pulled money
out of your paycheck, money you needed to feed your family,
then you might get a sense of the rage involved. Waiters have one
of the few jobs where their compensation depends on the whims
of their customers.

And believe me, waiters get stiffed. I can't tell you how many
times I've seen patrons walk out of the restaurant without leaving
a gratuity. When it happens to me, I usually grin and bear it. I've
come to the conclusion that waiters have to put up with the bad
tips if they want to be around for the good ones. But not all waiters are as patient as I am.

A few years ago I was working a slow weekday shift at The
Bistro with Allie, my girlfriend at the time. Two young women
were seated in Allie's section. Allie, who was a very good waitress, doted on the young ladies. Running Allie ragged, the girls
ended up ordering a hundred dollars' worth of food and wine.
After they finished their meal the girls asked for the check, hur-
riedly stuffed a wad of bills into the check holder, and raced out
the front door. Allie, sensing something was amiss, ran to the
table and frantically counted the money they had left.

"Did they leave enough to cover the bill?" I asked, following
close behind.

"Yeah," Allie said, her face flushing an angry red. "But no tip!"

"Goddamnit," I said, pissed that Allie was going to be in a bad
mood the rest of the night. "If they can't afford to leave a tip, then
they can't afford to eat out."

Allie wasn't listening to me. Allie was running toward the
front door.

"Wait a minute," pleaded Brian, our old assistant manager, putting himself between the homicidal server and the front door.

Allie pushed Brian aside, opened the front door, and ran into the street. I followed her outside and yanked her back onto the sidewalk.

"Allie," I pleaded, "don't get run over because those two cows stiffed you."

Allie spied her customers sprinting down the street. Jumping up and down, she screamed, "THANKS A LOT, YOU CHEAP BITCHES!"

It might be my imagination filling in details after the fact, but I swear all activity froze mid-motion at that instant. Even the cars stopped rolling down the street. Faces captured in a moment of time, every pedestrian on the street was looking at Allie.

"You cheapskates!" Allie bellowed. "Never come here again!"

The young women laughed, flipped Allie the bird, and continued on their way. I pulled on Allie's arm, worried that she was going to run those girls down and beat them into a puddle. She could do it, too.

"Not worth it," I cautioned. "Not worth it."

"I could *kill* those bitches!" Allie said, her voice cracking. At that moment her anger transformed into tears. The financial consequences of not being tipped suck, but there's an emotional and psychic toll as well. Not getting a tip *hurts*.

I can relate to Allie's pain. A few weeks ago, following house policy, I added an 18 percent tip to a ten top's check. The host, who had seemed happy with the service all night, got upset when he saw the automatic gratuity.

"You're not worth eighteen percent," he sneered.

I remember how much that man's words stung. That man assigned me a monetary worth and felt that he didn't owe me a penny more. He must've confused the practice of tipping with bidding for an item on eBay. I felt objectified and demeaned. I somehow maintained my composure and informed the gentleman he could discuss alternative payment arrangements with the local constabulary. The man left my 18 percent.

"Let's go back inside," I said to Allie, who was crying on my shoulder. "It's all over."

After work I took her out to a bar and medicated her with several Chardonnays. Several patrons who witnessed Allie's earlier meltdown came up to offer consolation and support. One of the well-wishers told us an interesting fact—our tip-challenged girls were *waiters* at a nearby restaurant. Sigh. No one brings it to you like one of your own kind.

Servers don't always remember good tippers, but we sure as hell remember the bad ones. The emotional pain and embarrassment of getting a bad tip burns that customer's face into our brains—much the same way a trauma fuses the most trivial details surrounding an accident into a victim's memory.

When I started working at The Bistro, I had a customer who always tipped me 8 percent. It wasn't just me or something I was doing—he tipped all the waiters 8 percent. After one abysmal tip too many, I confronted him.

"Excuse me, sir," I said. "Was there a problem with the service?"

"No," the man replied. "Why do you ask?"

"You left me an eight percent tip," I replied. "The customary tip is fifteen percent. I naturally assumed I was doing something wrong."

"Gee, Dad," said the man's teenage daughter, looking embarrassed.

The man glared at me like a bully who's just discovered that the person he's picking on has a black belt in karate.

"I'm sorry," the man said, quickly pulling his wallet out of his back pocket. "I made a mistake figuring the tip." The man dropped a few dollars on the table, dragging my tip total up to 13 percent. I took it.

The next day Fluvio got an angry e-mail from that customer, claiming that I had embarrassed him in front of his daughter and a restaurant full of people. Bullshit. I had called the guy on his cheap-ass ways, and he didn't like having his character exposed for all to see. Fluvio and I had a big fight over that one. To make a long story short, Fluvio posted a directive that any server who complained to a customer about a tip would be fired. Fluvio was right, of course. It's a no-win scenario. They'll just spread their special brand of parsimonious misery at another restaurant. After that incident, I never directly criticized customers over their cheapness again, except when they ask me to.

One night I served a young couple on a first or second date. The man, a take-charge sort of guy, ordered a mess of expensive food and a pricey bottle of wine. I gave the couple great service, so when I saw the 9 percent tip the man left me, I was slightly aggravated. As the couple got ready to leave, the man excused himself to use the men's room. When he was out of sight, his date waved me over to the table.

"Can I ask you something?" asked the woman, a very sexy redhead.

"Of course, madam."

"Did my friend tip you enough?"

Smiling, I opened the check holder and showed it to her.

The girl's face turned redder than her hair. She reached into her small purse and pushed a crumpled twenty-dollar bill into my hand.

"Sorry about that," she said.

"Thank you, madam," I replied, slipping the money into my pocket.

The man returned from the bathroom with a bounce in his step. Stupid bastard thought he was getting lucky that night. I knew better. As soon as the couple stepped outside the girl said something to the man and quickly walked away, her arms folded across her chest. The guy stood in the middle of the sidewalk looking like an artillery shell just landed on his head. Served him right.

Listen up, guys—sometimes girls will ask the waiter how much you tipped. They use it as a litmus test. They think that if you're not generous with the waiter, that means you won't be generous with them—whether that generosity is financial or emotional. Besides, bad tippers suck in bed.

Why do people tip what they do? Why are some people good tippers? Why are some people bad tippers? Studies conducted by sociologists suggest that the quality of service a customer receives isn't the biggest factor determining a waiter's tip. Roughly 70 percent of what predicts a customer's tipping behavior is the social norm of tipping itself. Society tells us that the standard tip is 15 to 20 percent. Since people usually follow the herd, the odds are good that 70 percent of all diners will leave the socially accepted monetary amount. Any waiter who's ever given a customer bad service but has still gotten a good tip knows this dynamic's at play. If tips were based solely on quality of service, then waiters would've gone extinct a long time ago.

I know what you're thinking. Seventy percent of a waiter's work is done before we even get near a table. So why am I bitching about bad tips? I'm bitching because there's still that other 30 percent of the dynamic that influences tipping to deal with. Think about it. If you get a 70 on a test, you're getting a D! Having only 70 percent of your customers leave average tips is like you're getting a D, too. A server has to get 80 to 90 percent of his customers to leave tips in the 15 to 20 percent range. To do that, a waiter has to have a firm grasp of the oddities, pressures, and subtle expectations that might increase or decrease a gratuity.

A few years ago a study claimed that if waiters employed certain subtle nonverbal tactics, they could increase their tip percentage. The study suggested drawing a smiley face on the customer's check, gently touching a patron's shoulder, or kneeling at the table, ostensibly to be at eye level with the diners.

When I read that study, I dismissed it out of hand. First off, touching the customer and adding saccharine artwork to the check works only if the server is a girl—and a blond, big-titted girl at that. Yes, the Cornell School of Hotel Administration spent good money on a study which proved that blond female servers with low body fat and large cup sizes made more money than their less-endowed female counterparts or male waiters. Never mind that if a guy draws a smiley face on the check, it's just plain creepy. And kneeling at the table? That shit might fly at Applebee's or the Outback but not at a high-end place. Can you imagine a waiter copping a squat next to a table at Gordon Ramsey's London? Gordon would rip the server's balls clean off.

The other 30 percent of what determines a waiter's tip boils down to how customers view themselves as people. If patrons perceive themselves as generous persons, and a waiter nurtures that feeling by treating them like a million bucks, then they will leave a good tip. Some customers like to think they're in touch with the plight of the workingman. If waiters properly exploit that bourgeoisie guilt, then they're going to pick up some extra cash. Then you get the customers who are snobs, people for whom owning brand names, wearing the right clothes, drinking rare vintages, and maintaining social standing are all that matter. If waiters project a subtle sense of deferral commingled with a slight hint of obsequiousness, these customers will view them like servants who've been in the family for generations and tip accordingly. Ass-kissing maître d's are especially good at this. The surest way for a server to increase his or her tips is to follow the biggest vein of weakness in a customer's personality and mine it for all it's worth.

A good waiter needs to push the right buttons in order to seduce a customer. In order to find those buttons, a server, like any good salesman, has to have a firm grasp of human weakness. Don't think I'm immune, either. I like to be coddled, flattered, and made to feel like I'm the only person in the room, too. That's why those lap dancers have so much of my money.

Waiters also have to contend with the dreaded customer who's never going to leave a good tip. Tight-fisted patrons incapable of generosity, these people are so afraid of losing whatever they have that they are unable to part with the tiniest piece. Giving gifts or money to others is painful, although they seldom have problems spending money on themselves. Chronically self-centered, they live in a world where they think people exist to serve them for little or no compensation.

Case in point: I once had a man who started choking at one of my tables. He waved off all attempts for assistance, but when he started to turn blue, I stepped in and Heimliched him. (It wouldn't do to have a customer die in my section.) I applied a few quick abdominal thrusts and the bolus obstructing the man's airway projectiled out of his mouth and splattered onto the table. Can you guess what kind of tip the man gave me after saving his life? Eight percent! I also found out from the name of the credit card that this guy was a doctor. Next time I let him die.

Customers like these are never going to change. The best way for a waiter to deal with these patrons is to fuck with them so they never darken the doorway of his establishment again. I know what you're thinking. You think I should have more sympathy for my tip-challenged customers. "Maybe he or she grew up poor and fears growing broke?" That's bullshit. Working-class people with far less money than their well-heeled counterparts with generosity issues are often the best tippers. I've known plenty of wealthy people who started out in life with nothing and are good tippers till this day. Shitty tippers are bad for business, and they've got to go. If you think I'm being callous, remember, a restaurant is a business—it's not your dining room. I'm an independent contactor trying to make a living. If you have a business and you've got customers who chronically underpay or have invoices 90 days late, do you want to do business with them in the future if you don't have to? No? I rest my case.

Since tipping is a social behavior it should come as no surprise that patterns emerge regarding how people tip. I've noticed that patrons can be classified into several categories when it comes to tipping. For the sake of convenience, I've listed them for your perusal. See if you fit into any of these categories.

✔ THE VERBAL TIPPER

—Heavy on praise but cheap with the cash. I'm surprised they don't put happy-face stickers on the check. I got enough of those cheap rewards in grammar school. Waiters don't want hugs. Show us the money.

✔ THE ACCOUNTANT

—Customers who tip on the amount of the check *before* tax. If forced to split a check of $100.01 between two credit cards, one guy will tip $7.50 and the other will tip $7.49. Always asking for duplicate copies of the check and complaining about the prices, these people enjoy a special place in hell. Oh, who am I kidding? These tightwads would ask Charon for a receipt before he ferried them across the river Styx.

✔ THE COMPENSATOR

—Usually cocaine-snorting, hooker-squiring, wealthy Neanderthal types who heap abuse on the waitstaff. These patrons, almost exclusively men, tip lavishly as a way to apologize for their boorish behavior. Waiters tend to have ambivalent feelings toward these patrons. We love how they pass out the cash but don't like how they make us feel like whores.

✔ THE FLAT TIPPER

—You could spill hot soup on their baby or treat them like the sultan of Brunei, they'll always tip you 15 percent.

✔ THE INGRATIATOR

—People (usually rich) afflicted with bourgeoisie guilt who want to demonstrate to themselves and everybody else that they're "down with the workingman." They give nice tips, encourage you to call them by their first names, and sing your praises to the owner. But if you start dating their daughter, they'll freak the fuck out. Guess who's coming to dinner?

✔ THE SUGAR DADDY

—Out-of-shape, wealthy Lotharios who try securing sexual favors from waitresses by giving them embarrassingly large tips. These mono-browed guys, who should be popping Zoloft instead of Viagra, think cash is going to make that hot-bodied twenty-five-year-old overlook their shocking lack of social graces, three ex-wives, personality disorders, and the wily thicket of hair growing out of their ears. Repulsed at the thought of being purchased like cattle, most waitresses can spot these guys coming a mile away. They'll take these men's money, of course, but just when the guys start licking their lips in anticipation, the waitresses'll turn around and tell them they have a boyfriend, are married, are lesbian, are transgendered, or are some combination thereof. Sadly, not all waitresses are immune to this nonsense. We've all seen nebbishy-looking rich guys squiring unbelievably hot babes while the much better-looking waiters, doormen, and busboys burn with envy. Money can create an alternate sex appeal. Every server knows at least one waitress who gave it up to a rich guy. Yes, I know I'm being a tad misogynistic, but don't be outraged. Male waiters are far worse. They'll screw anything that moves for free.

✔ THE AVERAGE JOE

—They tip 15 to 20 percent when they go out to eat. Average pains in the ass, these people constitute 70 percent of the dining public.

✔ THE 10 PERCENTER

—These diners still think it's the 1950s, Eisenhower's president, and waiters still get 10 percent. Usually senior citizens.

✔ THE FOREIGNER

—Customers who come from other countries and feign ignorance about American tipping customs so they can save a few bucks. The worst offenders are the Russians and the British. Don't laugh, Frenchy, you're not far behind. Italians and Israelis aren't that great, either. The Germans? They're not bad tippers.

✔ THE NICE CUSTOMER

—These patrons respect you as a professional and treat you like one. They tip 25 percent and up. Valued regular customers. Not enough of them.

✔ THE CHEAPSKATE

—Pricks who are incapable of generosity.

✔ THE FORMER WAITER

—Those who've ever waited on tables usually leave a good tip. Kudos if they don't announce their former waiterhood status (I hate that). Former waiters who leave bad tips are doomed to repeat working as waiters in all their subsequent reincarnations until they get their karmic shit together.

✔ THE WHORE

—The female equivalent of the Sugar Daddy. Usually attractive women who think flirting with a waiter and shaking their moneymakers will count as a tip. They don't—unless we're talking blowjobs.

Another thing people don't realize is that servers don't keep all of their tips. Depending on where they work, servers could be giving away 20 to 40 percent of their money to the busboys, food runners, bartenders, maître d', or hostess in what's called the "tip-out." That's normal procedure. Sadly, many corrupt owners and managers demand a percentage of the tips as well—a practice that is illegal in most states. Most servers, especially if they're working in a fancy place making serious money, usually cave in. Depending on the restaurant, between tip-outs and bribes, waiters need to earn $125 to $150 in order to take home an even $100.

Waiters aren't above a little larceny, either. A common restaurant scam is something called the "double tip." Most restaurants tack on an automatic gratuity for parties larger than six people. If they don't, they're assholes. Large parties take up valuable space for longer than two or four tops. If waiters get stiffed by a large party, they might end up working the entire night for peanuts. The added tip is an insurance policy against that happening. Unscrupulous waiters will snag some extra cash by employing a little grift.

Sometimes customers, often drunk, are unaware a gratuity has been added to the bill, so they *tip on top of it!* Waiters "facilitate" this error by writing the total with the automatic gratuity included in big script *on the back of the check.* Then the waiter presents the check to the customer itemized side down, hoping the sucker—ahem, customer—will just glance at the circled total and tip on top of it. It's dishonest. It's wrong. When I worked at Amici's, I did it all the time. The lesson here? *Always examine the check!* There are other little scams waiters can employ to jack up their tips—but I'm not giving away all the secrets.

I'll bet you didn't think tipping was such a complicated issue. My friends, I've just scratched the surface.

CHAPTER 10

Why Be a Waiter?

Waiters depend on tips to survive. As you've read, it can be a fairly irregular source of income. You might think it's a miracle anyone wants to wait tables in the first place, but, trust me, there's usually never a shortage of applicants. Waiting tables is as addictive as crack cocaine.

It's the quiet zone between lunch and dinner service. I'm spread out in the back with an espresso and my copy of the *New York Times*. The staff's clustered around me, chattering away as they eat their midday meal. The door chimes. The sound of silverware scraping against plates comes to a halt. I look over the top of my paper, half expecting to see another adulterous couple skulking around the front door.

Standing in the doorway, however, is a fresh-faced kid no older than nineteen. He's not eating here. The staff breathes a sigh of relief. Lunch break uninterrupted, the noise of people eating refills the air.

"I'll bet he's looking for a job," Imelda says, digging into her pasta.

I sigh deeply. I had a busy morning and was enjoying my little moment of Zen. Annoyed, I fold my paper, place it on the table, and walk toward the front.

"Hi," the kid says, extending his hand. "Are you the manager?"

"I am," I acknowledge. I tell the kid my name and shake his hand.

"I'm looking for a job," the kid says. "Do you have any openings?"

"We do. Let me get you an application."

"Thanks."

I kneel down behind the hostess stand and rummage through the plastic filing cabinet where we keep the applications. Fluvio is terribly disorganized. File pockets overflow with scores of forgotten résumés and applications. Fluvio doesn't look at 10 percent of applications people drop off. The secret to getting hired at The Bistro is catching Fluvio on the odd afternoon when he's actually here. If he likes you, you're hired.

I find an application and ask the young man to fill it out.

"You make good money here?" the kid asks, as he fills in the required fields.

"Depends on the day," I reply.

"Oh," the kid murmurs. "Which days are good money?"

"Fridays and Saturdays. We also have a strong Monday and Wednesday night."

"I'm available on weekends."

"We assign shifts based on seniority. It takes a while for new people to get to the really good shifts."

The kid looks crestfallen.

"But you never know," I say, trying to end the conversation on a light note. "I've got a waitress having a baby. Maybe something'll open up."

"Thanks," the kid replies. After a few minutes he stops writing and hands me the application

I skim over it. The kid's a student at a local college looking for extra money. He's worked summers at a deli but has no fine-dining experience. Sometimes not having experience is a plus. A newbie to the restaurant world's a tabula rasa that can be trained to do things just the way The Bistro wants them done. The downside's the amount of time you have to invest bringing the restaurant virgin up to speed. I've spent weeks training new servers, only to watch them throw in their apron to become professional yogis or Pilates teachers. That's a pain in the ass.

That's why we normally hire people with a couple of years under their belt. There's a downside to hiring experienced staff, of course—they often come in full of piss and vinegar and try to change the way things have been done for years. I'm not against reform or new ideas, but hotshots like that are usually after my job. They don't last long. Eventually they quit. Trust me, I have my ways. Fluvio isn't the only one who can act like a bastard.

"Okay," I say. "I'll give your application to the owner. If he's interested, he'll call you."

"Thanks," the kid says. "Any idea how long that'll be?"

I feel for the kid. He needs money, but he's not a good fit for The Bistro. It'd be cruel to hire him.

"If you don't hear from him in two weeks," I reply, hoping the kid reads between the lines, "then he's not interested."

The kid shows a flicker of disappointed understanding. "Thanks, sir," he says sheepishly.

"Good luck."

I watch the kid walk down the street. I feel bad for him, but I have to think about what's best for the restaurant. I keep my eye out for competent and quiet professionals, the smart waiters who keep their mouths shut and their eyes open. When jumping to another restaurant, these people don't rock the boat. They know patience is the key. Within months talent and good work ethics push them to the top of the heap. Grateful managers feel compelled to award them with moneymaking shifts. If that doesn't happen, a professional waiter looks for greener pastures.

My espresso's gone cold. I head into the back to brew another one. As I listen to the steam press through the grounds, I wonder for the millionth time why anyone would want to become a waiter. The University of Chicago recently did a survey of twenty-seven thousand Americans about job satisfaction and happiness. Clergy and firefighters were at the top of the job-satisfaction list. Waiters were at the bottom. Considering the shit we put up with, that's no surprise. For me, that survey's findings are laden with personal irony. Like most little boys, I wanted to be a fireman when I grew up. When I got to college, I studied to be a priest. Now, at thirty-eight, I'm a waiter. I started out heading for the top of the list, only to end up on the bottom. Where did I go wrong?

People who become waiters fall into three distinct categories: people trying to become something else, people whose lives are falling apart, and people stuck somewhere in the middle. Tucked within those categories is a small and distinct subgroup, the professional servers, people who make waiting tables their life's work. I'll admit those three categories are kind of broad. Waiters often find themselves with one foot in one category and one in the other. I've personally been in all three categories simultaneously.

The first type of server is the one you're most accustomed to seeing. These are waiters who, when not fetching lemon for your water, are busy trying to become something *else*. They're going to college, pursuing dance careers, writing the great American novel, sculpting, drug dealing, modeling for pornographic Web sites, and, of course, *acting*. Lifelong waiterdom holds little appeal for these individuals. The only reason they're working in a restaurant is because the money and schedule allow them time to achieve their long-term goals.

Because university registrars take perverse pride in design-ing Byzantine class schedules that offer mandatory courses available only when Neptune's orbit intersects Pluto's during a leap year, students' academic calendars are notoriously chaotic. Since restaurant jobs have more flexibility in scheduling than other jobs, many waiters are college students. It's a natural fit; students take classes during the day, work in the evening, and party into the wee hours of the night. Sleep? You've got to be kidding me.

Money is also a big factor. There are few jobs outside waiting tables where workers can make so much money in such a short amount of time. A normal evening shift usually lasts eight hours. A good waiter working an upscale establishment can clear $200 a night, sometimes more. That's $25 an hour! Not all servers reach this level, of course, but even if they clear only $100 a night, that still works out to almost $13 an hour. That beats the hell out of working at the college bookstore or delivering pizza for minimum wage. Outside of drug dealing, dorm-room prostitution, and creating Web sites like MySpace, waiting tables provides the biggest financial bang for the least temporal buck.

After the students comes the artistes—the endless procession of models, painters, writers, and actors—who struggle to make ends meet as they chase their *American Idol* dreams. I remember one waiter, an aspiring screenwriter, who shamelessly pitched his script to every unwilling customer he thought might get him a shot at Hollywood. He had a brilliant idea, so it was tough to watch his zeal turn into measured optimism, devolve into cynicism, and finally ossify into "c'est la vie."

I've encountered a few "actors" along the way as well. One girl I worked with did foot-fetish films and cable TV porn on the side. She won't be winning any Academy Awards, but hey, you can't knock a girl for trying. It's small wonder why so many struggling actors wait tables—it's a great place to hone your thespian skills. You try selling "Chilean sea bass garnished with endive marmalade" with a straight face. Think of it as culinary method acting, complete with imperious Europeans screaming at you. All this talk about waiters and acting reminds me of that old joke.

"My son's an actor in New York."

"Really? What restaurant?"

That underscores the bitter reality many artists who wait tables struggle with on a daily basis. When asked what they "do," they usually reply, "I'm an actor," or "I'm a writer." For the first couple of years that's okay—but, after several years working in the restaurant biz, if the bulk of your income still comes from waiting tables, you're a waiter. Don't get me wrong. I admire people who struggle to pursue their artistic dreams, but when a guy claiming to be a writer has been a server for years and is still working on the draft of his first novel, he's living in the deluded zone.

Sometimes when aspiring photographers or sculptors realize they've been waiting tables for too long, that's the kick in the ass they need to get out there and hustle up their own luck. Many waiters, through effort and by dint of hard work, leave the restaurant behind to pursue their dream careers. Occasionally lightning strikes and a waiter goes from waiterhood to superstardom "overnight." My favorite story is of Erika Sunnegårdh, a forty-year-old aspiring opera singer who spent eighteen years waiting tables in the Bronx, hoping for her big break. Eighteen years is a *long* time to wait. Singing at funerals to keep her voice in shape, Erika was getting close to throwing in the towel. Having never appeared onstage in any opera *anywhere*, she tried out for a role in Beethoven's *Fidelio* at the Metropolitan Opera. Awed by the majesty of her voice, the producers asked her to understudy for the performer singing the title role. In classic Hollywood fashion, the star fell ill on the day the performance was being broadcast to 10 million radio listeners, and Erika stole the show. Now she's an opera star. I wish every aspiring singer and dancer I've met in the restaurant business could hit it big, but, as Simon Cowell mercilessly informs us every week, that can't always happen.

The next category of server, people who don't know what do with their lives, is the type of waiter I most closely identify with. It starts out innocently enough. You lose your job, have a nervous breakdown, get paroled, or have a midlife crisis, and you have no idea what to do next.

I think there are many waiters like me, sitting on life's fence and trying to figure out what they want to be when they grow up. Before age and limitations start creeping up on you, waiting can be a fun life. When you're in your early twenties, it's a blast, but then, when you're in your forties, it can be horrifying. I partly blame my predicament on that crack-cocaine quality of waiting tables. Here, the schedule and easy money are important. Whereas with college students it's a means to an end, for the

Hamlet waiter it's a narcotic, seductive influence. If you skip college and go into the restaurant business, the odds are good that you'll be making more than a college graduate for quite a while. I made more as a waiter than I ever did as a low-level flunky in corporate health care. After a few weeks of profitable shifts you begin to think, Hey, this isn't too bad. Of course, as time goes by, your friends' incomes will outstrip yours and leave you in the dust. Out of all my college-educated friends, I earn the least amount of money. Don't even talk to me about 401(k)s.

The schedule's also a biggie. If you're a night owl like me, you'll take to the restaurant business like a duck to water. I like getting up at eleven o'clock and going to bed at three. Night is my natural element. My synapses fire up when the moon's hanging in the sky. Since most people are off when I'm working and vice versa, there's never any line at the movies, and finding a parking spot at the mall's a snap. Waiters begin to pity nine-to-five wretches with their miserable traffic-filled commutes and weekends spent running errands. Living outside the normal flow of the workweek, waiters get to see how crazy American life can be. Of course, we can develop a smug sense of superiority about how we're somehow above it all. I certainly did.

Being on the outside of the mainstream, however, is fun only when you *choose* to be on the outside. When it's no longer a choice, when you wake up one day and realize that you have to wait tables to survive, the "waiter mystique" wears thin real fast. Most people who waited tables in college look back on their serving days with a twisted sense of nostalgia. That's because, in the back of their minds, they knew they were getting out. Longtime waiters who successfully escape to other professions look back on their time in the restaurant trenches the way shell-shocked vets look back on heavy combat. "Yeah, I met a few good men along the way—but I'd never want to go back."

Of course, some waiters do very well in this situation. My brother springs immediately to mind. He's been in the restaurant business since he was sixteen—almost twenty years. Along the way he's done it all. He's been a dishwasher, busboy, server, head-waiter, and manager. He's hired and fired people and gotten fired and hired himself. He's been punched, kicked, groped, insulted, and kissed.

My brother never planned on being in the restaurant business for so long. Like me, he's still trying to figure out what he wants to do when he grows up. Unlike me, however, he didn't wait to get on with his life as he tries to figure it out. It took several years, but he finished his college degree, got married, bought a house, and had a baby—all while being a waiter. This guy didn't sit around and cry "woe is me" and wait for the perfect situation to start his life. He threw himself into life's slipstream and ended up doing all right.

The sad truth is that some waiters are *wasting* their lives. Too busy having fun and reveling in hyperbolic bitterness, these losers pretend they're somehow above the fray of ordinary life, living a bonhomie existence that allows them to critique everyone's life choices but their own.

This appellation of loserdom doesn't apply to all waiters trying to figure out what they want to do. Many waiters, like my brother, are using the restaurant business as a safe haven to venture out and build a life. Some waiters are just hiding. If you've worked in the restaurant business, you've seen the type of waiter I'm talking about. The ones who always talk about opening a restaurant, going back to school, starting a business, or touring Europe—only to spend year after year stuck in the same place. They're all talk.

There are a few rare individuals who make waiting tables a career. Usually hardy souls from parts of Europe where waiting is considered an honorable vocation (complete with formal schooling and internships), these servers are blessed with iron feet, steel legs, and an almost religious dedication to professionalism. The waiter I think of as the epitome of the career server is Wolfgang Zwiener, the former headwaiter at Peter Luger's steakhouse in Brooklyn. Zwiener came to New York from Bremen,

Germany, after he completed a three-year apprenticeship. (Most waiters today train for three days and watch a sexual harassment video.) After a stint at Lüchow's on East Fourteenth Street in the early 1960s, Mr. Zwiener ended up at Peter Luger's, becoming the headwaiter in 1968. Over the decades, between all the double shifts and parties, he got married, had two sons, and, on a waiter's salary, put them both through college and bought a retirement home in Florida. It didn't hurt that almost all the tips were in cash.

After almost forty years at Luger's, Wolfgang decided to move up in the world. Instead of retiring, Wolfgang took his sons' advice and parlayed his lifetime of restaurant know-how into his own restaurant—Wolfgang's—the highly regarded steakhouse on Park Avenue. Since its grand opening in 2004, he's opened another location in the Tribeca section of Manhattan. I guess he's doing okay.

Over the years I met a few people like Zwiener, people who toiled for years at some of the fanciest restaurants in New York City and made a comfortable living for themselves and their families. These guys were dealt a hand, and they played it to the best of their ability. Waiters like these are the heroes of the profession, servers for whom hospitality, refinement, and good service are an almost priestly vocation. Deep down, I know I could never muster up the commitment to the restaurant business possessed by Zwiener and others like him. Compared to waiters of that caliber, I am but a humble amateur. But compared to the next group of waiters we're going to examine, I'm Michael Jordan.

Quite a few waiters have lives that are train wrecks. A famous chef once observed that the restaurant business is a haven for people who don't fit in anywhere else. That's true. The restaurant business can be like the French Foreign Legion—without the heavy weaponry. But think about it, if all these people don't fit in anywhere else, that usually means there's something *wrong* with them!

The restaurant business is a fluid and chaotic environment.

Many hiring decisions are made under pressure. Managers need warm bodies to work the grill, wash dishes, chop onions, and bring food to the table. Owners often rely on instinct when hiring people, and references are rarely checked. With this kind of screening system fuckups can breed like cockroaches. Anyone who's ever worked in the restaurant industry has encountered results of these bad hires—the anxiety-producing drama queens, the falling-down drunks, the borderline nymphomaniacs, the hardcore drug addicts, and the depressed guys who cry on every waitress's shoulder. These aren't just people with problems. Heck, we all have problems at some point. These individuals are so problematic they make working in a restaurant harder than it has to be. Over the years I've noticed wacko servers share some common characteristics.

- Divorced (usually twice, and they have *bad* relationships with their exes)
- DUI (multiple)
- No car (see above)
- Serious substance abuse problem (hence the DUI)
- Transient living situation (always crashing at friends' or strangers' houses, living out of cars, motels, or boarding homes)
- Show up to work dirty (why spend money on laundry when you can buy crack?)
- Always trying to borrow money; always owing coworkers money
- Never wanting to work the shifts they're scheduled—then crying because they're broke
- Always wanting to leave early
- Crying at work; nervous breakdowns in the walk-in fridge; bipolar behavior; nymphomania; subject to rages
- Talking to themselves (okay, I'll admit I've done that)
- Always whining and seeking sympathy; attention seeking
- And, for some reason, always have *bad teeth*

Don't worry, if you're a divorcée or you've had a DUI, you don't automatically qualify as a screwup. (I've needed two root canals since I've been a waiter!) Yet, if you've waited on tables, you've met servers who've had several of the above conditions operating simultaneously. There are servers out there who've worked every restaurant in the yellow pages, never stayed more than three months at any one place, and walk around looking like they're heavily medicated. Their résumés usually reflect a steady downward spiral in terms of job responsibility and income. These are the people you pray don't own guns.

Some managers and owners *love* hiring these kinds of people. Instead of trying to get them help or lending an understanding ear, they ruthlessly exploit them. Mentally ill or compromised people are vulnerable. People with drug problems, burned-out single moms, downsized tech workers struggling with depression, people with financial problems, or the average alcoholic are easy to manipulate. These are the waiters who won't complain when management steals from the tip-out, engages in discriminatory hiring practices, indulges in sexual harassment, or hurls sexist and racial invectives at the staff. Some restaurant managers go out of their way to hire messed-up people. Why? *Because they're easier to control.* If the staff's easy to control, then it's easier for management to rip them off to line their own pockets. Restaurant workers are basically disposable. Because waiters tend to be a self-involved lot, mentally ill coworkers often go unnoticed or are ignored until they decompensate and can't perform. Since there's usually no health insurance in the restaurant industry, getting these people any kind of psychiatric help is expensive and well nigh impossible. When these workers flame out, they end up quitting or getting fired. If you start working at a restaurant and discover that 80 percent of the people are beyond nuts, you're in a toxic work environment. Get out before you end up going crazy yourself.

The espresso machine finishes brewing my demitasse. I place it on a saucer and head back toward the front of the restaurant.

As I sip my coffee I look out the front window and think about all the people I've worked with in the restaurant business. They're mostly faces not matching up to any names. Some of them worked in this business briefly and ended up doing something else. One of them died.

When people ask me what I do for a living, I tell them I'm a waiter. But I also want to tell them I'm a man who dreams of living a different life. My writing has been giving me hope that I'm a waiter working toward becoming something else. On my darkest days, however, I feel like a train-wreck personality that's going to stay in this business forever.

I sip my coffee and sigh. Maybe I should have been a fireman.

CHAPTER 11

A Little Knowledge Is a Dangerous Thing

The customer at table 17 is taking forever to make up her mind. As I wait patiently I idly think that, if I had become a fireman, I'd never have a problem getting laid. What is it about those guys that gets girls all hot and bothered? Man, the four-year-old me wasn't thinking that when he wore his fireman's cap to bed.

"Might I suggest the salmon, madam?" I offer, finally breaking the silence. "It's quite good here."

"I don't know," the woman says, furrowing her brow as she peers at the menu. "I'm a fussy eater."

No kidding, I think to myself.

It's Saturday night. I have other tables to attend to. This lady's consumed one cocktail, twenty minutes, and most of my patience while contemplating her menu. Her husband's getting antsy. I can feel my other customers' eyes running up and down my body, their telepathic cries for attention rattling off the back of my skull like hail on a tin roof. The part of my brain that runs on autopilot, my waiter's sixth sense, which lets me know drinks are running low or appetizers need to be cleared, starts tugging at my conscious mind.

"Let me give you a few more minutes," I say, turning to leave. "I'll be right—"

"Don't go anywhere," the husband groans, "or she'll take even longer."

"Yes, sir," I reply, stopping in my tracks.

The woman's lips move like she's silently reciting the menu items out of a prayer book. Fussy eaters are an interesting evolutionary paradox. How did they manage to survive the primordial jungle and pass on their DNA? Didn't they just eat what was available or die? When haute cuisine was still a long way off, our appendixes might've been used to digest grass. You ate what you could when you could. I can just imagine some Stepford cave-wife getting mauled by a saber-toothed tiger because she dithered between picking free-range mastodon and dietetic tree bark. Picky eaters seem like an evolutionary dead end, but they're here anyway. I'm sure some academic will find a reason.

"Madam?" I prod gently. No response. Damn. There's never a saber-toothed tiger around when you need one.

The woman stares at the menu. This is taking way too long. I feel anxiety start to tickle my stomach. My blood pressure shoots up.

"Is the salmon farmed or organic?" the woman finally asks.

"It's organically farmed," I reply.

"There's no such thing as organically farmed," the woman snaps. "It's either wild or raised on a fish farm."

"These are farmed," I reply, "but the supplier doesn't use pesticides or antibiotics."

"Then it's not organic," the woman harrumphs.

I want to tell this lady she's wrong. She's operating under the misconception that all organic fish is caught in the wild. Organic produce, by definition, is raised in a controlled environment that eschews the use of chemical pesticides, nonorganic feeds, and synthetic fertilizers. Because wild fish are not raised in such a controlled environment, hence the name "wild," many of them don't meet USDA requirements to be labeled organic. But here's the real kicker: under the current rules only vegetarian fish like tilapia and catfish can be labeled organic. Salmon are carnivores. Unless they've been raised on a fish farm eating nuts and twigs instead of little fish, they can't be considered organic. What my customer's asking for is an impossibility. Don't blame me. Blame the Department of Agriculture.

"I assure you, madam," I say, "the salmon is excellent."

"When was it delivered?"

"Friday."

"Not today?"

"No, madam."

"Ugh," the woman says, wrinkling her nose in disgust. "Frozen fish. I never eat frozen fish."

I catch the annoyed look threatening to spread over my face. This lady has no idea how restaurants operate. Most restaurants freeze their fish. If a restaurant gets a fish delivery twice a week, what are they supposed to do the other five days? Not sell fish? You can't run a restaurant that way. Fish is delivered to The Bistro on Tuesdays and Fridays. The guys clean the fish, cut them into filets, wrap the measured portions in Saran Wrap, and freeze the suckers solid. Even Nobu, New York City's temple of sushi, sometimes uses frozen fish. The chefs use a special deep-freeze process that transforms succulent fish into rock-hard slabs. When the frozen tuna needs to be pressed into service, all they need is a band saw, ten minutes, and a bowl of warm water to return the fish to its pristine red state. Fish purveyors have spent millions of dollars building gigantic freezers to freeze tons of premium tuna with sophisticated technologies that preserve the texture and flavor of the fish. Done right, tuna can stay fresh for two years! Imagine telling my finicky customer *that*.

"I'll have the spaghetti Pomodoro then," the lady says, angrily shutting her menu.

"For chrissake, Marjorie," her husband says, "you can make that at home for a dollar."

"They don't have anything organic," the woman pouts. "I'm fine with pasta."

"At least try the salmon."

"No!"

"It's a great price for salmon, Marjorie."

"It's farmed!" the wife says. "Forget it."

Marjorie's husband has stumbled onto the reason why The Bistro uses farmed salmon. Farmed fish is *cheaper*. That's why the salmon we serve is $22.95 instead of $35.95. Restaurants serving super–high-quality fish have to pass the food costs along to their customers. That might work for Nobu, but the average restaurant can't risk buying super-premium fish and not moving it. Customers zealously demand the best, but when faced with the prices in black and white, their fervor often cools. Restaurants have to balance food quality with a healthy profit margin.

"Marjorie . . ." the husband groans.

If I don't get away from these people, I'm going to go into the weeds. I decide honesty's the best policy.

"Folks, I'm sorry," I say. "But I've got other customers."

"She'll have the salmon," the husband says, waving me away.

"Very good, sir."

"But . . ." the wife sputters. "He can't order for me!"

I decide to stymie the progress of women's liberation and run away from the table.

I go to the POS computer and ring in the woman's salmon. She's going to be fine. The salmon's excellent. Besides, if she knew better, she'd want the fish to be frozen. Some fish, like salmon, contain parasites that are killed during the freezing process. If the fish wasn't frozen in the hold of the ship, you better pray it was frozen in the restaurant. People get sick from improperly stored fish. No one ever died from frozen fish. We all survived fish sticks, didn't we?

A few minutes later I encounter another animal lover.

"Do you serve free-range chicken?" she asks.

"No," I answer honestly.

"Why not?"

Fluvio told us to tell the customers we use organically raised chicken. Then again Fluvio automatically tells the customers whatever they want to hear. Fluvio almost told a Jewish customer we were a kosher place. Luckily, I intercepted that faux pas. I've learned not to listen to Fluvio.

"You'd have to talk to the owner about that," I reply. "I don't know why."

"I only eat chickens that were allowed to roam free and drink clean water," the customer says. "I think a happy chicken tastes better."

I shudder at the thought of happiness becoming a flavor enhancer. I wonder if chickens from industrial farms and free-range pastures appreciate the differences in their upbringing when facing the farmer's ax. Is the free-range chicken thanking the farmer for the nice living conditions as its head's being lopped off? I don't think so.

"Might I suggest pasta, madam?"

"How's the steak?" the lady asks.

"Excellent."

"Is it free range," the woman asks. "Like in Argentina?"

"Happy cows, madam?" I deadpan.

"Exactly," the woman says. "In Japan they feed their cows beer and massage them so they're really happy. Keeps the flesh tender."

There is some truth to what the lady's saying. If cows experience anxiety before they're slaughtered, they can release hormones that degrade the taste of the meat. I'm all for making a steer's end as painless as possible, but there's something about this lady's attitude that's creeping me out. Her desire to see animals humanely treated has less to do with compassion and more to do with her taste buds. It's like she won't be happy until every petting zoo's been turned into a death camp.

"That's Kobe beef, madam," I say.

"Do you have it?"

"No."

"Why not?"

"Because we're an Italian restaurant."

"Oh."

I finally persuade the woman to get the striped bass. Luckily, she doesn't inquire about its pedigree.

I sigh to myself. When I was a kid, customers never asked these kinds of questions. Gone are the days when patrons blindly ordered off the menu and took the chef's word as gospel. Things like free-range chicken, organic fish, and the stuff hemp-sandaled hippies ate was unheard off. Kobe steak? A sybaritic rarity. Nowadays customers armed with information gleaned from the Internet and television shows fancy themselves as apprentice chefs. Just because they read chef biographies and watch Bobby Flay, they think they know everything there is to know about restaurants and cooking. Trust me, they don't. In my seven years as a waiter I haven't learned a tenth of what there is to know. Do you watch *Grey's Anatomy* and think you can perform surgery? I hope not. Customers often think they're entitled to second-guess a chef's judgment.

Don't get me wrong, in the long run an educated customer's a good thing. I'm happy to see palates becoming more informed and adventurous. No one ate raw fish when I was in high school. When I was a kid, Tuesdays meant meat loaf and Fridays meant pizza. On Sundays Dad would try his hand at making something out of a thirty-year-old cookbook. One time he made something I call fish heads and oatmeal to this day. Dad tried calling it bouillabaisse, but I still don't believe him. He warped my tender culinary mind. I can't blame my father, though; he tried exposing his kids to a bit of culture. In the end he just couldn't overcome the Irish meat-and-potatoes genes.

Now American tastes are much more sophisticated. High school kids eat sashimi, college kids churn their own tofu, and adults daydream about opening vineyards in Napa. We have twelve-grain bread, frozen Thai food, twenty-dollar mustards, gourmet chocolates, and more places to eat out than ever before. Restaurants, food, and kitchen equipment are a multibillion-dollar industry, and every industry needs a PR network. Today the most visible propaganda arm of that industry is the Food Network.

The Food Network is, quite simply, the Death Star of American cooking. Born in the crucible of cable television, it gradually assumed the level of influence that once belonged to Julia Child and the James Beard Society. Long before *American Idol* and the rest of the reality TV craze, television executives stumbled upon the idea to pluck relatively unknown chefs out of obscurity and turn them into television superstars. These mad geniuses realized they could operate a television show with low overhead and make massive profits off food-industry ad dollars. You don't even have to be a chef! Look at Rachael Ray! The Food Network took its low-overhead shows and did what the news channels did—broadcast twenty-four hours a day, 365 days a year. Why watch a cooking show once or twice a week when you can watch one all the time? It's a great American tradition—take a fun activity and dedicate twenty-four hours of programming to it. It works for NASCAR and the Golf Channel, so I'm not surprised it works for food. Salivating over the free exposure, chefs and restaurateurs clamor to cook in the network's studio kitchens. The restaurant industry has always been an incestuous business. Chefs, owners, suppliers, dining-out guides, and food critics fall over one another with ass-kissing cross promotions, each trying to become the next Emeril, *Gourmet* magazine, or *Zagat*. I just wish waiters could get a reach around once in a while. We seem to have been left out of the loop.

Now there have always been cooking shows. Food on television is nothing new. I remember watching the Galloping Gourmet getting soused, trying to decipher Chef Tell's impenetrable accent, and Julia Child dumping wine into everything. Americans love cooking shows. Come to think of it, how many of us are eating when we watch a cooking show? As we watch the chef perform his or her magic, the humble ham sandwich we're gnawing on briefly transubstantiates into whatever the chef's preparing. There's always a small communion between viewer and chef, only you don't get to eat what they're making. It's like watching a Catholic mass on TV.

But the Food Network's evolved beyond mere cooking shows. When a channel has that much airtime to fill, it desperately needs *content*. The development guys have given us chefs battling in culinary Roman arenas, dragged viewers across the world looking for exotic flavors, and offered us a never-ending assemblage of toothy domestic goddesses teaching us how to whip up fantastic meals in fifteen minutes.

There's nothing wrong with learning about food, and there's nothing wrong with learning how to cook. In that regard I think the Food Network's a cool thing. You just have to remember those telegenic chefs massaging olive oil into rump roasts are also trying to move cheap aluminum cookware with their name on it out of a warehouse in southern China. I worry food is being sexualized into a sort of status symbol in the service of profit. What happens when these messages are constantly inculcated into people's psyches? I'm not saying they're doing anything deliberate, but after watching the Food Network's on-air personalities wax orgasmically in reverent tones about grilled this and sautéed that, the pickings in my average cupboard start looking shabby in comparison. I know—food's been a status symbol ever since the lords of the feudal manor ate meat while the peasants ended up with offal and the hooves. Fast-forward a thousand years. Today we drool over elaborately filmed platters on television the way chubby teenage girls look at the skinny fashion models. People think TV life is real life. Everyone wants to be a rock star. People want to eat like a rock star. We're starting to become convinced that everything that passes our lips has to be sexy, fresh, wonderful, and exciting. A peanut-butter-and-jelly sandwich doesn't cut it anymore.

One time I had a couple come into The Bistro long after the restaurant was closed. They said they were hungry and asked me to open the kitchen especially for them. I said I couldn't. When they asked me if there was another place open at that late hour, I suggested a diner down the street. They looked at me in shock. Diner food was beneath them. I'll never forget what the woman said as she walked out the door. "Where are we going to find a quality place to dine at now?"

People forget food is first and foremost about survival. Everything else is secondary. Some people believe the impetus of eating to stay alive has faded from our consciousness. Oh, yeah? Go three days without food. When you're starving, all the niceties about food presentation and theories about social communion, free-range this, and organic that go out the window. Remember the hungry refugees at the Superdome clamoring for food after Hurricane Katrina? Try being in their shoes. You'll remember very quickly that food's about survival. What did the man say? The only difference between civilization and chaos is three meals and twenty four hours? Chilling.

Despite all my bitching about the Food Network, I have to admit I watch it myself. I've always enjoyed watching Mario Batali huff and puff while competing on *Iron Chef*. I'm going to get no end of shit for saying this, but my favorite program is Rachael Ray's cooking show. I like how she whips up nice little meals using the stuff average people have lying around their kitchen. No, I don't like the cheap-ass tips she hands out on her show *Forty Dollars a Day*, but I understand that's a conceit designed to make for an interesting program. Besides, I always thought she was kind of cute. Did you see her in that layout in *Maxim*? Anthony Bourdain may bitch about her not being a chef, but somehow I don't think he'd look as good in a bikini.

As the night progresses I get seated the most difficult kind of customers a waiter has to deal with—foodies. Foodies are usually middle-aged people who fancy themselves experts on food, wine, and the finer points of table service. There's nothing wrong with being a gourmand, but foodies are not gourmands. They're gourmand wannabes. Like anything else, culinary knowledge takes time to learn. Foodies think they can watch one TV show and become the food critic for the *New York Times*. They're the culinary version of the guy who's had one karate lesson. They clutch their *Zagat* guides like Mao's Red Book and quote Frank

Bruni like brainwashed members of the Weather Underground. *Gourmet* magazine's their spank mag and the Food Network's their Spice Channel. Right off the bat, I know these four guys are going to be trouble.

"Excuse me, waiter," one of the men says. "Where's the bread from?"

I tell him it's from a commercial bakery.

"Oh," the man says, putting the bread back in the basket. "I thought it was artisanal bread."

"Sorry, sir."

"Do you have any other bread?" his companion asks.

"We don't, sir."

"Well, bring me some balsamic vinegar to dip this bread in."

"It's in the bottle next to you, sir," I say.

The bread lover picks up one of the bottles of balsamic vinegar we have on the tables and holds it up to the light.

"What kind of balsamic is in here?"

I tell him. It's a good commercial brand you can find in the supermarket.

"You don't have *super-fancy balsamic vinegar*, do you?" the man asks.

"I beg your pardon?"

"It's balsamic vinegar that costs two hundred dollars a bottle," the man says. "I have it at home. You can put it on ice cream."

"I've never heard of it," I say. "But then again, I learn something new every day."

"You should know about it," the man sniffs. "You're a waiter in a Tuscan restaurant."

"I don't think the management would be offended if you brought your own balsamic vinegar in, sir."

The man looks at me like I slapped him. "Just tell us the specials," he says dryly.

I tell the men the specials. We have a rib-eye-steak entrée for thirty dollars.

"I'd like the steak," the balsamic connoisseur says, "but I'm worried about mad cow disease."

"Our steaks are excellent," I reply. "But if you're really worried, I'd suggest you eat something else."

"But I'm in the mood for a steak," the man says, smiling slyly at his companions. This guy's putting me on for his amusement. Okay, pal, let's play.

"The steak's very good here, sir," I say.

"But how can you guarantee there'll be no mad cow disease in my steak?"

"No one can guarantee anything one hundred percent, sir."

"So it could have mad cow?"

"That's a very *remote* possibility."

"You sound so sure," the man says, smirking. "How can you be so sure?"

"I can explain it. I'm just not sure if you'd want me to."

The man stares at me. "By all means," he says. "Go ahead."

"Sir . . ."

"Tell me."

Okay. You asked for it.

"Well," I say, assuming a professorial air, "mad cow disease affects the spinal cord and neurological tissue of cows. When they butcher a cow in Europe, they sometimes process the whole carcass. When they remove the cow's brain, the nearby meat can get contaminated with the organisms that cause mad cow disease. Sometimes it's transferred from the brain into the meat by using contaminated knives."

My customer turns a lovely shade of green.

"In the United States," I rattle on, "we don't have that problem because we usually lop off the cow's head almost as soon as we kill it."

"Oh," the man says.

"So the odds that brain and spinal matter will get into your steak are small. And quality control would probably prevent a sick cow from being processed into food anyway."

"You didn't need to tell me all that," the man says.

"I warned you."

The newly minted vegetarian glares at me. "There was no need to get graphic."

"It's a graphic thing."

"I'll have the fettuccine Alfredo, Mr. Wizard," the customer says.

"Very good, sir," I say, keeping the grin off my face.

CHAPTER 12

Filth

If you thought the cow thing was disgusting, skip this chapter.

It's nine o'clock on Sunday evening. Facing Monday morning reentry, my customers have already settled up and are saying their good-byes. I'm happy. This is my favorite kind of night—regular customers coming in at a slow, steady, lucrative pace. I didn't break a sweat and I'm pocketing $200 bucks. Righteous.

"Thanks again," one of my favorite regulars, a burly man with an Amish-style beard, says. "Everything was wonderful, as always."

"Thank you, sir," I reply.

"Thanks for always taking such good care of us," the man's elegant wife says. "We appreciate your service."

"My pleasure."

"See you next week," the man says.

"Looking forward to it, sir."

"Good night."

I sigh as I watch my regulars walk out of sight. If all my customers were as polite and generous as these two, I'd be able to retire to Tahiti within a year. Oh well. I walk to the back of the restaurant and start doing my end-of-the-night paperwork.

Just as I start tabulating my receipts, the front door chimes. I groan inwardly. Technically The Bistro's open for a few more minutes. I don't need any last-minute diners keeping me here for another two hours. Besides, the kitchen guys are tired. Plastering the happy smile on my face, I get up from my seat and walk toward the entrance.

When I see who's waiting at the door, I'm both relieved and turned on. It's not a new customer. It's the hot twenty-something blonde who ate in my section with her three equally hot girl-friends at the beginning of the night. That table was a waiter's letter to *Penthouse*. The blonde and I flirted with each other shamelessly throughout the entire meal. I was a bit disappointed that she didn't leave me her phone number. But now she's back, looking for a little waiter love. *Oh yeah . . .*

I swap out my waiter smile for the real deal. As I get closer, however, I see that the girl's pale beneath her makeup. Some-thing's wrong. She's not showing me her bedroom eyes—she's showing me her pissed-off-customer look.

"Miss," I say, "is everything all right?"

"No," she says. "Everything is not all right. I got sick and threw up an hour after I left here."

"I'm terribly sorry to hear that."

"It was my tuna. There was something wrong with it."

Uh-oh. A customer's blaming The Bistro's food for making her sick. This can be a tricky situation.

"When did you start feeling sick?"

"Actually, I started feeling queasy at dessert," the girl says. "And I threw up the minute I got home."

"What time did you get sick, miss?" I ask.

"Around eight-thirty."

"And you finished your tuna around . . . ?"

"Seven-thirty?" the blonde says. "Maybe? What's with all the questions?"

"I'm just trying to understand what happened."

"You guys gave me food poisoning!" the blonde says, loudly. "And I want my money back!"

"Miss . . ."

"I got sick on your food! I want the entire bill refunded."

"Are your friends sick?" I ask.

"What does it matter?"

"I'm trying to determine if—"

"They're fine," the blonde says. "I think one of your cooks forgot to wash his hands after he went to the bathroom and infected my tuna! I want my money back."

Oh man, I hope none of the customers caught that visual.

"How are you feeling now?" I solicit gently.

"I'll be fine," the woman says. "I think it all came up when I puked."

"I'm glad to hear you're feeling better."

"I'm glad, too," the girl snorts. "You going to give me back my money or what?"

"Allow me a few moments, miss. I need to call the owner."

"Why?"

"He's the only one who can authorize a refund," I lie.

"Fine."

I head over to the waiter's station and disappear from the blonde's view. The odds that this girl got sick off her medium-well tuna are slim to none. I'm not a doctor, but I know from experience it normally takes seven to forty-eight hours for offending microbes to incubate in your system and make you sick. Even though there's a slim chance some superbug could have made her sick this quickly, it would still need two to three hours to start working its magic. This young woman claims she started feeling ill twenty minutes after swallowing the last bite of her yellowfin tuna. That's impossible. Of course, chemical poisoning could explain her rapid-onset symptoms, but since she's telling me she's feeling better and none of her friends are sick, the odds that ammonia or industrial-strength degreaser got into her food are remote. It's possible that the symptoms she experienced were caused by something she ate twenty-four hours earlier, and, since she just left our establishment, she's blaming it on us. Of course, it's also possible that she drank too much and simply threw up.

You can't tell this stuff to a customer who's blaming your establishment for food poisoning, though. They don't want an epidemiological lecture—they want justice. And, if a restaurant could possibly be at fault, even though it's unlikely, the best thing to do is pay up. No restaurant wants to get a reputation for serving cuisine you taste twice.

But something about this girl's story seems, well, fishy. She never looked sick when she was flirting with me. She also made a big show of picking up the tab and leaving me a nice fat tip. My theory is that when she got home the buzz from her Pinot Grigio wore off, and she had an episode of buyer's remorse. Quite a few of the twenty-something women (and men) I serve really can't afford the *Sex and the City* lifestyles they're living. They spend all their money on fancy clothes, expensive shoes, and dinners at trendy eateries so they can live some outsize Candace Bushnell fantasy. After their fancy cocktail soirees, you'll find half these girls slinking back to rat-trap apartments anxiously looking up their available credit on the Internet. I once dated a cute Manhattanite who was always dressed to the nines and ate every meal out. A few weeks into the relationship she hit me up for money to help cover her share of the rent in an apartment she shared with three other girls. I declined and suggested she move to Jersey. She told me she'd rather die.

I'm thinking this lady's claiming she's a victim of food poisoning to make The Bistro subsidize her evening's festivities. That probably explains why she's back here an hour after she left. If this was the real deal, she would have called from home the next day to complain. Quite a few customers have tried to pull this stunt over the years, and I'm not about to let this girl skate on a $300 bill. I don't care how cute she is. I return to the front and explain what I'm prepared to do.

"Madam," I say, "The Bistro runs a very clean and safe kitchen. All personnel have been trained in safe food-handling practices."

"Now wait a minute—" the young woman interjects.

"But," I say, talking over her, "we *are* sorry for your discomfort. Even though we're not admitting responsibility, we value your patronage as a customer. Therefore, the owner's going to refund *your* dinner and dessert. That will remove seventy-five dollars from your bill."

"But I want the *whole* bill refunded," the girl says.

"That we cannot do."

The girl tries giving me her best cold stare. While she's wasting her time, I enjoy looking at her green eyes. I notice they're flecked with gold. I start wondering how candlelight would reflect off her naked skin. . . .

"Okay," the girl says, interrupting my Spice Channel moment. "I'll take the refund."

"Thank you, miss," I reply. "I'm glad we were able to come to an accommodation."

I go to the back, perform some digital sleight of hand, and refund the girl's $75. My tip? That remains unchanged.

"There you are, miss," I say, handing the girl her altered credit card receipt.

The girl takes the receipt, turns on her heel, and walks out the door. So much for manners, but at least I get to scope her ass on the way out.

Since Fluvio will want to know about this, I leave a note in the shift log explaining what happened and what action I took. Then I go to the kitchen and confer with Armando.

"It wasn't us," he says, starting to get defensive. No chef likes being accused of making a customer sick—unless he meant to do it.

"I know you didn't do anything wrong," I say, soothingly. "But you need to know what she said."

"She wanted her tuna cooked to death!"

"Some people," I mutter.

I'm not saying customers have never gotten sick from something they ate at The Bistro. When a restaurant cranks out thousands upon thousands of meals a year, the odds are good *some-*

thing bad will happen. If a restaurant follows safe food-handling practices and keeps things clean, this reduces the odds that bad things will happen—but it doesn't eliminate them.

Some restaurants are better than others. The Bistro's a very clean place, but I've been in restaurants where I've seen things that would make your skin crawl.

I once had the misfortune to work in a restaurant where the owner was so cheap that there was never any hand soap in the dispensers. Sometimes there wasn't even toilet paper. The owner also felt that some of the health code rules were optional. For example, waiters were expected to foist a $2 house salad consisting of cheap greens, overripe tomatoes, and moldy red onions on every customer. Well, there were never any *gloves* at the station where we made these little salads. (Now think about the no-toilet-paper thing.) At the end of the night, after all the waiters had scrounged through the lettuce and tomatoes with their bare hands (there were no tongs either), we were told to put the produce back in the fridge and reuse it the next day! The next day the tomatoes would be slimy. If a waiter threw them out, however, one of the busboys would rat the server out to the chef. What a place.

What I'll never forget was that place's staff bathroom. Like Amici's, staff were expected not to use the customer toilets. While not as small as the "phone booth of sodomy," this staff bathroom was also a windowless cube that reeked of farts, body odor, and the cheap cologne the kitchen guys doused themselves with before hopping on the bus to go home. Illumination was provided by a solitary plastic lamp wobbling uncertainly on the side of the cheap, dirty sink. The underpowered toilet? It shifted when you sat on it. Finding used tampons and feces floating in the bowl was not uncommon. One night the bulb in the lamp blew out. Of course there were no replacement bulbs. The owner's solution was to take a candle off the table and put it on top of the toilet tank. The wind from the door opening and closing, however, blew it out. I know what you're thinking. What about using flashlights? These cheap bastards didn't have any of them, either. People were pissing in a pitch-black bathroom. They missed.

When I went into the darkened bathroom to take a leak, my shoes couldn't get traction. The floor was slick with a congeal-ment of urine and tracked-in kitchen grease. I decided to use the customer bathroom instead. When the lighting was finally restored later that evening, we discovered that some guy, possibly aggravated at the poor conditions, decided to lodge a protest by hosing down the wall with a golden shower. He didn't even try aiming for the toilet.

Here's a tip for you, dear reader. If a restaurant's bathroom is nasty, the odds are good that the kitchen doesn't bother main-taining Health Department mandated levels of hygiene either. Sure, customers can be pigs and mess up a perfectly good rest-room in five seconds, but look for these details.

- No hot water in sink
- No hand soap in dispensers
- Cheap rub-your-ass-raw toilet paper
- No paper towels
- Overflowing garbage cans
- No toilet paper dispenser, just a tattered roll on top of the tank
- A toilet seat shifted off its base
- Graffiti
- Semen stains *anywhere*

In addition to the skid-row bathrooms this restaurant pos-sessed, it also had those awful strips of fly paper hanging down from the ceiling in the service area behind the kitchen. There have been great advances in pest control since the 1930s, but the owner of this place, in a never-ending quest to save a buck, obvi-ously had never heard of them. Whipped by the breeze generated from constantly opening and closing doors, the fly strips flut-tered in the artificial wind like glistening black-studded pennants hung by primitive tribesmen trying to scare outsiders away from some kind of sacrificial burial pit. The mice writhing in agony on the floor as they tried to free themselves from sticky paper traps helped complete the forbidding effect. I wouldn't be surprised to hear that this restaurant's customers were dying from the Ebola virus, much less garden-variety gastroenteritis. I quit after a couple of months.

And, since we're on the subject of viruses, let's discuss another nicety of the restaurant world, working while sick.

I remember reading somewhere that chefs have developed this macho ethos that compels them to work even when they're injured or sick. Unless you're dead, lost your hand in a meat-grinder accident, or are actively exsanguinating from a severed artery, you had better show up for work—you pussy! To some extent, that's true. I've watched Fluvio cook in near delirium with a 102-degree fever and sweat as his sciatic nerve sent waves of racking pain up and down his legs and back. Armando pops so many antihistamines and Tylenol when he gets a cold I worry that his liver will pop out his navel before the end of the shift. Of course everyone in the restaurant works injured. Every cook has burns and scars tattooing his hands and forearms, testifying to his job history the way a junkie's track marks bear witness to his addiction. I once saw a waitress come into work with a nasty hot-oil burn festering on her inner thigh. (I know because she showed me. Don't ask.) I once sliced my finger open on the foil when opening a bottle of wine and bled all over a table. The outraged customers, fearing I had the Hanta virus or something, stormed out of the restaurant. I finished the shift with a bandage dripping Betadine on my thumb.

But I think that the Bushido kitchen code, if it ever existed, has been supplanted by something far less romantic and much more cynical—there are almost never any sick days in the restaurant business. If you don't work, you don't get paid. I'll concede that higher-paid chefs might drag themselves into the kitchen because of old-school work ethics and fat paychecks, but those of us operating on the lower end of the totem pole come into work sick because we need the money. A busboy with a kid to support isn't going to stay home and miss out on $100 because he's got a case of strep throat. What's more, he's probably fearful he might lose his job. Fluvio's good when his staff gets sick, but other, less-scrupulous owners will just fire that dishwasher with pneumonia and get a new one. Why not? There are plenty of guys waiting to take his place.

Most restaurants do not offer health insurance to their employees. Some waiters like me *might* have coverage, but among immigrant staffers, it's practically unheard of. So when people get sick, they don't get the medical attention they need, and whatever's sickening them gets worse or lasts longer than it has to. When cubicle warriors fall ill, they have insurance to cover their prescriptions and doctor's visits. They have sick days to subsidize recovering on the couch while watching Nigella Lawson's breasts bounce as she bakes a pie on TV. Bus people, dishwashers, and most waiters, however, don't have that luxury. And don't kid yourself; in America, health insurance and sick time have become a luxury, not a right. It's a vicious circle—staff member gets sick, can't afford to go to the doctor or take time off, he gets sicker and can't work and is forced to pay for a doctor he can't afford; now he has to work harder to make up the shortfall, straining his already tapped reserves of strength and setting him up for more illness.

And these are the people cooking and handling *your* food! You shouldn't be surprised. Let's face it: economics, politics, and lack of proper access to health care are creating a nation of potential Typhoid Marys that is going to weaken this country with disease from the inside out. Uninsured restaurant workers are just the tip of the iceberg. There are many lower- and middle-income Americans in the same boat. Go to a hospital. See how many of the outsourced nurses' aides who do the bulk of patient care have access to sick days and quality health care. Not many. Sure, if you've got money and resources, you have health insurance, but the people serving at your favorite restaurant might not. You see, it's back to that Potemkin village thing I was talking about earlier.

Luckily, at The Bistro hand washing is practically a religion. There are soap dispensers, antibacterial cleansers, and plenty of paper towels at every sink. We may come into work sick, but at least we are trying to use universal precautions. Safe food handling, like using gloves when making salads and resisting the urge to recycle old produce, helps keep the customers safe—most of the time. But sometimes the threats don't come from human beings. Sometimes they come from God's little creatures.

The day after the tuna incident the restaurant's packed and people are waiting at the door. Fluvio and I are arguing over the seating chart when Saroya interrupts us.

"Guys," she says, "I've got a problem."

"What's up?" I reply.

Saroya leans forward and whispers, "We have a bug."

"What?" Fluvio says a shade too loudly. "Where's the bug?"

"Quiet!" I hiss, looking around nervously.

"Where is it?" Fluvio says, his voice dropping several decibels.

"It's crawling along the wall by table twelve," Saroya says.

"Did the customers see it yet?" I ask.

"I don't think so."

"I just had the place sprayed," Fluvio groans.

"They see that bug, and it's free dinners for everybody," I say. "For your sake, I hope they're eating pasta."

"Always bugs when we're crowded," Fluvio stammers angrily. "Never when no one's around."

"I guess they like Italian," I say.

"So what're you guys gonna do about it?" Saroya asks.

"Just kill it, sweetie," I reply.

"And how am I supposed to do that without attracting attention?"

"Think of something."

"You're the manager," Saroya replies. "*You* think of something."

"Great. Throw the manager thing in my face."

"Kill it, you big sissy."

I give Saroya a dirty look and walk toward table 12. I glide by casually, furtively scanning the walls, trying not to look *too casual*.

There, in all his fat, glistening brown glory, an example of the species *Periplaneta americana*—the American cockroach—defiantly clings to the wall. It's as if he's shouting "Screw your pesticides and delicate sensibilities. I've been around for three hundred fifty million years. I was here before you, and I'll be here after you. I can survive a nuclear holocaust, a month without food, and a week without my head. Sorry to disturb your dinner, but nature doesn't stop because you're paying thirty bucks for an entrée. And don't worry, I brought friends."

I sigh. The cockroach's a big motherfucker. I have to get rid of it.

I take a linen napkin out of my apron and approach the table. The customers are drinking white wine. The wine bottle's in an ice bucket. I pull the bottle out of the ice water, wrap the napkin around the wet bottle, and pour a little into everybody's glass. I may be acting like a courteous waiter, but my tactical goal is to maneuver close to the bug. Fluvio watches anxiously as I play commando and use my body to block the cockroach from the customers' view. Any second someone might shout, "Eeeck! A bug! FREE DINNER!" The stakes are high.

No one freaks. I put the bottle back in the ice bucket. Now the bug's positioned directly behind me. I unfold the napkin and transfer it to my right hand. In my mind's eye I have an idea of my target's position on the wall. I raise my napkined hand and prepare to turn on my heel. I have to strike swiftly. Everyone's counting on me.

"Thank you, waiter," one of the patrons says.

"My pleasure, sir," I reply.

Engage target.

I spin around and, in a natural fluid motion, pluck the cockroach off the wall. I do it so smoothly no one thinks anything's up. As I depart from the table I feel my prisoner struggle inside the napkin. For a moment I wonder what karmic sins it committed to deserve coming back as a cockroach. Maybe he was a concentration-camp guard, a serial killer, or a politician. Maybe he was a chef.

I crush the bug inside the napkin. It dies with a satisfying crunch. I drop the napkin into the trash. Fluvio looks relieved.

"Good job," he says.

"Double O Waiter," I say proudly. "Licensed to exterminate."

"Why do you think they're back?" Fluvio asks.

"I don't know, Fluvio," I reply. "Those critters can soak up radiation and not breathe for forty-five minutes. They're invincible."

"Great."

"Let me check something."

I head to the basement and go to the fuse box to test out a theory. I heard on TV that cockroaches are attracted to electromagnetic radiation. When I open the box, dozens of brown bugs scatter for safety. The things are everywhere. The fuse box is covered with brown flecks of cockroach shit. Lovely.

I head back upstairs to tell Fluvio the problem's worse than we thought. I try looking on the bright side: I always knew watching Animal Planet would pay off one day.

Some of you might think The Bistro's a health hazard, a disgusting place you'd never eat at. Well, I got news for you—there've been cockroaches in every restaurant you've ever eaten in. *Every single one!*

All restaurants (you hope) have contracts with pest control companies to keep their bug and varmint problems under wraps. Think about it. You've seen ants, cockroaches, and the occasional mouse scurrying across *your* kitchen floor. They're after the food in your pantry, the wet sugar you forgot to wipe off the counter, and the crumbs on your floor. Now imagine your kitchen's a whole lot bigger, pumps out hundreds of meals a day, has dozens of people tracking through it and tons of food lying all over the place. Even with the most conscientious bagging, sealing, and sweeping, one of God's creatures is going to come crawling in. Sometimes they hitch a ride in a produce crate, crawl in through a crack in the wall, or secret themselves in the customers' clothing. Yes, people sometimes bring their own bugs into restaurants.

You just can't stop the most successful species in the world from making an appearance. I read somewhere that if you took all the insect life in the world and placed it on a scale, it would outweigh all other life-forms on the planet *combined*. That includes the elephants. You're gonna run into them from time to time.

Of course, that doesn't mean you give up and let them run all over the place. The Bistro has a contract with a pest-control company. Every month the exterminator puts his John Hancock on a form that the health inspector had better see hanging in a prominent place. But pest control's expensive. Some restaurants that are hurting financially will cut back on some niceties—like the exterminator. That's when trouble starts.

Just behind the cockroaches are the mice. And right behind the mice are the rats. Think of cockroaches as force recon, the mice as light infantry, and rats as tanks. Throw in some flies for air support, and you've some serious shit and awe on your hands. And fecal matter is bad news, people. I don't think I need to explain that there are some nasty parasites in that stuff. And fleas on the rats and mice. Bubonic plague, anyone? Yummy.

Okay, maybe I'm exaggerating. I don't think anyone's gotten a dose of the black death at Per Se, but there's likely been a mouse or two in that kitchen. Conscientious cleaning and pest control keeps the critters under control, but believe me, it's only that, under control—not eliminated. As you're reading this, you're being watched by a dozen pairs of eyes peeking out of the dark corners of your house. There are mice under your floorboards right now! Sometimes, however, something larger than your ordinary mouse finds its way into a restaurant.

It happened during the Sunday lunch rush a few years back. A commotion broke out by the front tables. Plates started smashing to the floor. A lady began shouting unintelligibly.

Perched on her table was an American gray squirrel. He didn't look happy.

"Holy fucking shit!" I shouted. In retrospect, it seemed the most professional response at the time.

The squirrel, frightened by the patron's shrieking, tried to escape through the plate glass window. Mistake.

The rodent smacked its head on the window. Dazed by the impact, he leapt on top of the frantic woman, elevating her screams to a new degree of urgency. The squirrel bounded onto the floor and scurried under the hostess stand. Another female customer, an obvious animal lover, ran over crying, "It's just a baby! Don't hurt it!"

The squirrel started hissing malevolently at its erstwhile rescuer. I'm thinking, *This lady gets bitten, this lady gets rabies, this lady sues our asses off.*

"Madam, please let me handle this," I said.

"Oh, I'll get him," she cooed. Here's where watching Animal Planet gets you into trouble.

"MADAM, STEP AWAY FROM THE SQUIRREL!" I yelled.

With a hurt expression the animal do-gooder returned to her seat. Tough shit, lady. This is a restaurant. Not a petting zoo.

A busboy rushed up with a broom, and we tried sweeping the little bastard out the front door. The rodent dashed from under the hostess stand and made a beeline for the back of the restaurant. After he succeeded in horrifying most of our customers, he sought refuge underneath a four top sitting on one of the banquettes in the back. I was in hot pursuit.

"I don't mean to alarm you," I said politely to the four top, "but a squirrel has run under your table. Could you please get up?"

I will never, till my dying day, forget the look on their faces.

"What is a squirrel doing in here?" one woman said, performing a rapid egress from the table.

"I assure you, madam," I replied, "he is not on the menu."

When I got under the table, I discovered that the glorified rat had crawled through a hole under the seats. I could hear him scuttling under the banquettes. He'd taken up residence, and he wasn't coming out.

With the exception of one very cool couple, the back of The Bistro had to be evacuated and seated at other tables. The give-away-free-shit parade was in full swing. After dispensing drinks and desserts gratis I called the police and asked them to send an animal-control officer.

"Somehow a squirrel doesn't seem to fit the ambience of a Tuscan bistro," the desk sergeant said. I could hear other cops laughing in the background.

"No kidding," I replied.

The cop gave me the number of an exterminator and I called him. The guy came over in twenty minutes with a trap and instructions on how to set it. Later, when all the customers left, I was on my hands and knees rigging the filthy device. I wanted to ask Fluvio when animal trapping became part of my job description.

Of course, the squirrel didn't take the bait that night. The next day we had to pretend like he wasn't there and seat the back section anyway. I spent the whole night waiting for him to reappear. I dreaded hearing, "Waiter, there is a squirrel in my soup!" I feared he might bite some yuppie on the ankle and give him rabies. With my luck it'd be the food critic from the *New York Times*.

That night I reset the trap and had better luck. Fluvio called me at home after midnight. The squirrel set off the motion-detector alarm, springing the trap. When Fluvio entered the premises with the police in tow, our little buddy was freaking in his cage. The next morning the exterminator picked him up and released him in the woods. Problem solved.

Later that day a curious customer who witnessed the rodent incident popped his head in the door and asked, "Whatever became of the squirrel?"

"We had him for lunch, sir," I replied.

Then there's the stuff that falls into the food. I once had a customer hand me a plastic pen cap and ask if that was a standard ingredient in tortellini en brodo. Occasionally a staple from a wooden produce crate or a button that popped off a server's shirt finds its way into a salad and results in a broken tooth. Errant hairs, of course, are my favorite.

"Excuse me," a silver-haired lady asks as I walk by the table. "Are you the manager?"

"Yes, madam," I reply cautiously.

"There's a hair in my salad."

"I'm terribly sorry, madam," I say, picking the offending plate off the table. "I'll get you another one right away."

"Don't bother," she says. "To tell you the truth, I've completely lost my appetite."

"Oh dear."

"Cancel our orders," the woman's outraged husband says. "We're going to leave."

"I'm very sorry about this, sir."

"You should be," the husband says. "I've never seen something so awful in a restaurant."

If this guy thinks a stray hair's bad, he'd never be able to stomach the squirrel story. Maybe I should tell him about the "phone booth of sodomy." No. Better to leave him in ignorance. He couldn't handle the truth.

"Again, sir," I repeat. "My apologies."

The couple get up and leave. I take the salad back to the kitchen for a postmortem. Moises and Armando gather around and watch as I pluck the hair out of the salad and hold it up to the light. For a moment I feel like David Caruso on *CSI Miami*. The hair's long and silver. It's the crabby woman's own hair. Case closed.

"Bitch," Armando grunts.

When customers complain about a hair in the food, it's often one of their own. If you see a short and curly one? Well, that's one of ours.

"What about their entrées?" I ask. "Can we give them to someone else?"

"No," Armando says, shaking his head. "No one else ordered the same thing."

"Shit."

Armando cooks up the trichotillomaniac couple's food and offers it to the kitchen staff, but everyone's too busy to eat it. The food grows cold and eventually gets thrown into the garbage.

Now that's disgusting.

CHAPTER 13

I Hate Mother's Day

hen the Italian poet Dante described the center of hell in his poem *The Divine Comedy*, he got it wrong. The epicenter of Hades isn't Satan trapped in a block of ice munching on Judas Iscariot like an everlasting carrot stick. The center of hell is a restaurant on Mother's Day.

"I want the window seat," the man says, flanked in the doorway by his wife and mother. It's hard to hear him over the din of a busy restaurant.

"I'm sorry, sir," I reply, powering my voice over the noise, "but that table's been reserved."

"I'm friends with the owner," the man says. "Tell him I'm here."

I fight the urge to roll my eyes. Friends of the owner don't negotiate with waiters. Friends of the owner wordlessly slip under the velvet ropes and slide into the best seat in the house. If you have to say "I'm friends with the owner," you've already told me you're out of your league.

"I'm afraid Fluvio's not in," I reply, keeping my voice friendly but firm. "And the people who reserved the window table made their reservations months in advance."

The uptight trinity of husband, wife, and mother stare at me like I just sold a busload of Jerry's Kids to white slavers. I can tell they're not used to hearing the word *no*.

"But Mother wants that table," the man snaps.

"I can't give you that particular table, sir," I say. "But I do have some lovely tables in the back."

"Unacceptable," the man says, panic shading his voice. "Mother wants to sit in the window."

I wince internally. Whenever I hear a guy refer to his mother in this way, the theme music from *Psycho* starts playing inside my head. This guy is in his late forties and is still hungering for his mother's approval. He probably always will be. I toy with the idea of telling the man it's time to cut the cord but decide that would be out of line.

"I'm sorry I can't accommodate your request, sir," I say.

The man's gray-haired mother lets out a disgusted snort. A brittle, skinny woman with black button eyes, she probably dressed her son up in sailor outfits.

"This is ridiculous!" her daughter-in-law hisses. "We said we're friends of the owner. Give us the table."

The man's wife impatiently taps the spiked end of her high heel against the hardwood floor. She looks like a younger, Botoxed, and overdieted version of her mother-in-law.

"Sorry, madam," I reply sweetly. "But that's not possible."

The daughter-in-law stops tapping her shoe. Three sets of eyes start drilling holes in my skull. They probably think that staring will cause me to cave in and give them what they want. That's the modus operandi of customers when they realize they can't bully you.

I pick three menus off the hostess stand. "Please follow me."

"So you're giving us the window?" the man asks with deluded hopefulness.

"Sorry, sir, I'm giving you a table in the back."

Face registering disappointment, the man looks at his mother and shrugs.

"I guess we'll take it."

"This way, please."

As the unhappy procession trails behind me, I listen as the wife laces into her husband.

"You should have made reservations earlier!"

"It's not my fault, Mary Anne."

"We should go somewhere else! Look at your mother. She's so unhappy!"

"There's nowhere else to eat at this hour."

"Goddamnit, Roger. You can never do anything right."

After I seat the happy family I cast a glance back at the table. The mother's clutching her purse to her chest defensively, regarding her environs with barely concealed disdain. I feel a small surge of sympathy for the man sandwiched between two hyper-critical women. He's screwed.

I sigh inwardly. I'll be dealing with many more uptight people before my shift's over. Mother's Day, you see, is universally despised by waiters. It's not that we hate motherhood, but this calendar-mandated paean to the virtues of motherhood has a tendency to make people's unresolved childhood issues bubble to the surface. For an endless variety of reasons, people harbor powerful and ambivalent emotions toward their mothers. We've all met people with sky-high psychotherapy bills who complain incessantly about their maternal figures. But, as Sigmund Freud pointed out over a century ago, negative emotions directed toward Mom have a tendency to induce tremendous guilt. The floral and greeting-card industries gleefully exploit that guilt in order to separate us from our money. The psych-op warfare specialists who design Mother's Day commercials have got us all brainwashed that we're horrible people if we don't load Mom up with flowers, cards, and expensive gifts on the big day. Like Christmas, Mother's Day has become a socially and economically mandated display of forced goodwill and cheerfulness. Not taking Mom out to a restaurant on Mother's Day is like Ebenezer Scrooge pistol-whipping Tiny Tim on Christmas morning. By the time the second Sunday in May rolls around, people are caught up in a near-religious frenzy, hoping to expunge a year's worth of guilt by being extra nice to Mom on this *one* day. Mother's Day has evolved into a Yom Kippur for guilty children everywhere. Taking Mom out to brunch used to be an appreciative gesture. Now it's a guilt-expiation liturgy. Because of this dynamic, customer expectations have become so outsize and unrealistic that restaurants are under immense pressure to make everything perfect.

Customer expectations have to take a backseat to the cold reality that Mother's Day is the busiest restaurant day of the year. Restaurant owners, eager to make killer profits, often overbook reservations and extort customers with overpriced holiday menus that make price gouging by the oil industry look benign in comparison. So when customers' hopes of childhood redemption break upon the rocks of a noisy, overpriced, and crowded restaurant, they have a tendency to take out their frustrations on their server. On Mother's Day, waiters become psychological punching bags.

A short while later I'm standing near the POS computer printing checks when something small and soft thumps into my leg. I look down. It's a four-year-old boy. He's as cute as a button and grabbing his crotch.

"Batroom," the child gurgles.

"The bathroom is in the back to your right, sir," I reply, talking to him like an adult. Hey, it works with my friend's kids.

"I need to go pee-pee," the boy insists, making a face. I look around for the kid's mother. No dice.

I forgo traumatizing the little tyke with my thousand-yard stare and escort him by the hand into the men's room.

"Can you get on the toilet by yourself?" I ask.

The boy replies by dropping his pants and hopping on the porcelain bowl. He's wearing Spiderman Underoos. How cute.

"I'm okay," the boy says, swinging his stubby legs in the air.

"Very well, sir," I say, closing the door. "I'll be outside."

Back at the POS computer I watch the men's room out of the corner of my eye and silently pray the kid doesn't fall in the toilet.

That's the last thing I need today. By the time my last check prints out the little boy pokes his blond head cautiously out the door. I walk over to him.

"Everything all right, sir?"

The boy points to the sink. "Can't reach."

"This," I mutter to myself, "is not in my job description."

I open the faucets, make sure the water temperature's safe, and pick up the little boy. When he's done washing his hands, I put him down and hand him a paper towel. Hands dried and germ-free, I lead the little boy back into the dining room so he can reunite with his mother. She isn't hard to find. She's the most frantic-looking woman in the restaurant.

"Here you are, madam," I say soothingly, putting the child back into his booster seat. "He was a big boy and tried to use the bathroom himself."

"I'm so sorry," the mother says, looking incredibly relieved. "He was playing under the table. I didn't notice that he was gone."

"No problem, madam," I reply. "I'm keeping my radar set low today."

"Thank you, waiter."

"You're very welcome," I say. "Happy Mother's Day."

When I turn around, Beth is waiting for me.

"We're running out of champagne flutes," she blurts.

"How can that be?" I reply. "We cleaned thirty of them this morning."

"Beats me, all I know is I don't have any for my tables."

"But we only seat fifty people. Did we break half of them?"

"Your guess is as good as mine."

"All right," I say. "I'll go downstairs and find some more."

"Thanks."

I take a quick look around the restaurant and figure out why we don't have any champagne flutes. Every adult customer is drinking a mimosa. The waiters must've gotten confused. I said only *mommies* were supposed to get complimentary mimosas.

Oh well. It's cheap sparkling wine and no-frills OJ anyway. It won't break us.

I race downstairs and pull a box of champagne flutes out of storage. Since I know they're filthy, I hand the box to Felipe, the dishwasher.

"Amigo," I say, "I need these glasses *ahora*."

Felipe pulls a flute out of the box and holds it up to the light. The glass is crusted with brownish spots. I wouldn't be surprised if they're mimosa remains from last year.

"*Mierda*," Felipe grunts. "*Cinco minutos cabrón.*"

"Fast as you can, brother."

"*Dios mio*," Felipe mutters angrily. I don't blame him for being miffed. The pile of dishes in the sink's taller than he is.

When I return to the front of the restaurant, I discover that the hostess is seating a couple with two teenage sons in my section. After introducing myself and making the obligatory "how nice you look today" noises, the mommy of the hour asks if we serve eggs Benedict.

"I'm sorry, madam," I reply. "We do not."

"How can you not have eggs Benedict on Mother's Day?" the woman's husband sputters angrily.

"Oh honey," the man's wife says, placing her hand on his arm. "It's okay."

"We've never made that dish here," I explain apologetically. "But we have lovely pancakes, omelets, French toast, and our regular lunch menu as well."

"You have eggs, right?" the husband asks me.

"Yes, sir."

"You have butter?"

"Yes, sir."

"Bacon?"

I can see where this conversation's going.

"Not Canadian bacon, sir."

"But you have regular bacon, right?"

"Yes."

"Then I don't see what the problem is. Tell the chef to make my wife eggs Benedict with regular bacon."

"Sir, I . . ."

"Just do it."

I feel the man's impatience break over me like a wave. My smile starts to buckle. My emergency waiter programming kicks in and instructs my auxiliary systems to redirect psychic energy to my emotional shields. After a second my waiter smile reenergizes.

"I'll ask the chef if he can accommodate your request, sir," I reply.

"Thank you, waiter."

I look over at the man's teenage sons. They appear to be looking for a hole to swallow them up.

I head into the kitchen. It's a madhouse. Everyone has an intense look of concentration on his face. It always amazes me how the kitchen staff keeps track of fifty orders simultaneously. I could never do it. Fluvio, of course, is nowhere to be found. He was in early this morning to go over the seating chart but escaped under the pretense of taking his wife and son to brunch. I don't blame him for running away. I'd've bailed, too, if Fluvio had let me. I actually tried to get the day off, but Fluvio just chuckled evilly when I asked.

"Yo, Armando!" I shout. "Can you make eggs Benedict?"

"Today?" Armando asks, not looking up from the entrée he's plating.

"Yes, today."

"No fucking way."

"That's what I thought, Armando," I say. "At least I can tell the customer I talked to you."

"Tell that asshole to make eggs Benedict at home."

"I will."

I march back to my four top and deliver the bad news. I edit out Armando's commentary.

"That's ridiculous," the man says.

"I'm sorry I can't accommodate your request, sir," I reply. (That's waiterspeak for "you're shit out of luck.")

"Now listen here—"

"Honey," the man's wife says firmly. "Let it go. Remember your anger-management exercises."

"Yeah, Dad," says one of the man's sons. "Chill."

The father takes what's probably a series of court-mandated deep breaths while the mother orders for the table. Bacon and mushroom omelets for everybody. Thank God. I smooth everything over by delivering extra mimosas to the table. Now I understand why my waiters are giving away so much free booze—they're medicating the customers. Now that I think about it, that's a good idea. Next year I'll put Thorazine in the orange juice.

I look at my watch and grimace. It's only one o'clock. Truth be told, I could use some medication myself. I've got eight hours and three hundred customers to go. I don't know how I'm going to make it. I head over to the kitchen to fix myself a little pick-me-up.

Beth is way ahead of me. Sitting on her haunches with her back pressed up against the kitchen wall, she's drinking urine-colored liquid out of a pint glass filled with ice.

"Let me guess," I say. "Red Bull and vodka."

"Just Red Bull," Beth replies, trying to look all innocent.

"Sure."

"You don't believe me?"

"Nope."

"I'm hurt." Beth pouts.

"So how much Grey Goose did you put in there?" I ask, pointing at the pint glass.

"About two shots," Beth replies, her face breaking into a mischievous smile.

"That's what I thought."

"You're not mad, are you?"

"Not today."

Normally I don't like waiters drinking on the job. I remember how Inez used to slurp Chardonnay and 7-Up out of a pint glass until she got a serious buzz going. I'm sympathetic to the fact that servers occasionally have to medicate their aches and pains while on the job. I wouldn't have minded Inez's drinking so much if she hadn't gotten drunk and combative with the customers all the time. Normally I never drink on duty, but today, with my knees and soul crying out in pain, I decide to make an exception. I pull a cocktail shaker off the shelf, fill it with ice and Bloody Mary mix, and add a liberal helping of vodka.

"You're drinking?" Beth asks, astonished.

"Sssshhhhhh," I say, putting a finger to my lips.

"You know one of the Uncle Toms is going to tell Fluvio."

"I don't care," I say. "That's what he gets for being AWOL on the busiest day of the year."

"Way to be, brother," Beth says, clinking her glass against mine. "Way to be."

I guzzle my Bloody Mary and head back onto the floor. As I'm running around I notice many brand-new mothers are celebrating the holiday with us today. I grin inwardly. I served some of these women before they started dating their husbands. I even hit on a few of them. When I started at The Bistro seven years ago, they were fresh-faced college graduates determined to take the world by storm. Now they're married and having babies. How time flies.

"Excuse me, waiter," one of the new mommies asks me. "Would you mind taking a group picture?"

"Certainly, madam," I reply. "It would be my pleasure."

The woman hands me one of those impossibly complicated digital cameras. After giving me a brief tutorial she instructs everyone to gather around.

"Lean in, everybody," I say, peering through the viewfinder. "Say cheese."

After I snap the picture the young mother hands her baby, a pink-swaddled little girl, to the octogenarian woman sitting next to her.

"Could you also take a picture of us around the great-grandmother?" the mother asks.

"Sure."

Everyone clusters around the wizened matriarch. As she looks at the baby squirming in her arms, a voice in the back of my head tells me this might be this old woman's last Mother's Day. Suddenly I think about my own mother. I better not forget to call her.

Despite the numbing effects of the ethyl alcohol, the hours tick by with agonizing slowness. As soon as one table gets up a demanding set of new customers takes its place. The noise level in the restaurant's gotten so bad I feel like I'm working inside the turbofan of a 747. If I couldn't read the customers' lips, I'd never be able to understand anyone's order. Suddenly I realize that I'm sweating. I walk over to the thermostat and look at the display. The temperature's inched up to almost 85 degrees. I remember learning from a television show that sound can create heat. On the sun, a hot place to begin with, explosive processes within the interior interact with the star's magnetic field lines and create acoustic waves of tremendous power. These sound waves are so intense that they superheat the atmosphere just above the sun to a temperature of 1 million degrees Celsius. I smile inwardly at the thought of my customers suddenly glowing incandescent and vaporizing from the sound waves emanating from their jabbering mouths. Maybe if I told them to shut up, it'd get cooler in here. I decide to turn the air-conditioning on instead.

"Holy shit," Louis says, walking past me, his shirt soaked through with sweat. "It's hot in here."

"I know," I reply. "I just turned on the AC."

"Thank God."

"Louis," I say, "I can't even believe you're here. I thought you'd find some way to scam out of Mother's Day."

"Believe me, honey, I tried."

"Run out of dead grandmas?"

"Kiss my ass," Louis snaps prissily.

Louis is a bit of a drama queen. Whenever he doesn't feel like working, he calls in with some fictitious medical or family emergency. Once, on a slow night, he told me he was having a heart attack and asked if he could go home. He made a miraculous recovery when I picked up the phone and started to dial 911 instead. I guess spending the night in an ER was too high a price to pay to save face and make good on a fib.

"Don't feel bad, Louis," I say. "I tried to get out of working, too."

"Fluvio didn't buy your excuse?"

"He just laughed when I told him I wanted today off."

"That bastard."

"And he's not even here."

"Figures."

"I'm telling ya, Louis," I say, shaking my head. "This is the last Mother's Day I'm going to work."

"You said that last year," Louis says. "And the year before that."

I think about my own mother, enjoying retirement with my father in the hinterlands of Pennsylvania. I miss her. I think about the great-grandmother I took a picture of earlier. People aren't always around forever.

"I know," I reply. "But this time I mean it."

"Sure you do."

A few minutes later I'm telling a new table the specials. As I'm explaining to a blue-haired old lady what a frittata is, the sound of breaking dishes fills the air.

"Mazel tov!" a drunken patron shouts.

The restaurant erupts in laughter.

My head swivels toward the source of the noise. Kelly, a new server, is standing near the entrance to the kitchen, staring at the floor in shock. She's dropped an entire table's worth of food.

"Will you excuse me a minute?" I ask my customers, failing to keep the homicidal gleam out of my eye.

"Uh-oh," the blue-haired woman says. "Someone's in trouble."

By the time I reach the crash site the bus people are already efficiently cleaning up the mess. After performing a quick check to make sure no patrons or staff were injured, I ask the server what happened.

"The plates were too hot," she whines.

Kelly's been on the job only a couple of weeks. Something tells me she won't be here much longer.

"What table was the food for?" I ask.

"Fifteen," she replies.

Annoyed, I push past Kelly and head into the kitchen.

"Yo, Armando!" I shout.

"What?"

"You gotta recook table fifteen."

"What the fuck?" Armando says. "It just went out!"

"Kelly dropped the whole order."

"You're shitting me."

"I wish I was."

Armando closes his eyes, takes a deep breath, and exhales. When his eyes open, he smiles. "Give me ten minutes," he says.

As I walk out of the kitchen I say a prayer of thanks that Armando's so graceful under pressure. For most chefs, verbally bludgeoning Kelly into emotional catatonia would be the normal course of action.

"Your table will get their food in ten minutes," I tell the hapless server. "Don't drop it this time."

"I won't," she says sheepishly.

"Now I've got to go over to fifteen and smooth things over," I say. "Thanks a lot."

"Sorry."

I walk over to four adults seated at table 15. One of the women already knows what I'm going to say before I say it.

"That was our food that hit the floor," she says. "Wasn't it?"

"You must be psychic, madam," I reply.

The table's aggravated that their food's going to be delayed. Before their aggravation can turn into anger I employ the most powerful customer-service tool at a restaurant manager's disposal—free booze. After a round of free drinks all is forgiven. If Fluvio knew how much booze got wasted washing away waiter fuckups, he'd have a conniption.

Eventually Mother's Day ends. Because I've been running

around all day, my underwear's soaked through with sweat. All the moisture and chafing has invited a nasty rash to take up residence on my ass.

"Why are you walking so weird?" Beth asks me.

"I've got a case of Waiter Butt," I reply.

"Ouch."

"You wouldn't have any Gold Bond powder on you, by any chance?"

"Sorry," Beth replies. "I'm fresh out."

After an extensive cleanup Beth and I start walking over to Café American for a well-deserved drink. As I hobble up the street I call my mother to wish her a happy day. I decide not to mention my current dermatological crisis.

"My God!" squawks Arthur, the bartender, when we walk in the door. "You're still alive!"

"Barely," Beth mutters.

Arthur's a part-time actor with two ex-wives and three kids. Thin, with a shock of unruly black hair, he's a handsome fellow who usually has a bemused expression on his face. Like all good bartenders, he's quick with a story or a piece of gossip. Today, however, he looks like a beaten man.

"How'd it go here?" I ask, gingerly lowering myself onto a bar stool.

"Hell on earth, brother," Arthur says, dramatically shaking his head slowly from side to side. "Hell on earth."

"Sounds like you had a bad day."

"The worst," Arthur replies. "We had a party of ten stiff us on the tip for a five-hundred-dollar check."

"How'd that happen?"

"The guy who paid for the party thought the tip was included in the bill. When we told him it wasn't, he claimed the person he made the reservation with misled him, and he refused to pay it."

"Sounds like a scam."

"Probably," Arthur says. "But he was making such a scene we let him go."

"You should've made him pay."

"Whatever," Arthur replies, waving his hand dismissively. "Life's too short to worry about pricks like that. Now, what do you two want to drink?"

"Two dirty Ketel One martinis," Beth asks.

"Coming right up, darling," Arthur says. "And these are on the house. Waiters drink free today."

"Thanks, Arthur," Beth says.

Arthur mixes our drinks and rests them on top of the bar. Beth and I drink them quickly. We like them so much we order two more. The alcohol mercifully numbs my gluteus maximus.

"So I heard a funny story about Mother's Day," Arthur says, as he's mixing our second batch of martinis.

"Tell me," I say. Arthur always has great stories.

"Did you ever see the movie *Heat*?" he asks.

"The one with De Niro and Pacino?" I reply. "Great movie."

"Remember the gun battle?" Arthur asks.

In the movie's most cinematically intense scene, cops and robbers battle it out with fully automatic weapons in the middle of a crowded downtown Los Angeles street. Violent, loud, and very scary, it's one of the greatest gun battles ever captured on film.

"Yeah," I say. "What does that have to do with Mother's Day?"

"I was watching it on DVD the other day and listening to the director's commentary."

"And?"

"The section of L.A. where they were filming the gunfight only allowed them to shoot on Sunday mornings."

"So?"

"Guess which Sunday they did some of the filming?"

"Mother's Day?" I say, a big grin spreading over my face.

"Yeah," Arthur says, grinning. "They filmed that gun battle outside of a restaurant serving Mother's Day brunch."

"Awesome," I say. "Just awesome."

"Can you imagine M-16s blasting outside while you're trying to hustle French toast?"

"I'd be tempted to swipe a gun from one of the actors."

"Waiters and machine guns," Arthur chortles, "on Mother's Day. That's not a good combination."

"You ain't kidding."

A couple of hours later I arrive home. The martinis I drank earlier have worn off, and my rear end is throbbing with pain. I peel off my clothes and examine my posterior region in the mirror. My ass is as red as a boiled lobster.

I shake my head in disgust and head into the bathroom. Grabbing a package of oatmeal bath powder I keep around for these situations, I start filling the tub with warm water. While the water's running I go into the kitchen, throw ice into a rocks glass, and fill it to the brim with chilled vodka. Returning to the bathroom, I lower myself into the soothing water, close my eyes, and start sipping my drink.

The minutes pass. The house is quiet. The only sound is water dripping from the faucet. I plug it with my big toe. The melting ice shifting inside my glass reminds me I have a drink in my hand. I take a long swallow and think about how much I drank today. Staring into my glass I imagine a tiny Satan trying to free himself from one of the ice cubes. Hmmm . . . maybe I did drink a bit too much.

I put the glass down on the edge of the tub and close my eyes. My rash still burns and the bathwater's growing cold. I hate Mother's Day.

CHAPTER 14

Vengeance Is Mine

aiter," my customer says, "my coffee is not hot."

"I'm terribly sorry, madam," I reply.

"Make it hotter."

"But of course, madam."

"Remember," the woman says, "I'm drinking decaf."

I take the coffee to the back and dump it out. I steep a new cup with boiling water to warm it up. It's an old waiter trick. I toss out the water, fill the cup with piping-hot decaf coffee, and return it to the table. A minute later the customer calls me back to the table.

"Waiter," she says, "my coffee is still not hot."

"Terribly sorry, madam."

"Are you stupid?" the woman says. "How hard is it for you to give me a hot cup of coffee?"

"A thousand pardons, madam," I say. "I'm new here." (I've been new here for six years.)

"Get me another cup," the lady says. "And remember . . ."

"It's decaf," I say. "Understood, madam."

I return to the back and refill the lady's cup with regular. I brew a strong espresso and dump it into the lady's coffee. I take the cup and place it in the oven. After two minutes at 400 degrees I take the cup out with a pair of tongs and place it on a cold saucer. I bring the bubbling cauldron of java back to the ill-mannered woman's table.

"Madam," I warn, trying not to be a total dick, "please be careful. This beverage and the cup are extremely hot."

"Good," the woman says. "Just the way I like it."

As I walk away from the table I hear the woman cry out when she grasps the cup handle.

"Ouch," she yelps. "It burns!"

I walk away from the table, struggling to keep the self-satisfied smirk off my face. *Vengeance is mine, saith the waiter.*

Yes, dear reader, we've come to the scary part of the book. This is the chapter where I talk about waiters spitting in your food.

Adulterating food or drink is a convenient way for servers to exact covert vengeance. Waiters can and do spit in people's food. Personally, I think spitting in someone's food is unimaginative and rude. Dropping sputum into someone's fettuccine Alfredo may give the goober in question a momentary burst of satisfaction but not much else. I'm proud to say we're above such petty bullshit at The Bistro. No server has ever adulterated a customer's food with foreign matter or bodily fluid. (Or at least they haven't told me about it. I'd rather live in ignorance on this one.) I prefer more elegant methods of revenge.

Of course, not all restaurant personnel are as classy as me. One day, when my friend Sal was working at a chain restaurant, he had a very abusive customer. The customer kept sending back his hamburger saying it tasted bland. On the burger's *third* return trip Sal and the cook decided to play floor hockey with the man's meat. Using greasy brooms as hockey sticks, they passed the char-broiled puck around the filthy kitchen floor for several minutes. I think the goal post was a dustbin. They hosed off the burger in the sink, threw some heat on it, and brought it to the table. The abusive customer dug into it and pronounced, "Now it's good." Dust and floor cleaner were just what it needed.

Some of you reading this are probably horrified that anyone

would seriously consider messing with your food. Usually such antisocial behavior is a reaction to abusive customer behavior. It's an unfortunate fact of life, but customers can really piss us off. Complaints about food or service I can deal with—that's the job. But when customers cross the line, when their dissatisfaction devolves into personal attacks, waiters are sorely tempted by thoughts of revenge. Many of my patrons are a few pills shy of psychiatric commitment. They have so many personal problems it's hard for them to keep their shit together in public. They consume most of their psychic energy trying not to freak out at work or in front of the kids. When they get to my restaurant, they have little restraint left. Often customers are angry at someone in a position of power over them, usually their boss or a client. Unable to express anger at the people responsible for their incomes, many customers redirect that anger toward us. Since waiters are perceived to be in a subservient position, customers think yelling at us is safe. We're only servants, after all. We become a cheap substitute for therapy or a punching bag. I've had people call me a loser, faggot, asshole, cocksucker, and shithead *to my face.* How would you react if someone at work talked that way to you? When you lose respect for my dignity and call me names, my inner serial killer comes bubbling to the surface. When that happens, watch out. Revenge is inevitable.

I'm a big fan of the psychiatrist/gourmand/serial killer Hannibal Lecter, the fictional maniac who ate his victims with fava beans and a nice bottle of Chianti. I always liked Dr. Lecter because he dispatched his prey with *panache.* (And, if you didn't notice, all his victims kind of deserved it.) My favorite scene in the movie *Hannibal* was when a tuxedoed Lecter, looking like a deranged James Beard, removes the top of a man's skull, digs out some gray matter, and flambés the guy's brains tableside— *while the guy's still alive.* After I saw that film I'd found myself measuring the circumference of obstreperous yuppies' heads and wondering where I mislaid my cranial saw. "What's the special tonight? Why, my dear sir—*you are.*"

You probably think I'm crazy, but I've never actually indulged in my little cathartic fantasies. I have an aversion to long periods of incarceration. Actually, I'm quite mentally healthy. Some people in this world would like you to think a negative thought has never furrowed their brow. Those are the people who snap. Have you ever wondered why, when the police are digging up the graves in the back of a serial killer's house, the neighbors always say, "But he was such a nice man! He was so quiet!" Uh-uh. Too quiet. Everyone, no matter what kind of job he or she has, fantasizes about freaking out at work. How many corporate drones, stuck in a boring staff meeting, have had the sudden urge to jump on top of the conference table and start screaming obscenities? Strip off their clothes? Kiss the woman or man next to them? We all have. How many employees joke about shooting the boss or blowing the place up? I'm not suggesting we do any of these things, mind you, but let's not kid ourselves; we all have a little murder in our heart. Why should waiters be any different?

In 2003 a woman dining at a Sizzler Steakhouse asked her waiter if she could have vegetables instead of potatoes with her meal. There appears to have been a disagreement between the waiter and the Atkins dieter over this legitimate request. The waiter, hoping to get that coveted employee-of-the-month plaque, defended the restaurant's no-substitution policy. I can understand where the waiter was coming from. Corporate restaurants are notoriously inflexible when it comes to making substitutions, and I have no doubt the waiter in question was sweating what his manager would say if he acceded to the woman's request. In the end the woman prevailed and got her veggies. The waiter, however, lost his mind.

According to the police report, the waiter, with two accomplices, went to the woman's house and daubed it with eggs, syrup, sugar, toilet paper, and instant mashed potato flakes. The authorities were summoned. Recognizing her attacker, the woman told the 911 operator, "Oh my God! It's the waiter from Sizzler!"

Luckily no one was hurt. The waiter went away for a nice long rest. Let me go on record saying I don't condone his behavior.

But I understand.

It's a miracle more waiters don't go postal. They're surrounded every day by whiny, spoiled customers and supervised by power-mad control freaks. Toss in the workforce's penchant for substance abuse and poor impulse control, and you've got a recipe for disaster. When you look at workplace homicides, however, the number of waiters turning into deranged killers is low. There aren't too many news reports about waiters shooting up the joint. Waiters must have an unknown safety mechanism that keeps them from going completely apeshit. I think it's cursing like sailors.

People who abuse waiters are taking a big chance. We don't need to drop phlegm into your entrée to exact vengeance. (But if you do, get the two-pack-a-day smoker to do it for you.) We can just subtly exercise our power and wreck your life.

When I was at Amici's, we had a regular customer who was serially cheating on his wife. We nicknamed him Lothario. Silver-haired, imperious, and rude, Lothario would start screaming at the restaurant staff if he had to wait a single minute for a drink. Everyone, even Caesar, experienced the lash of his razor-sharp tongue. One day Lothario brought his much younger mistress to the restaurant. Blond, twenty-five, with high heels and long legs that disappeared up into a plaid miniskirt, she was a real piece of eye candy.

"I hope that's his daughter," groaned Rizzo, the headwaiter.

"Probably not," sighed Scott, the resident drunk. "Oh shit, he's sitting in my section."

The moment Lothario's ass hit the chair he started yelling for the waiter. Passive-aggressive Scott took his sweet time getting to the table. Lothario took it upon himself to conduct a customer-care in-service. After dictating his order, Lothario's hand resumed its roaming underneath his date's skirt.

"Man, he took his wedding ring off," Scott whined. "I mean, what is he thinking? He comes here all the time."

"The rich live in an alternate reality, my boy," Rizzo observed.

"It's amazing how competent people can be in some areas of their lives," I remark, "and so incompetent in others. If you're going to cheat, at least be discreet."

We watch as the girl plays the coquette, laughing and tossing her hair, gazing at Lothario with unabashed admiration. She's at that age when a girl transitions from ingenue to womanhood. I had a sinking feeling that Lothario was going to accelerate that process.

The meal went as expected. Lothario shouted for more water and wine, sent his entrées back twice, and doled out dirty looks and unkind words for everybody.

Scott, after a long life of suffering the slings and arrows of outrageous yuppie scorn, finally snapped. Dropping off the dessert menus, he inquired in his most obsequious voice, "Would your daughter like some ice cream?"

The girl tittered. Lothario's face flushed bright red with anger, or maybe it was the Viagra.

"No ice cream?" Scott asked innocently.

"That's not my daughter," the man stuttered.

"Terribly sorry, sir."

The man got upset but, in the end, he realized that making a scene was not in his best interest. He never should have taken his chippie to his wife's favorite restaurant. One slip of the tongue by a disgruntled waiter, and he'd wind up in divorce court while his wife banged the cabana boy at some fancy resort on an exotic island.

On another occasion I had a corporate blowhard hosting a big business dinner. Before the guests arrived he pulled me aside and gave me a pep talk.

"This meeting's very important to me," the man says.

"Yes, sir."

"If you screw this up, I'll make sure you're fired."

"Yes, sir," I reply. "Thank you, sir."

"Are you being funny?"

"No, sir."

The dinner went smoothly. All the diners were happy with their food and the service. I am a professional, after all.

When dessert plates have been cleared and the coffee finished, the man hands me his credit card.

"Ring it up," the man says. (Please note the absence of the words "please" and "thank you.")

I pretend to run the card. After a minute I return to the table and whisper in the man's ear, "I'm sorry, sir, but this card seems to be experiencing some difficulty."

The man turns as white as a sheet. "That's impossible," he hisses. "Try it again!"

"Problem, Bob?" asks one of the clients he was desperately trying to impress.

"There's no problem," Bob says smoothly.

"Do you have another card, sir?" I ask.

"No," Bob says. "Try it again."

"I'll have to call the credit card company, sir," I say. "It'll be a few minutes."

I go to the phone and pretend to call American Express. Actually, I check the messages on my answering machine and call up a few waiters to set up a cocktail run later that night. I enjoy watching Asshole Bob rub his stomach while his ulcer grows exponentially. I go back to the terminal, ring up the sale, add a twenty percent tip, and hand the receipt to the Bobster.

"Sorry for the delay, Bob," I say.

Bob examines the receipt. "A twenty percent tip?" he exclaims, looking up quickly.

I say nothing and skewer the man with my thousand-yard waiter stare.

"Here's a pen, sir."

Bob signs the bill. As the party leaves I notice the client Bob was trying to impress regarding him a bit more cautiously. Did I screw up the business deal? Probably not, but maybe I gave that prospective client a moment of pause. Did Bob lose sleep that night? Who cares? At least I didn't give the cops his license plate number and tell them he was driving drunk. *I've done that.*

Don't ever think waiters and restaurant staffs are helpless victims. We're not. There are Web sites popping up on the Internet where waiters can list bad tippers by name. Sure, some unimaginative servers will adulterate the food. Not me. I prefer something more elegant, something with *panache*. I prefer the emotional version of flambéing your brains. I engage in psychological warfare. I'll subtly embarrass you in front of your girlfriend or client. Instead of putting hair in your pasta, I'll slip into my arrogant waiter persona and make you uneasy. I'll lose your reservation, make your steak medium instead of medium rare, put too much vermouth in your martini, and seat you next to the men's room.

But sometimes I'll employ a nifty chemical weapon that's at every waiter's disposal—flatulence.

Sure it's lowbrow and crude, but it works. A waiter can zip in, drop a silent and deadly fart next to a problematic table, and then zip away. By the time the victims know they're under attack, the waiter is long gone. Suspicion turns to the next table or each other. Most of the time people are too embarrassed to say anything, so they just eat through the stink. And if a waiter is pissed off at every customer in the restaurant, he can just fumigate the entire place with his love. I call this little maneuver "crop-dusting." It's one of the little things that help me get through life.

Yes, I can be bad. And I have a long memory. I might not exact vengeance right away. I can wait till your next visit, or the one after that, but don't kid yourself, eventually vengeance will be mine. Like Dr. Lecter, I have infinite patience. I've never spat in a customer's food, but I don't claim I never will.

Be afraid.

CHAPTER 15

Snapshots

I sigh and stare out The Bistro's front window. I didn't get much sleep last night. For the past few months I've been spending every spare moment getting that book proposal together for my agent. Before and after every shift, I sit down at my desk and try coaxing words and sentences into doing my bidding. We're supposed to start submitting to publishers this summer, but I'm suffering from a case of writer's block. That's not a good thing. I have a deadline. The pressure's on. I stifle a yawn. I was up until 2 A.M.

On the other side of the plate glass it's a bright Sunday afternoon. The restaurant's doing a brisk business. Customers swilling wine and smoking cigarettes crowd the outside tables. Teenage girls with exposed midriffs cluster by the pizza joint across the street and pull shaggy-haired boys off their skateboards with the gravity of their adolescent abdomens. While the boys posture and playact being cool, I notice the girls swing their hips with an awkward tentativeness, like they're carefully acclimating to their new bodies' power. Claude, the neighborhood homeless guy, stands next to them, oblivious to their presence. Wearing an army field jacket despite the early June heat, he slowly chews a slice of pizza and stares off into space, quietly contemplating some distant part of his private universe.

I tell one of the bus girls that I'm running to Starbucks for a cup of coffee. When I step inside, my favorite barista, the redhead with the ponytail and ivory skin, pours me a small coffee without my asking. Another young girl, an obvious trainee, is standing next to her.

"How are you today?" the redhead asks, smiling broadly.

"Good," I reply, pushing two singles across the counter. "How are you doing?"

"Same old stuff," she shrugs, handing me my coffee. "Different day."

"Tell me about it."

I take a sip of coffee. The hot liquid feels good going down my throat.

"Coffee," I sigh gratefully. "The lifeblood of tired men everywhere."

"Why do you say that all the time?"

"I read it somewhere, and I liked how it sounds."

"Oh . . . How are things across the street?" she asks.

"Not bad. How's things here?"

"You work across the street?" the trainee interrupts.

"Yeah."

"At The Bistro?"

"That's right."

"You're the sad man in the window!" the trainee exclaims.

"Excuse me?"

"Whenever my mom drives past that restaurant, she calls you the sad man looking out the window."

Flummoxed, I stare at the girl for a moment. Then I recover. "Nice to know I'm a local legend," I say.

"Oh," the trainee blurts, "I didn't mean anything by it."

"It's cool," I say reassuringly. "Good luck."

"Thanks, mister."

I nod at the redhead and wink. "Take it easy on the newbie."

"I will," she replies. "Have a good night."

The moment I walk back into The Bistro, Beth runs up to me. "Can you void something for me?" she asks.

"Whaddya screw up this time?" I reply, my mind elsewhere. *Sad man in the window?*

"I put all my new table's appetizers on the wrong check."

"Outstanding."

"Please fix it for me."

"If I had a dollar for every void I did for you guys, I'd be driving an Aston Martin."

"Please . . ." Beth pleads.

"What table?" I ask.

"Twelve."

"I'll get right on it," I say, waving her away.

"Thanks."

I walk over to the POS computer and open up the program to fix Beth's mistake. I make just as many screwups ordering food as any other waiter in the place—but I have the manager codes, so they never notice.

As my fingers fly across the touch screen I watch Beth recite the specials to a table. Even though she's only a few years older than the teenage girls outside, there's nothing awkward about how she moves inside her own skin. Aware of her feminine power and careful how she wields it, Beth carries herself with a quiet dignity that seems to have escaped many of her peers in this era of Internet gonzo porn. This may stem from the fact that Beth almost wasn't pretty. When she was a small girl, a dog mauled her face. It took several reconstructive surgeries to put her back together. Today the only evidence of Beth's trauma is a tiny scar above her left cheekbone. Her plastic surgeon should get the Nobel Prize for Medicine. I think that incident taught Beth, on some level, a lesson about what truly constitutes beauty. When they're young and beautiful, some girls get lost inside a self-centered world. I think Beth learned early that physical beauty is fleeting, and that, in an odd way, made her more beautiful.

"Can I get on the computer now?" Saroya says grumpily behind me. "I've got three tables to put in."

"Sure," I say, keying a few more commands into the system. "I'll be done in a sec."

Saroya lets out a long, controlled sigh. She does that whenever she's impatient. With me, that's often.

"Chill, baby," I say. "I'm almost done."

"Chill this," Saroya says, digging her sharp nails into my biceps, "I need to get in there."

"You know I love it when you grab me like that," I say, my voice dropping to an Elvis Presley bass.

"Hurry up."

"Why so grumpy?" I ask casually. "Trouble in paradise today?"

"What you mean?" Saroya replies.

"Problems between you and lover boy?"

"Ugh," Saroya says, throwing up her hands. "He's acting like an asshole."

"I guess the honeymoon's over then."

Saroya just glares at me. Knowing I've said enough, I exit out of the computer and give her a wide berth.

Saroya's been having a tough time. Eight months ago she and her daughter moved into Armando's condo. Even though everything seems to be going well, I know there are some serious readjustments going on in that household. Armando's become an instant daddy, the girl is sharing her mother with another man for the first time, and Saroya's relationships with the most important people in her life are changing. Conflict is inevitable and normal.

Saroya and Armando, however, are very connected to each other. Besides the obvious physical attractions, I suspect there's something deeper at work. Armando's mother died when he was a baby. It's a subject he never talks about. Saroya's father was a policeman in Nicaragua. He was shot and killed when she was five years old. It doesn't take Sigmund Freud to understand that these types of events have an effect on people. It's not surprising that a little boy who lost his mother hooked up with a little girl who lost her father. That may sound a little pat, but I've found that many successful relationships have a bit of shared trauma at their center. They both have good heads on their shoulders. I think they'll be fine in the long run.

Felipe, The Bistro's dishwasher, hustles past me, carrying a bus tub of onions up from the dry goods area. Felipe's a major pain in my ass, literally. Whenever my hands are full, he takes advantage of my defenselessness and tries sticking his finger up my butt. Since I'm wearing pants it's not going to happen, but I swear to God, I think I've had my sphincter tickled more times than a two-dollar Bangkok whore. Now Felipe isn't gay, mind you: this is just another example of the homophobic grab-ass games Spanish kitchen workers love to play. I do get my revenge. Like a patient sniper waiting for the perfect shot, I wait until Felipe's in a position of utter vulnerability—usually when he's carrying dishes or standing on top of the stove cleaning the ventilation grates. When the opportunity presents itself, I grab a pair of tongs or a pepper mill and . . . well, you know. I smile inwardly. If the customers knew where that pepper mill had been, they would never bug me for fresh ground pepper. I'll skip the obligatory salad-tossing analogy.

But Felipe's got a story, too. Leaving his wife behind, he's working in the United States so he can help pay for his son's legal studies in Honduras. Sometimes he gets terribly lonely, and sadness gets the better of him. Once he got so depressed that he didn't show up to work for a week. Sometimes Felipe goes over to the dance halls in Corona, Queens, to have a few *cervezas*, dance in the arms of a pretty girl, and try to forget that home is two thousand miles away. I always laugh when I hear radio commentators blab about how "easy the immigrants have it up here." Work in a restaurant for a couple months. You'll think differently.

As I return to the front I exchange greetings with a high-powered yuppie couple eating salmon and tuna at table 16. They're good regular customers who've always been nice to me, but I'm worried about the woman. When I first met her three years ago, she was an adorable, sexy, and vibrant-looking blonde. Back then she was dating a distinguished-looking, if a tad arrogant, man a few years her senior. After they broke up, however, something inside this lady went off the rails. Even though she's still pretty, she's become one of those joyless, obsessive-compulsive health nuts who tracks every calorie in and out of her body and lashes herself to a StairMaster seven hours a day. Maybe adipose tissue is the vital ingredient missing from this woman's life.

Eventually she hooked up with another distinguished-looking, if a tad arrogant, man a few years older than her. No surprise there. But the blonde's old boyfriend still eats at The Bistro. Whenever he comes now, it's with his wife and kids. His children are preteens, so the old boyfriend must have left or cheated on his wife and family to be with the blond woman, and now he's returned to them. But what's really interesting is that this man's wife looks like an older version of what his ex-girlfriend is now becoming—an intense-looking, scarily thin, über-fit blonde. I wonder if that occurred because type attracts type or because there's something about the old boyfriend that induces this reaction in women. I can't help but wonder, *What's the story there?*

I might never find out. Since I get to watch people only during the time it takes them to eat a meal, all I get to see are snapshots of their lives. Sure, I observe people's expressions, listen to their conversations, maybe even glimpse a bit of their past, but I'll never know the fullness of who they are. I see scores of people every day, and most of what makes them who they are remains a mystery. And I love a good mystery. Like Philip Marlowe, I love figuring out people's stories.

I guess that's why I've been a big reader since I was a kid. My father and mother certainly encouraged me. My dad, a high school teacher, was always thrusting books into my hands. Somewhere in the family photo albums there's a picture of two-year-old me sitting in my father's lap as he's reading aloud from the *New York Times*. Of course, I couldn't understand anything

Dad was telling me about Richard Nixon, but I understood early that there was something magical in the power of words. To me, words were like incantations that could conjure fantastic worlds in the mind and take me to places I had never been. I devoured books, hunted words in dictionaries, and was a library junkie by the time I was eight. I read *Star Wars* before I saw it in the movies and devoured all of Ian Fleming's books by the time I was thirteen. I picked up most of what I know about grammar and usage by osmosis. I also had two great English teachers in high school. They taught me that reading literature could teach you about the "universal human experience." Maybe you'll never hunt another man through the jungle, my teachers told me. Maybe you won't climb Mount Kilimanjaro or watch a bullfight in the afternoon— you don't have to. The world's a big place. You can't do or be everything, nor should you. Life is bigger than any one man. But when you read about other people's lives, when you read their *stories*, you catch a glimpse of a world bigger than your own. You may never travel a hundred miles from where you were born, but if you read stories, you'll get to see the entire world. You'll enter into the Great Mystery.

Inspired by their lessons I toyed with the idea of becoming a writer when I was in college. In my naïveté, I thought I could tell some stories myself. I penned several chapters of the Great American Detective Novel in my dorm room and showed it to a person whose opinion I valued highly. He told me my writing wasn't very good. Crushed, I never tried writing anything more complicated than a term paper or business report.

Then life did what life did, and I became a waiter. At first it didn't occur to me to write down the stories that came through The Bistro's doors every day. Sure, I had read *Kitchen Confidential* and Debra Ginsberg's *Waiting*, but those people were *writers*. My college critic's words still burned in my ears. *This isn't very good.* Who was I kidding?

Then I discovered the Internet.

I didn't go online until long after everyone else had jumped

on the digital bandwagon. In 2004 I discovered a new phenomenon called blogs, online diaries containing mostly mundane
but occasionally fascinating tidbits about people's lives. Loving
stories, I couldn't get enough of them. Then an idea began ger-
minating in my head. I have a million stories from the restaurant. Maybe I should start telling them. So I opened an online
account, and Waiter Rant was born. For the first time since college I began to write.

My initial foray was less than successful. Like most bloggers
toiling unappreciated in the needle-in-haystack vastness of the
Internet, I became frustrated that no one was reading my stuff. I
think three or four people came to my site a week. My comment
counter was firmly set at zero. I figured that my college critic was
right. I must suck as a writer. I gave up.

Then, five months later, for some unknown reason, I started
writing again. Blogging, with its diarist orientation, turned out
to be ideally suited to recording those little snapshots of life that
flash past me inside The Bistro. Within a month my writing got
noticed. I was linked on a popular Web site, and, before I knew
it, my Web site was getting hundreds, then thousands, then tens
of thousands of hits a day. I was interviewed by the BBC and the
New York Times. I had a real audience. People were also telling
me something I never heard before—"You're a good writer." It
was nice finally to get some encouragement, and from thousands
of people. By the time I wrote my three hundredth story I began
to figure out why I had resumed writing.

William Hurt, the Academy Award–winning actor, is one of
my regular customers. The day after I saw *A History of Violence*,
he came to The Bistro to eat. As I served him I pondered the
weirdness of seeing someone getting his brains blown out on the
silver screen one day and then eating risotto in my section the
next. So, as a goof, I started watching all the movies William's
ever starred in. As I made my way through the William Hurt
filmography, I stumbled across a jewel of a film called *Smoke*.

Made in 1995, the movie revolves around a Brooklyn cigar

shop and its colorful proprietor, Auggie Wren, played by Harvey Keitel. This film has special resonance for me because I once worked in a cigar shop to earn some extra money. Auggie's character, a raconteur and amateur photographer, has taken a picture of the same street corner outside his shop at the same time every day for fourteen years. Assembling all the pictures into a series of photo albums, Auggie can't explain why he does it; he just knows he has to. When he shows the photos to William Hurt's character, a blocked writer and grieving widower named Paul Benjamin, he notices the author flipping through the album a bit too quickly. "You'll never get it if don't slow down, my friend," Auggie says. When Benjamin remarks that all the pictures look the same, Auggie points out the differences in the seasons, the expressions on people's faces, how the light plays on the buildings. It's then the viewer realizes what Auggie's done. Put together, all those snapshots combine to create time-lapse photography on a massive scale. By slowing down and focusing on something as small and mundane as a street corner, Auggie has created something beautiful. By staying in one place, Auggie's created a work of art. Auggie sums up his philosophy when he says, "People say you have to travel to see the world. Sometimes I think that if you just stay in one place and keep your eyes open, you're going to see just about all that you can handle."

Until The Bistro, I never worked at anyplace longer than two years. After walking the restaurant's floorboards for several years, however, I think I unconsciously realized I knew enough about something to start writing about it. Like Auggie's street corner, the sameness and stability of The Bistro focused me so I could appreciate the little stories that waltzed into my restaurant every day. Staying put inspired me to write. Two years after starting my blog, when I flipped through the hundreds of the stories I had written, I realized I was doing what Auggie did. I was taking snapshots of The Bistro with words.

But, as the barista at Starbucks pointed out, people have also been taking snapshots of me. To many people, I'm a great waiter and a friendly person. To others, however, I'm that slightly arrogant, reserved guy who corrects customers when they mispronounce their entrée. There are even a few customers who despise me—calling me the rudest waiter in the neighborhood. And to a lady who only catches a glimpse of me through the plate glass, I'm the sad man in the window.

Later, in my car heading home, the events of the day flicker under my eyes like the dashed white lines in the middle of the road. I think about Beth and how she almost lost her beauty. I think about Saroya's struggle to build a family and Felipe's efforts to do the right thing by his. I think of all the things I've seen and what people have confided in me—their hopes, their dreams, and their confessions of sin.

Within The Bistro I've seen people get married and divorced. I've seen babies being born and parents mourning the loss of children. I've waited on people celebrating birthdays and grieving at funeral repasts. I've helped people when they had heart attacks and seizures. I've witnessed customers being kind and cruel. I've met the rich and famous and the poor and common. I've spoken to nuns and priests, rapists and pornographers, criminals and cops. I shook hands with soldiers and politicians. I've looked upon the beautiful and the ugly. I've been felt up, fucked, smacked, assaulted, lied to, and abused. To borrow a phrase from Bob Dylan, I've seen people busy being born and people busy dying. Auggie was right: if you stay in one place long enough and keep your eyes open, you'll see all you can handle. It was just like my English teachers told me—if you read stories, you get to see the entire world. And not just the stories you find in books and film, but the stories of strangers sitting next to you on the subway or in an ordinary restaurant. You can find the world in your own story, too—you just have to keep your eyes open.

I pull into my parking spot, fumble with my keys, and let myself into my apartment. My joint-custody dog Buster races around the house, thrilled that I'm home. I leash him up and take him for a walk in the cooling evening air. I idly wonder where Claude and the other homeless are bunking down for the night. When Buster finishes with his business, we go back inside. I refill his water bowl, give him a treat, and fix myself a drink. I power up my computer, take a sip of my Johnny Walker Black, and once again try coaxing words into doing my bidding. I have a deadline. The pressure's on.

CHAPTER 16

Heaven and Hell

The next Saturday The Bistro's packed. A line of customers waiting for tables snakes out the door and into the street. As my first round of tables finish their desserts, the frustrated people milling around the front entrance glower at the lingering customers with impatient hatred. Sensing the negative energy being transmitted their way, my remaining patrons hurry up and slow down—taking their sweet time to sip the last dregs of their coffee. I love passive-aggressive shit like that.

"Can you tell these people to hurry up?" one of the waiting customers, a shrill woman with a baked-in tan, asks the hostess. "We've got reservations for seven o'clock. It's seven-ten now."

"I'm sorry, madam," the hostess replies primly. "I can't control how long people take to eat."

The woman obnoxiously taps the thin, expensive watch strapped to her wrist. "I was guaranteed a table at seven," she yelps. "I'm a friend of the owner!"

I sigh inwardly and shake my head. Fluvio wouldn't recognize this lady if his life depended on it. The tanning-booth junkie's behavior doesn't surprise me, however.

"Madam," the hostess replies, "when your table's free, I'll seat you right away."

"Unacceptable," the lady says icily. "I want to speak to the owner."

"Fluvio's not available," the hostess replies automatically. "He's on vacation."

Sensing I'm going to be drawn into the fray, I decide to be proactive and walk over to the hostess stand. Before I can get there I hear a woman scream.

"Help! Oh my God, help!"

My brain instantly triangulates the location of the scream. Customers sitting at the back tables are covering their eyes and jumping out of their chairs. Louis is running toward me with a terrified expression on his face. Something has gone horribly wrong.

"The lady on table eight!" Louis shrieks. "She just threw up and keeled over!"

"Call 911!" I tell the hostess automatically.

I cross the length of the restaurant in record time. At table 8 I find a slim, delicate-looking lady in her mid-sixties, one of The Bistro's regulars, slumped against the shoulder of the man sitting next to her. White as a sheet, with vomit rolling off her chin, the lady lets out an agonal groan as her eyes roll toward the back of her head. She looks like she's going to die right here.

The man supporting the stricken woman looks up at me. I know what he's going to say before he says it.

"The ambulance is on its way, sir," I say.

"We knew this might happen," the man says softly, gently stroking the woman's hair, looking confused. "It's not totally unexpected."

"Sir?"

"She's at high risk for strokes."

"Yes, sir."

As my eyes take in the scene, it looks like someone fired a shotgun loaded with recently masticated risotto all over the table. A stroke would explain it. This lady didn't just throw up; she projectile-vomited. The splatter effect is widespread. I'm not a doctor, but things look very bad. My emergency health care training automatically kicks in. *Maintain airway. Prevent aspiration.*

"Sir," I ask. "Is your wife breathing?"

"Yes," he says.

"Is there anything in her mouth she can choke on? Any food?"

"I don't . . ."

"We have to look, sir," I say, pressing in.

Saving me the trouble, the husband sweeps his finger inside his wife's mouth. Some vomit drips to the floor.

"Her mouth looks clear," he murmurs.

"Good," I say. "Make sure she keeps breathing."

Entering restaurant-manager-crisis mode, I step away from the stricken lady and tell the hostess to update 911 that we have a female in her mid-sixties suffering from a possible stroke. I ask Beth to cover my section, and, knowing the paramedics will need room to work, Louis and I throw all the customers from the back section into some recently vacated tables on the aisle. Great, I think to myself, now the hostess's seating plan has been blown to pieces.

Suddenly, the interior of the restaurant is bathed in strobing red and blue lights. The Bistro transforms from cozy restaurant to downtown emergency room in the twinkling of an eye. The Puccini playing on the overhead speakers is drowned out by blaring police radios squawking commands in the staccato language that only cops understand. As the paramedics trundle a large gurney down the length of the restaurant, I feel sorry for the customers. They all came here to have a good time, not to see this. But, when you serve over forty thousand people a year, statistically, one or two nights like this are bound to happen.

"Hey," a bespectacled man waiting with three people by the door calls out to me, "are you in charge?"

"Yes, sir," I reply. "I'm the manager."

"We have a reservation at seven-thirty for a table in the back. Can we get seated?"

"I'm terribly sorry, sir," I reply. "We're experiencing a medical emergency. The back is unavailable right now."

"What!" the man yelps. "I want to sit in the back!"

"I'm sorry, sir—"

"When I called, I specifically asked for a table in the back!"

"What's the matter, George?" asks a woman standing behind the man.

"He won't give us a back table," the man says over his shoulder.

"Why not?"

"It's not that I don't want to give you the table," I try explaining. "I can't. The medics need room to work."

Oblivious, the man squints at me from behind his thick glasses. "You're gonna sit us in the back, right? You're gonna sit us in the back like we want, right?"

"Don't you see the paramedics working in the back?" I reply, aghast.

"Phyllis and I don't want to sit anywhere else, George," the woman, obviously George's wife, warns ominously.

"Well, we want that table when it clears out," the man huffs.

I point to an empty table near the door. "I have that table available," I say.

"Unacceptable," the man says.

I look toward the back. The paramedics are busy stabilizing the woman. The entire Bistro's ground to a halt. I don't have time for this shit.

"Listen, sir," I say, putting steel in my voice. "You can either sit at what I have available or dine with us another night."

The man looks flabbergasted. "B-but . . ." he stutters.

"I'm sorry, sir, but that's the way it has to be."

"I don't want—"

"I need to keep this door clear," I order. "You need to sit down *now*."

The self-involved four argue among themselves but finally do sit down. After a few minutes the medics bundle the woman onto a stretcher and tear out the front door. The cops and I talk outside as the lady, looking like a wounded and frightened bird, is loaded into the rig. I feel for her husband. When he and his wife were young and vibrant newlyweds, I doubt if he considered their end might come like this. No, probably not.

With a blast of sirens, the ambulance streaks off into the night. I head back inside, the bus people clean up the mess, the waiters resume serving the food, and I make my way around the restaurant, thanking the diners for their patience. George's wife glares at me from her substandard table, but I don't care. It's all over.

I'm not surprised at this woman's reaction, however. It seems customers are never happy with where they get seated in a restaurant. I constantly overhear customers asking others in their party if the table is "okay" or if they want to sit somewhere else. Every hostess has horror stories about patrons throwing temper tantrums if they can't get the exact table they want. Why do people get all bent out of shape over a table? Simple—survival of the fittest.

The incessant jockeying for the best table is all about competition for resources. Once, in our primordial past, we'd bash in one another's heads for scraps of mastodon meat, breeding partners, fur pelts, and a nice cave near a clean water supply. If you didn't, you wouldn't be able to pass on your genetic material. That impetus to survive is hardwired into our brains. We see unscrupulous businesspeople exhibit this instinct all the time—when they character assassinate each other in the press, acquire and dispose trophy spouses with astonishing rapidity, buy fur pelts (still), and get into frenzied bidding wars over a nice cave, I mean condo, in a trendy neighborhood. Of course, this crap isn't solely the province of rich customers. You should see me in a mall parking lot during the Christmas holidays. Talk about competition for resources! I become like one of those digitally six-pack-abed warriors from *The 300*. Cursing the cowardice of handicapped people and expectant mothers with their preferred parking slots, I want to cry out, "Wimps! Fight it out like everyone else! Now where's my spear?"

It's a tough world out there. We all want to have our little piece of the pie and our shot at happiness. Struggle is part of life. Sometimes you have to be aggressive to get what you want. Occasionally, we stiff-arm people with ambition or trample over them in pursuit of our goals. We don't set out to hurt people; sometimes we just do. Of course, we get elbowed and ground into the dirt, too. Life can get rough. At some point we will all know what it feels like to lose. You have to learn to take it on the chin gracefully and figure out how to win the next time. That's the great lesson of sports. Getting a good table in a restaurant, however, isn't essential to one's survival or happiness.

In order to achieve their goals, some people have internalized knocking people around psychologically, economically, and sometimes even physically to get what they think they deserve. They're like people with a faulty adrenal system or an overabundance of testosterone—it's always game time, it's always time to be aggressive, it's always time to battle for any little thing they think they deserve. When I tell these people they can't have the primo table they want, they act like I'm threatening their very survival. I may not be withholding food or shelter, but I'm holding out of their grasp a valuable "psychological resource"—the illusory feeling that they're somehow better than everyone else. That's what a seating chart at any high-end restaurant is all about. Ask any reservation manager or maître d'. She'll tell you it's a sensitive social/economic pecking order, and no status-conscious customers want to be on the bottom of the pile—or near the men's room. That would mean, *gasp*, they're somehow inferior. And if they're inferior, they won't survive! That explains why those four people were willing to step over a woman having a stroke so they could get the table they wanted.

Of course, those four people will survive not sitting in the back—just like I'll survive parking three miles from the mall entrance the day before Christmas. And don't think I've got some prejudice against rich and successful people hustling to make it—far from it. Nonwealthy slackers aren't immune from this craziness either. Middle-class America—secure in the knowledge that at least they're better than *that* guy—loves watching people make complete idiots of themselves on national TV. Many of my wealthier customers are the nicest people I've ever met. I've never bought into the fiction that the rich are evil and that poor people are romantic souls always struggling for justice and equality. Talk to any cop. There are poor assholes in this world, too.

But there's got to be more to life than just survival. There's got to be more to life than being better than everyone else. You have to survive for *something*. My godfather, a Catholic priest, once told me, "You may be the strongest and survive—only to win a life not fit for living."

Late the next morning Beth and I are sitting by the front window drinking coffee and kibitzing. It's early, and we're not expecting customers for an hour. I take a sip of my coffee and sigh. Like Grand Central Station when it's empty, The Bistro hums with potential, as if it knows that being empty is an unnatural state.

"So did you hear how that lady's doing?" Beth asks me.

"The woman from last night?" I reply.

"Yeah."

"I called the hospital, but they wouldn't tell me."

"What a shame. That poor lady."

"Yeah," I murmur. "It was terrible."

"Well, the paramedics got here fast."

"Thank God."

"You know what, though?" Beth asks.

"What?"

"I'm still pissed at those assholes."

"The four top who wanted to sit in the back?"

"Yeah. Can you believe how insensitive they were?"

"I believe it."

"It's almost criminal."

"'Hell is other people,'" I say, quoting Jean-Paul Sartre.

"You ain't kidding," Beth replies.

"I wish I was."

Beth and I are quiet. We continue to sip our coffee and watch the world go by. Outside, people bustle along with faces set to grim purpose, running around like so many rats in a cage. *Gotta hustle. Only the strong survive.* I think about that four top and how coldhearted people can be. And not for the first time I remember that indifference to the suffering of others is the ingenuity of evil. When that whole survival-of-the-fittest thing goes haywire, it can damage the part of our soul that makes us care about other people. When you don't care, when you're wrapped up in your own selfishness, man's inhumanity to man becomes that much easier to ignore.

A few hours later the front door chimes. Two parents and their daughter walk in for an early dinner. My face brightens. I remember the father is a good tipper. After I seat them and bring their cocktails, they order expensive entrées and a $200 bottle of wine. It's my lucky day.

They polish off their appetizers and tuck into dinner. In the middle of their entrées the little girl waves me over.

"Yes, miss?" I ask.

"Who's that?" she says fearfully, pointing toward the window.

I look over. Claude, our local homeless guy, is outside looking in. I wave to him. He waves back.

"That's just Claude," I reply. "He's harmless."

"See, dear," the mother says reassuringly. "I told you it was okay."

"Why is he out there?" the girl asks.

"He's always out there," I reply.

"Is he a bum?"

"Claude is homeless, miss."

"Homeless?"

"Yes."

"Where does he sleep?"

"I don't know."

"Why doesn't he have a home?"

"That's a good question, young lady," I reply. "And the answer is very complicated."

"Does he ever ask you guys for food?" the mother asks me.

"On occasion."

The little girl looks at her father. He looks at her. Something passes between them.

"Listen," the father says, looking uncomfortable, "give Claude dinner on me."

"That's very nice of you, sir," I say, mildly surprised.

The father gazes at his rack of lamb. "It's the least I can do," he mumbles.

"Do you know what he likes to eat?" the girl asks me.

"I know what Claude likes, miss," I reply. "Don't worry."

I go to the back and order some food for Claude. When it's ready, I wrap it up and take it out to him.

"Hey, Claude," I say, "one of the customers bought you dinner."

"Oh boy," he says.

"Your favorite dish," I say, holding out the bag.

"Mmmmmm."

I watch as Claude peers into the bag. He looks very happy.

"I'm set for life," he says, grinning.

I smile at the irony of his statement. "Enjoy, Claude."

Claude starts to walk away. Then he stops and turns around. "Thank those people for me," he says, staring at a spot on the sidewalk.

"I will, Claude."

He walks away, holding the bag to his chest, and I go back inside.

"The gentleman says thank you for dinner," I tell the father.

"No problem," he says sheepishly.

"Enjoy your dinner, sir."

I walk back to the hostess stand. People in this country walk past guys like Claude every day and think he's a loser—just another guy who lost out on life's lottery. I know many people look at me and think the same thing. I see the looks. I'm thirty-eight years old and waiting tables. I can do the math. Every day I work among the successfully sleek and carnivorous beautiful people. Sometimes I wonder what these people have that I don't have. Are they better than me? Are they smarter than me? More ruthless? Was I out to lunch when the happiness and success genes were passed out? I'll admit it—sometimes I'm envious of rich guys with their expensive suits, artificially brightened smiles, and fit-bodied Robo-babe girlfriends. Sometimes I feel that, if life's a game of survival of the fittest, then I lost.

As I pause near the hostess stand, the image of the woman who suffered the stroke comes into my mind. I remember how frail and vulnerable she looked. I remember how cold those selfish table-conscious customers were. They didn't care if that woman lived or died. Maybe they viewed her being sick as a form of weakness. Jesus, next thing you know, dying will be considered a personal failure. I remember again what Sartre said about hell being other people.

I look out the window and see Claude sitting on a bench eating his dinner. He's having a hot meal because something in a little girl's eyes moved a father to feed a hungry stranger. That something was probably a mishmash of self-serving motivations and noble impulses. Maybe that dad felt guilty; maybe he was shielding his daughter from the coldness of the world; maybe he wanted to be nice.

I stand there and try to figure out what that something was. After a while I give up. I don't need to know. I content myself with something I read on a bishop's coat of arms long ago—"Love is ingenious." No matter how convoluted the motivations, love's impulses often triumph over our more selfish instincts. Maybe that's the very thing that makes life fit for living. With a start, I realize another great story has dropped into my lap.

And Sartre? I chuckle to myself. He was only *half* right. Heaven can be other people, too.

CHAPTER 17

Substance Abuse

Fluvio has finally made good on his promise to open a new restaurant. After months of dickering over the financing, he signed the lease and took possession of the keys for the new place a few weeks ago. Since he's been spending all his time prepping the new restaurant I've been working crazy hours at The Bistro. Because it's the busy season, idiot customers are breeding like cockroaches. The pressure of the extended hours coupled with trying to complete the book proposal is taking its psychic toll. It's Tuesday night. I feel burned out and lonely. Tomorrow's going to be a busy Fourth of July. I beg Fluvio to let me go early so I can get some time for myself. Fluvio hears the exhaustion in my voice and cuts me loose. Louis can play manager tonight.

I end up having a post-shift drink at Café American. It's a cozy restaurant housed in a Civil War–era building three blocks up from The Bistro. The café's bar is situated in what used to be the front room of an old government building. A set of large French doors opening onto an outdoor patio stand in for the front wall, while a scuffed mahogany bar running underneath a heavy glass mirror takes up the left side of the old anteroom. Nestled against the right wall are four high-topped wooden tables with padded leather bar stools. A cutout doorway with damask curtains separates the bar area from the dining room. The subdued light playing off the embossed tin ceilings gives the place a relaxed, lived-in feel.

There are cheaper places to drink, but there's nowhere I'd feel more welcome. Some high-end establishments don't like waiters from other restaurants drinking in their place. They'd prefer wealthier rear ends warming their bar stools. I've gotten the cold shoulder from many snooty bartenders in my time. Café American's owner, Rick, however, actually goes out of his way to be nice to waitstaff. He usually sends out free homemade desserts or mini pizzas, which are gratefully consumed by inebriated servers. After a hard night of waiting on entitled people the last thing I want is to feel unwelcome. Coming into Café American is like slipping into a comfortable pair of jeans.

I stare at my drink. A shallow pool of vodka and olive juice is all that remains of my martini. I drain it, place the empty glass back on the counter, and begin looking for Arthur, the bartender. He's busy flirting with a blond woman at the other end of the bar. That's okay. I've got plenty of time. I settle back in my chair and enjoy the feeling of 80-proof alcohol working through my system. I run my eyes across the bottles standing sentry on top of the bar's underlit counter. Gleaming like understated rubies and sapphires, they glow patiently, waiting to be called into action.

"Another?" Arthur says, interrupting my contemplation.

"Yes," I reply, pushing my empty glass toward him. "Please."

"Tough night?"

"Yeah," I reply, sighing. "Lots of assholes."

"Same here," Arthur says.

"I had plenty of bad tippers," I say. "But at least I got to leave early."

"Is the rest of the gang coming out tonight?"

"I think Beth and Dawn are coming later."

"Is Dawn still single?" Arthur asks.

"Dude," I reply, "how old's your daughter?"

"Fifteen."

"Dawn's twenty-one."

Arthur grins. "I know. That doesn't make me a bad person, does it?"

"It doesn't make you a good one."

"So'd you hear about the waiter at Café Foo Foo?" Arthur asks.

"What happened?"

"Heroin overdose," Arthur says. "Out cold on the bathroom floor."

"Did he die?"

"No," Arthur says. "But I heard the owner took his sweet time calling 911."

"Figures."

"I heard the needle was still in his arm," Arthur says. "A customer found him."

"Waiter!" I twitter in a falsetto voice. "There's a junkie in my soup!"

"That's cold, man," Arthur laughs.

"Aw, c'mon," I reply. "You know this business. Plenty of substance abusers. I'll bet the other waiters stole his tables before they even called the ambulance."

"You're probably right."

"You know I am."

"Hey," Arthur says, "do you remember when that chef in England started screaming that all the chefs were doing coke?"

"Jamie Oliver," I reply, nodding. "When I heard that, I was like, 'No shit, Sherlock.'"

"Did he just fucking wake up and notice there were drugs in the kitchen?"

"Blimey!" I yelp. "I don't believe it! There's cocaine here, mate! Help! Call me a news conference!"

"I'll bet his publicist put him up to it."

"Nothing like stating the obvious in the name of self-promotion."

"You're so young," Arthur says, "yet so cynical."

"I used to be in marketing."

"So any druggies work at your place now?" Arthur asks.

"No," I reply. "The usual potheads and drinkers, but no hard-core stuff."

"Remember Crackhead Pete?" Arthur asks. "He used to work for you."

"Oh my God," I grunt. "How could I forget?"

Pete was a neighborhood waiter legendary for his substance abuse. If you had it, he'd snort it, smoke it, or inject it. Pete, when he was sober, was an excellent waiter. But when he was on one of his benders, he'd forget things like taking a shower and doing laundry. His customers would complain that he smelled bad. Needless to say, he had a hard time keeping a job. He worked every restaurant in the neighborhood and earned the dubious distinction of being fired from every one of them. The neighborhood snarks started calling him Crackhead Pete. Soon, that's what everyone called him—even the children. If people assigned me the appellation "Crackhead" anything, I'd leave town. I guess I should be happy with "sad man in the window."

"He worked here one day," Arthur says, waxing nostalgically.

"What happened?"

"You know how we give employees a free drink at the end of their shift?"

"Sure."

"Pete showed up at ten in the morning on his first day and asked if he could have his shift drink early."

"That sounds like Pete."

"Rick fired him on the spot."

"You're lucky," I say. "Fluvio put up with him for a year and a half."

"That's crazy."

"Fluvio has a soft spot for drunks."

Substance abuse has always been a problem in restaurants. A recent study conducted by the Substance Abuse and Mental Health Services Administration states that 17.4 percent of all restaurant workers use illegal substances. And we're not even talking about the drinkers here. The combined number of coke fiends, potheads, drunks, and pill poppers has to be, conservatively, 25 percent of the workforce. I often wonder, Does the restaurant lifestyle turn people into addicts, or are addicts drawn to the restaurant lifestyle? Plenty of sober people work in the industry, but there's a healthy percentage of slackers who love partying into the night and sleeping in until noon. They're waiting for lives that never quite happen, reminding me of the alcoholic characters in Eugene O'Neill's play *The Iceman Cometh*.

Customers also drag their substance-abuse issues into restaurants every day. I once had a customer, Drunky Dave, who ate at The Bistro every week. I was always his waiter. Dave would always order two cocktails, drink a bottle of expensive red wine, and wash down his dessert with an Irish coffee and *two* grappa chasers. Grappa's disgusting stuff. I call it Italian lighter fluid. When someone uncorks a bottle of the stuff, I can smell it from across the street.

When it was time for Drunky Dave to go home, he could barely regulate his breathing, much less stand up straight. Once, when he was in a drunken stupor, he started throwing up. As he bolted for the door, vomit dripping from between his fingers while he attempted to keep his dinner from projectiling out his mouth, he clipped an old lady on her way to the bathroom. I caught the old lady before she broke a hip. The bus people cleaned off the table, and I called Dave a cab. When I was satisfied the contents of his stomach had been deposited onto the curb, I walked outside and presented him the check.

"But I'm not finished!" Dave protested.

"Yes, you are," I replied. "Come back when you're sober."

"Fuck you!" Drunky Dave screamed. "I eat here all the time. I drop a lot of money here."

"You're drunk," I said as the cab pulled up. "And the beauty of all this is that you're not going to remember a thing when you wake up."

"You're right," Dave acknowledged, in a rare burst of self-awareness.

"Good night, Dave," I said, pushing his head down as he got

inside the cab. I took his check inside and rang everything up. Of course I wrote in a 30 percent tip for myself.

Drunky Dave never said a thing.

Guys like Dave are just the tip of the iceberg. I've seen rich yuppie chicks pass out from overdosing on Special K; I've seen people snort heroin while waiting to get inside the restaurant; and I've caught sixty-year-olds smoking pot in the bathroom. I've had customers beg for napkins as they bled from deviated septums caused by cocaine abuse. From my vantage point, standing above the customers, I see track marks peeking out from under French cuffs. I notice the broken capillaries and the rheumy eyes. I see women rummaging through their purses looking for benzodiazepine candies. I notice the slightly jaundiced skin and detoxification tremors of men going mad as they try to space out their drinks in polite company. I know all the signs from having worked in a drug rehab. Sometimes I feel like I never left.

In addition to taking your order and delivering food, servers are often forced to play liquor cop. In the state of New York it is against the law to serve alcohol to a visibly intoxicated person. If you come into my place already drunk, I'm not going to serve you. But what if you get drunk inside my place? What if you're noticeably pregnant and drinking like a sailor? Do I fatten your check and my tip with high-priced booze or cut you off? Ah, the moral dilemma begins.

Many of my customers are drunks. They shouldn't be drinking. If they were members of my family, I'd give them AA literature, not booze. But they're not family—they're customers. They have a right to get fucked up if they want to. If I cut them off, they'll likely just go drink themselves stupid at home. If I see customers who've had too much to drink, I'll give them time and coffee until they sober up. If they're not sober, I ask how they're getting home and offer to call a cab. I'm sure some of my customers have gotten behind the wheel drunk. There's no way for me to know what they're going to do when they leave my restaurant.

Sometimes they go to another bar to drink. Late at night, on my way home from work, I've seen people I served a few hours earlier fighting and arguing in the street like stew bums fighting over the last drop of Four Roses.

"Did Crackhead Pete steal from you?" Arthur asks, breaking my train of thought.

"No," I reply. "He never took as much as a nickel. But he was always asking to borrow money."

"I think he owes everyone in town twenty bucks. He even hit me up once."

"You'll never see it again."

"I'll consider it charity."

"Talking about waiters and substance abuse," I continue, "what's the percentage of waiters who've gotten a DWI?"

"Oh, man," Arthur says, looking up at the ceiling like he's figuring a large sum. "We've got at least two waiters here who fit that bill. I'd say thirty percent."

"That sounds about right," I reply. "Ever notice a lot of waiters don't drive?"

"Their licenses have been revoked."

"Exactamundo."

A customer walks up to the bar and asks for a cosmopolitan. Arthur slips away to prepare the drink. Dawn and Beth, getting off shift from The Bistro, walk in the front door and grab the bar stools next to me.

"Finally," I say, looking at my watch. "You guys took your sweet time."

"My last customers were assholes," Beth says.

If you haven't guessed it by now, "asshole" is a cherished customer descriptive.

"What bad behaviors were on display this evening?" I ask.

"The lady gave her date a hand job under the table," Dawn says. "Can you believe that shit?"

Dawn's a petite twenty-one-year-old blonde with a cute body and green eyes. Arthur's in lust with her.

"I believe it," I reply.

"They took forever," Beth groans.

"The hand job took forever?" I ask.

"It took them forty-five minutes to order," Beth says, ignoring me. "The lady took forever to eat."

"Hard to eat with one hand," I say. Dawn giggles.

"I wish you were their waiter," Beth says. "With that stare of yours, they'd've cut it out immediately."

"Yeah," Dawn says. "Thanks for abandoning us."

"Hey," I shoot back, "how often do I get to leave before one A.M.?"

Arthur comes over, says hello, and gets the girls' drink orders. They both order mojitos.

"So," I ask after Arthur walks away, "did the couple retire to the bathroom and, uh, finish the job?"

"Yeah," Beth says, "but they took an awfully long time."

"Probably doing drugs, too," I say. "It's amazing how many people need to have their consciousness altered before they have sex."

"Whatever," Beth says, shrugging. "The night's over."

I sip my drink. Beth and Dawn chug down their mojitos and order another round. I think all servers drink their first postshift drink quickly. A waiter's first drink is medicinal, his second is relaxing, but his third is anesthesia.

"So you got 'em?" Beth says to Dawn, her voice dropping to a whisper.

Dawn fumbles in her purse and pulls out a medicine bottle.

"What's that?" I ask.

"Xanax," Dawn says.

"You're not gonna take that now, are you?" I say.

"What are you," Dawn says, "my father?"

"Xanax and mojitos don't mix."

"I have a prescription."

Beth and Dawn take their pills and wash them down with a rum and mint chaser. In a few minutes the drugs will kick in and they'll forget their own names. I've seen it happen before.

I shake my head and look down at my martini. It's still half full. I take another sip. The best advice I ever got about drinking was from my godfather. "Drink till you're mellow," he used to say. "After that it's all downhill." My father, never a big drinker, was another example. He'd have one beer every night, and that was it. I can count on the fingers of one hand how many times I've seen my dad tipsy.

Of course, I've skied booze's downhill slope more than once. I've done the blackout thing. I've thrown up on the subway. I've felt cold porcelain on my cheek while prostrate on the floor of a filthy men's room. I've acted just like some of my more difficult customers. Most of that shit happened before I turned thirty. Now I like to drink but hate being drunk. I try imbibing to the fine edge of happiness and then stop. Two drinks are my normal limit. If I go to a party, I ask for half-strength margaritas or light vodka and cranberries. At my brother's wedding reception I sucked on watered-down scotch-and-sodas all night. I hate feeling dizzy. I hate throwing up. I'm afraid of getting cancer and throwing up from the chemo. I've seen cancer patients driven mad by nausea. I'd probably kill myself before throwing up for hours on end. But I smoke cigarettes, so I'm just as full of shit as everyone else.

I take another sip of my drink. Lately I've been drinking past my limit. That worries me. After years of watching good and bad people suffering from addictions, I came to the conclusion that everybody, and I mean everybody, narcotizes their pain somehow. I don't care if you think the pain comes from insufficient parenting, frustrated dreams, the human condition, or the wages of Original Sin. Everyone tries to deaden it somehow.

I hear a woman laugh. It's a sexy, crystalline laugh that forces my head to turn. The laugh came out of a lithe woman wearing high heels and a leather miniskirt. She's sitting on one of the tables against the wall. A young guy's clumsily nibbling her neck. The woman's in her late forties and still a knockout. I know her. She's a bad drunk. She goes home with a different guy every other night of the week. Her conquests are usually younger men. She's slept with half the waiters in town. She made a play for me once. I felt sorry for her and shined her on. She called me a fag. I look at her carefully. Her good looks won't last forever. Eventually booze will ruin them. Men will stop being enchanted and start being repulsed. Soon she'll have only liquor to numb her pain.

I've seen people get addicted to crack and booze, religion and sex, money and power. People can get addicted to shopping and exercise, chocolate and soap operas, surfing the Internet, and even throwing up. When happiness and peace are scarce, people will turn to artificial means to shut off the jabbering in their brains. Waiters aren't free from pain. They suffer from aching joints, bad backs, bruised egos, tattered nerves, and emotional angst.

I look at my reflection in the mirror. A lonely-looking guy stares back at me. I never drank every day until I became a waiter. Doctors say one or two drinks a day are actually good for you. That may be true. Maybe I'm drinking more because I'm older. Maybe I'm drinking more because I'm a slacker waiter watching his life amount to nothing. I'm thirty-eight years old and waiting tables. This writing thing is a crapshoot. I'm still struggling with the proposal. If this doesn't work out, I'll have nothing going on, nothing to look forward to. That scares the shit out of me.

Beth and Dawn order another round of mojitos. They've gone from sober to trashed in half an hour. They're chattering away on their cell phones. They've forgotten I'm even there. That's okay. They're young girls. They like to party. They'll get annihilated, sleep it off, and go back to work the next day. I've always said you can't diagnose alcoholism in someone until he's twenty-seven. Before then everyone's a situational drunk. When you're in your late thirties, however, like Crackhead Pete and me, things are very different.

Crackhead Pete eventually met a pretty girl. They started a business, and he got most of his drinking and drugging under control. He's not the same desperate character I met years ago. It's a nice reminder that no one's beyond redemption.

I smile ruefully to myself. I gave Pete a lot of shit when I was his boss. I joined the chorus of people calling him a crackhead. Now he's got some of the things I want but don't have. What a kick in the ass that is.

"Arthur," I say a bit loudly, "another drink, please."

"You gonna go past your limit tonight?" Arthur asks.

"Yep."

Arthur makes my drink and slides it toward me. I know I'm breaking my own rules. I want to join Beth and Dawn in obliviousness. I feel like there's a dead zone in my brain keeping me disconnected from the human race. I want to get drunk like my customers. Behind me the sexy alcoholic laughs. Suddenly, I don't feel sorry for her. I realize I want to fuck her, too. When people are desperate and lonely, they'll try to connect with anything. I prop my head up on my elbow and start lapping my third drink. I'm in a bad place. The café transforms from a pair of comfortable jeans into a straitjacket. My head swims. The Iceman's coming. I need anesthesia.

I don't want to think anymore.

CHAPTER 18

The Fourth of July

Despite my hangover I show up early for my shift the next day. I have to. Fluvio is at Bistro Duetto getting ready for its grand opening. It's lunch on a beautiful Fourth of July. The Bistro's crowded. If it were up to me, I'd still be in bed. But since I never cut any other hungover waiters slack, I'll never hear the end of it if I call in sick. Waiters are like arrogant teenagers, always sniffing the air for the slightest whiff of hypocrisy.

Thick-tongued and feeling like someone stuck an ice pick into my occipital lobe, I try to ignore the clatter and bustle of a holiday lunchtime crowd. I try to imagine I'm cocooned inside a muffling force field that blots out the nerve-fraying shrieks of children and softens the pain banging inside my head. After a few minutes I realize my therapeutic visualization isn't working. The acetaminophen I took earlier isn't doing the trick, either. I've already exceeded the maximum adult dosage. If I take any more, my stressed liver's going to slither out my navel.

I look outside The Bistro's plate glass window. Crowds of people throng the sidewalks soaking up the vitality of the summer season. A beautiful woman in short shorts and a diaphanous T-shirt strolls past. As I covertly watch the muscles under the tanned skin of her legs stretch and contract, a couple of high school boys spoil my view by pausing midstride to gawk at her, too. I'm slightly annoyed. I've been looking at women longer than these boys have been alive. They need to learn a little discretion like me. Who am I kidding? On some level, men are always fifteen.

"Hey," Beth says, walking in the front door. She looks terrible.

"My, my," I cluck. "Look what the cat dragged in."

"Gimme a break," Beth grumbles. "You got hammered last night, too."

"Not like you, darling," I say. "I wasn't dancing on tables."

"Was I?"

"The video I took will be all over the Internet tomorrow."

Beth flips me the bird. "You're full of shit."

"At least you got home all right."

"I didn't get home," Beth groans. "I'm wearing the same clothes I had on last night."

"How delightfully skanky."

"I washed my shirt in a sink, so I'm not totally skanky."

"Don't sweat it," I reply. "I had no clean pants this morning, so I ironed the ones I've got on with Febreze."

"Ew."

"They're so dirty I thought they'd get off the floor under their own power and commit suicide."

Beth laughs. I like it when Beth laughs. Her face lights up with a radiance that could dispel the darkness of human sin. Even hungover she's still pretty.

"How many on the books tonight?" she asks.

"About one-fifty."

"Ouch," Beth says, wincing, "Why can't tonight be a slow night?"

"It's always busy when you're hungover," I say. "This business is like a merciless god."

"I don't know how I'm going to make it," Beth groans.

"The wages of sin is death, young lady," I say with mock seriousness. "Now hurry up and get ready. You just got a table."

"Already?"

"Like ripping off a Band-Aid, honey. Dive in and get the pain over with fast."

"Ugh," Beth says, shaking her head. "Can you believe it's July Fourth already?"

"I know," I reply. "Valentine's Day seems like last week."

"And I haven't even been to the shore yet," Beth says. "Where does the time go?"

"Tempus fugit, kid."

"I guess."

Beth heads to the back to get ready. She'll be all right. Beth has the best work ethic of any server at The Bistro.

The front door chimes. A young woman of twenty-five walks in. She's wearing a big smile on her face.

"Remember me?" she asks.

I flip through my mental Rolodex of faces. "Sophie?" I say carefully.

"You remember me!" the girl yelps.

I remember. Sophie. She was a bus girl when I started at The Bistro six years ago. She was nineteen back then, another college freshman hustling to make a few summer bucks. Much to my surprise, she had a schoolgirl crush on me. Fluvio used to tease me about it.

"Of course I remember you, Sophie," I say, coming around to give her a hug. "How've you been?"

"I'm great," Sophie says. "I'm starting my second year of law school."

"You're going to be a lawyer?" I say. "Good. You can defend me when I blow this place up."

Sophie laughs. We give each other a hug. I catch a whiff of her perfume.

"You look great, Sophie," I say, as we pull apart. "Very grown up."

"Ugh!" Sophie says, putting her hand to her cheek. "Do you remember the hairdo I had when I worked here?"

"Something with pink in it, I recall."

"Oh, you do remember."

"Hard to forget."

Sophie's hair is now long and professionally styled. I notice her clothes fit very well. When she worked at The Bistro, she wore bulky clothes that obscured her figure. Now, baby fat long dissolved, she moves with the grace of a self-assured woman. I feel my pulse quickening. I realize I'm feeling desire. There's a minor argument between my id and superego before the portcullis of my self-control comes crashing down. I try to remember that this girl's fourteen years younger than me. I'm feeling what all men feel when they realize the little girls they've known are growing into women. It's a feeling I'll be experiencing until they plant me six feet under. I try and remember Lew Archer's old adage. "When a man gets older, if he's smart, he likes his women older, too." That's good advice, though I wonder how Ross Macdonald's fictional detective would have fared working around nubile twenty-year-olds every day.

"Are you still with Allie?" Sophie asks.

"Oh," I say, waving my hand, "we broke up two years ago."

"You guys went out forever," Sophie exclaims. "What happened?"

"Things change," I say. "But it's all good. Allie's engaged."

"Really?"

"Yeah, the wedding's next year."

"Wow," Sophie says.

"How about you? Any boyfriends?"

"Yes," Sophie says, with a slight blush. "One guy. It's pretty serious."

"Good. I'm happy for you."

Sophie giggles the giggle all women giggle when they're in love. "Thank you."

"Listen," I say. "Go in the back and say hi to the guys. Many of them will still remember you."

"I'd like that," Sophie says.

"Go ahead."

As I watch Sophie walk toward the kitchen my stomach clenches. Seeing her happy and confident throws my constrained life into sharp relief. When I worked in mental health, the elderly patients always resented the younger ones. I'm beginning to understand why. Young people seem to have their whole life ahead of them. Their options seem limitless. As I get older my limitations are starting to pile up. I remember looking recently at an advertisement for the NYPD and realizing I was too old to apply. Not that I want to be a cop, mind you, I was just aggravated that I had become old enough to be excluded from something. But I try to look on the bright side. At least I'm ineligible for the draft.

Young people are starting to remind me that I'm caught up in the swift current of time. When I watch those girls outside The Bistro or see Sophie turning into a young woman, it's not just about sex. I'm beginning to grasp, not in an intellectual way, but in a deep-in-my-bones way, that I'm getting older. Sophie's another reminder that time is unstoppable, that life does not wait. Sometimes, when I consider this little bit of existential angst, I feel like I'm turning into a lonely middle-aged man. A poet once said that "time is the fire in which we burn." I'm not old by any means, but after seeing Sophie, I feel myself getting a little crispy around the edges.

Sophie comes back up front to say good-bye. We exchange e-mail addresses. We'll probably never see each other again. That's not because we don't care about each other. It's because our lives will travel on different trajectories. Sophie thinks we'll be buddies for her entire life. That's sweet. One day she'll realize that friends float in and out of your life with astonishing rapidity. This is especially true in the restaurant business. You can work next to people for several years, know all their aspirations and fears; but once you move on, the odds are heavy you'll lose touch. I've learned to be glad to have known people when I knew them. Artificially extending a relationship beyond its natural course is usually not a good idea. Ever wonder why girls dump their boyfriends after they graduate from college? That's why. As Sophie walks away I contemplate the fact I was in high school when she was born. Now I'm thirty-eight, and she's in law school.

Lately the passing of time has been very much on my mind. I'm scared that time's moving too fast. I think that's why I got upset in the bar last night. That's why I drank so much. I was trying to anesthetize myself. Maybe I'm having that midlife crisis I hear everyone talking about. I look at the summer tableau milling around outside The Bistro. The fact that another season's slipping by only accentuates my feeling of loss. I shouldn't be surprised I feel the way I do. I think time flows differently when you're a waiter. It flows faster.

Waiters live outside the normal time-space continuum. To waiters, people with nine-to-five jobs are alien creatures. When you're getting out of bed, we're just crawling into ours. When you're fast asleep, we've only just begun to party. Waiters are, when you think about it, creatures of the night. At first it's all very romantic, but after a while the evenings smear into a blur of darkness and neon, causing the months to pass by like days.

There are some benefits to this vampiric existence. Since we're off when most people are working we never have to wait in line at the mall, there's always a seat at the movie theater, parking spaces are bountiful, and we know all the cool places to be on a Wednesday night. As I mentioned earlier, we usually work evenings, we have the days free to pursue those romantic stereotypical interests like writing, acting, modeling, etc. The truth? A lot of waiters spend that free time sleeping.

Because of our schedule, it's very difficult for waiters to maintain relationships with so-called "normal" people. This is a problem for anyone who works in the restaurant industry. To give up working a Friday night in order to hang out with your nine-to-five buddies can be a painful hit in the wallet. A waitress friend of mine recently gave away a Saturday night shift so she could attend her friend's wedding. Not only did the waitress spend money on a dress that she could use only once, she also lost the bulk of her week's income. Because she was out so much cash, she couldn't afford to give her friend a big gift. She spent the wedding reception embarrassed that she couldn't give as much as the other girls in the bridal party. People who've never worked in the restaurant industry need to understand that when servers take time off to be with their friends, they're actually giving a gift worth hundreds of dollars—the gift of their time. When you factor in the lost wages, that waitress probably gave more financially to the newlyweds than all the other bridesmaids. Because that gift wasn't money stuffed into an envelope, the bridesmaids cattily said that my waitress friend was cheap, and the waitress was hurt by their comments. I consoled her by saying that that's what happens when women swim in the unmarried, bitter, and over-the-age-of-thirty pool. But I digress.

The converse of the time dilemma is also true. If waiters want to socialize on Monday or Tuesday night, they have to understand their friends might be stressed out after a long day at work. My friends understand my schedule and lifestyle, but when I visit them, they're half asleep by nine o'clock. I have to be conscious that our schedules belong in different universes. Sometimes they get angry that I don't attend some of the parties they throw, but they also realize every time I come on a work night I'm automatically losing $200. That's an expensive party.

The difference in schedules really hurts romantic relationships. Waiters often hook up with people in the restaurant biz because they're the only people who have the same kind of schedules. Waiters who become couples often try to get the same days off. If they work at the same restaurant, that can rapidly become a problem. If they decide to break up, the atmosphere on the dining room floor can quickly become toxic. Every restaurant manager's had to deal with this headache. Maintaining relationships is even harder when one member of the couple leaves the restaurant business or hooks up with someone outside our merry little clan. It's hard to maintain a relationship when you're working Saturday nights and your significant other's sitting at home alone. My schedule was one of the reasons my last relationship fell apart. My ex got sick of spending New Year's Eve alone and celebrating Valentine's Day a week late. I don't blame her. Besides, I was always cranky around the holidays.

When you're a waiter, you observe the holidays from a different perspective. You become part of the machine separating people from their money. After a few years waiting tables, commercialism hollows out the holidays and turns them into just another day on the calendar. That's a problem.

Since earliest recorded history humans have used holidays to mark the passage of time. The Druids celebrated the harvest, the Romans partied during the winter solstice, and the Incas commemorated the movement of the stars. People use significant days to orient themselves in time. How many of us have said, "I remember that happened before last Christmas" or "Was that before or after 9/11?" Holidays remind us where we are in the year. Desensitization to the holidays is another reason time flows faster for waiters than for regular people. Anyone who's ever waited tables has experienced the "Is it Mother's Day already?" sensation.

Sometimes I feel like I'm living in a different dimension, separated from normal reality by an imperceptible but impenetrable barrier. I can see what the normal people are doing. I see my friends getting married and their babies getting older. I see girls like Sophie growing into young women. I see the pages of the calendar turn. It's during moments like these that I hate being a waiter. I get paranoid, thinking that the restaurant business is a trap designed to bleed away the most productive years of my life. I feel like a jealous ghost watching the living. Sure, being a waiter has given me a different perspective from which to view life. In some respects having that different point of view has paid off. People often think of that perspective as living on the "edge," moving outside the boundaries of normal experience. But if you think living on that edge is an exciting adventure, try it for a while. It gets old fast.

I didn't always feel so divorced from time. When I was in the seminary, I felt time was holy. The principal liturgical seasons of Lent, Easter, Advent, and ordinary time gave structure to the year. The Liturgy of the Hours, the daily prayer of the Catholic Church, gave structure to the day. I'd shuffle into the chapel with my fellow seminarians to pray every morning, evening, and night. You always knew what season it was from the readings, songs, and antiphons being used. My favorite time was Night Prayer. Just before bed, when the world outside had grown quiet, we'd gather in our dark church and reflect on how we had spent our day. We'd ask for mercy. We'd pray for guidance. We'd cling to hope. When we were finished, we'd turn to the statue of the Blessed Mother and sing a hymn to her in Latin. The sound of thirty men quietly singing themselves a lullaby is something I'll never forget. I miss the sacredness of time. Time seems cheap to me now.

Soon I'm too busy to wax philosophical. Fluvio returns from setting up at the new restaurant and starts barking orders. Every year the local merchants sponsor a big fireworks show down by the river. Half an hour before the pyrotechnic display starts, The Bistro always fills up with customers. I hope I can get all my tables settled before the show starts. I love fireworks.

Of course, just as the first shells start exploding overhead, a couple gets seated in my section. Beth and the other servers are already outside. Most of the customers are outside, too.

"You," Fluvio says, pointing at me, "take those people."

I feel like a disappointed little boy. I want to see the fireworks, too. Fluvio doesn't stick around to listen to my protests. He goes outside to watch the fireworks. I go over to my new table. Two old people, disinterested in the commotion outside, peer at their menus.

"Good evening," I say, trying to be professional. "Can I get you something from the bar?"

"What are your specials?" the man says, not looking up from his menu.

As I recite the specials I watch the brilliant starbursts reflected in windows across the street. The kaleidoscope of fire high in the sky projects shifting patterns of color onto the onlookers' upturned faces. The Bistro shakes and rattles while the benign artillery barrage roars overhead.

I'm angry. I'm missing the fireworks. Another holiday's passing by, and I'm stuck inside The Bistro. I need to see those fireworks. I need to be outside celebrating with everybody else. I need to be a normal person, not a servant, for *one minute*. Seeing the fireworks becomes a psychological imperative.

"Excuse me," I say to my table. "Would you mind terribly if I go outside and watch the fireworks?"

"We want to eat!" the old man protests.

"It'll just be a few minutes," I plead.

The old woman reaches across the table and pats her husband on the hand. A communication passes between them. For some reason I think the old woman understands where I'm coming from.

"Of course, dear," the wife says, looking up at me. "We can wait. Go outside."

"Thank you, madam."

I run out the front door. The grand finale is just beginning. My eyes widen. For a moment I'm like a schoolboy. The night sky has blossomed into fire. The bass from the concussive blasts vibrates my chest and sets off all the car alarms in the neighborhood.

I feel a hand hard on my arm. It's Fluvio.

"What are you doing out here?" he shouts. "You have customers!"

"They're fine," I say. "Don't worry about it."

"Get inside," Fluvio orders.

I pull Fluvio's hand off my arm and look him straight in the eye. The smudged lenses of his eyeglasses dull the reflection of the fiery magnificence exploding above him.

"I'm gonna be a normal human being for a few minutes," I say.

Fluvio stares at me openmouthed. He starts to say something but then thinks the better of it. He storms off, muttering under his breath.

I spy Beth and the other waiters across the street and walk over to join them.

"Something, huh?" I yell over the din.

"It's beautiful," Beth shouts, jumping up and down excitedly.

I stand alongside my coworkers. The kitchen guys have come outside, too. For a moment we forget we work in a restaurant. We're regular people celebrating the Fourth of July. I smile to myself. My old sociology professor would've said that fireworks displays are a sort of "secular liturgy." Standing outside with the great swell of humanity, I feel the way I did when I was in the seminary chapel—connected to something bigger than myself.

Suddenly, I realize I no longer feel hungover. The explosions above are knocking time back into joint. I no longer feel alienated and disconnected. As the summer sky blazes I feel human again. The Chinese believed that fireworks chase away evil spirits. I think they were right.

The display ends. The air reeks of gunpowder. The crowds disperse as ashes sprinkle down from the sky like snow. I head back inside The Bistro and go to my table.

"Thanks for waiting," I say to the old couple. "I appreciate it."

"That's okay," the old woman says. "You only live once."

CHAPTER 19

Russell Crowe and Me

t's lunchtime a month later, and I'm half an hour late for work. Walking briskly toward The Bistro, I can see Armando peering angrily at me through the plate glass window.

"You were supposed to be here at twelve," he says as I walk through the door.

"Sorry, man," I reply. "I overslept."

"What a lame excuse," Armando grunts. "Why don't you talk about your lame excuses on your blog?"

"Maybe I will," I snap back.

"Be on time next time."

"Okay, little boss man."

Armando shakes his head and walks away. The sous-chef might be Fluvio's cousin, but under the restaurant's hierarchy he has no supervisory authority over me. Armando runs the kitchen; I run the dining room. But ever since Bistro Duetto opened a few weeks ago, I can feel the dynamic among the staff members shifting. It doesn't help that Fluvio's shanghaiing waiters from the old place to work in the new. Due to chronic understaffing, we're all stretched thin, and tempers are flaring. As I predicted, Fluvio's lack of organizational skills is hurting both restaurants. He has the cooks from Duetto sneaking into The Bistro after closing to swipe our supplies and pre-prepared food. Three waitresses who defected to the new restaurant are tearing out one anothers throat's in the quest to be Duetto's manager. And at The Bistro, long-simmering resentments that had been held in place by Fluvio's presence are now bubbling to the surface. The change between Armando and me has been sudden and profound. Armando's always been a hard worker, but he's never had to deal with ordering food or negotiating with vendors full time. Since Fluvio's been so preoccupied, Armando's been forced to take on extra duties. Couple this with a new live-in girlfriend, and Armando's a very busy man. I'm trying to be understanding.

Part of me is pissed at Armando, though. Ever since Saroya moved in with him, she's been getting harder and harder to deal with. While I'll admit I've never been the most punctual of workers, Saroya wins the booby prize when it comes to employee tardiness. After several months of cohabitation with the chef, she's been coming in whenever she feels like it, leaves the moment the money slows down, and almost never pitches in to help fellow servers when they need a shift covered. What's worse is that she won't listen to anything I tell her. Whenever I confront her behavior, she threatens to run to Armando and tell him I'm harassing her. And Armando's aggravated with *my* being late? Please.

I clock in to the computer and grab a cup of coffee. Beth is busy telling the lunch specials to a table. The Bistro is crowded. I catch Beth's eye and toss her a "Do you need help?" look. She shakes her head. Everything's covered.

The house phone starts clamoring for attention. I cover the distance from the computer to the hostess stand in eight paces and pick it up by the third ring.

"WHY YOU NO ANSWER THE PHONE?" Fluvio yells.

"But I am answering the phone," I reply matter-of-factly.

"It ring and ring . . ."

"I got it by the third ring. Relax." As I've mentioned before, Fluvio's got a thing with phones.

"You're late anyway," Fluvio says.

"And I'll leave here late, too," I reply. "Remember that."

"Whatever. What else is going on?"

"I sent my book proposal to the agent," I say brightly. "He's going to start sending it to publishers tomorrow."

"Uh-huh," Fluvio says.

"Aren't you going to wish me luck?" I ask.

"It's probably not going to happen."

"Gee, thanks."

There's a moment of silence. I listen as Fluvio breathes moistly into the receiver.

Then he blurts, "You're never going to leave here."

I pull the receiver away from my face and stare at it. Fluvio often speaks with the air of a man who thinks his words become law the moment he speaks them. That's characteristic of people with delusions of grandeur, but the armchair psychologist in me knows that Fluvio's pronouncements are a soothing technique. He's experiencing major stress in opening the new restaurant, so he's telling himself the things he needs to hear. He *needs* me at The Bistro. I've tried telling Fluvio that I will still be able to help him through this difficult time, even with all that's going on with me, but my assurances aren't stopping him from freaking out.

Many chefs and owners possess outsize personalities and demand David Koresh–like obedience from their employees. Like starry-eyed neophytes trapped in a culinary version of Jonestown, waiters and staff can find it hard to extricate themselves from the delicate web of abuse, reward, and guilt that can constitute a restaurateur's cult of personality. When servers try doing something for themselves—auditioning, studying, or spending time with their spouse and children—the control freaks often see it as a *betrayal*. Now smart chefs or owners, who are secure in their sense of self and scouting possible long-term strategic alliances, will encourage subordinates to develop their human capital. What's that old saying? Be nice to people on the way up so they'll be nice to you on the way down? Setting aside simply acting like a human being for a moment, from a strictly utilitarian point of view, it pays to be nice.

But Fluvio doesn't have that sense of perspective. His deep-seated control issues make him force everyone who works at The Bistro to be nervous, agitated, and dependent on him. He doesn't encourage people to follow their dreams. Since my Web site never made any money, it never impressed Fluvio and flew underneath his psychological radar. Now, when it looks like my hard work might finally pay off, Fluvio's secretly rooting for me to fail. People tell me about what he says behind my back. He's hoping I fall flat on my face. I suddenly remember how Caesar fired Fluvio when he started to want something for himself. Ah, how abuse perpetuates itself.

"We'll see, Fluvio," I reply. "We'll see."

On the other end of the line there's an indrawn breath and more silence. In the background I can hear the three waitresses arguing. Too many egos, not enough talent.

"I've got to go," Fluvio says, hanging up.

I cradle the receiver and close my eyes in silent prayer. I don't think I could stand it if Fluvio's proved right. Seeing his smug "I told you so" look would be intolerable.

A short while later Beth and I are in the kitchen drinking coffee. The lunch shift's drawing to a close. The restaurant's almost empty. Beth can't wait to go home.

"I've worked six doubles in a row," she groans. "I can't take any more."

"The craziness won't last forever," I reply. "Bistro Duetto will eventually stand on its own two feet."

"It can't happen soon enough."

"I hear ya," I answer. "I've worked twelve days in a row."

Beth and I sip our coffee quietly.

After a minute Beth asks, "So what's up between you and Armando?"

"We've got a mini power struggle going on," I reply.

"Things have gotten tense between you two."

"I've noticed."

Beth takes another sip of coffee. She looks pensive. "You know Louis and Saroya are talking shit about you," she says.

"That's nothing new."

"Yeah," Beth says. "But now they're saying your blog has given you a swelled head—that you're focusing on your writing instead of your job."

"I remember when they just crabbed about me stealing the best tables," I chuckle.

"It's not funny," Beth says. "Don't you ever worry that someone who works here might wreck your anonymity and screw up your blog?"

Beth's question sparks a tickle of anxiety. Ever since I started Waiter Rant I've taken great pains to protect my anonymity and the true name and location of The Bistro. But the blog isn't a secret at work. Everyone at the restaurant knows about the Web site. Initially, everyone got a kick out of it and chuckled at the names I assigned to them. It also helped that I never wrote any nasty or critical stories about the staff. I passed up some juicy stories, but I like working in a peaceful work environment. I've been less than kind to the customers, however, and if they found out about my Web site, I might be compelled to quit. Anonymity has shielded me from customer retribution and protected my job. Now that tensions between the staff and me are increasing, I'm beginning to wonder if someone might rat me out just to get rid of me.

"Everyone's been real good about it so far," I say optimistically.

"Let's hope your good luck holds." Beth says.

Suddenly I see a flash of red hair out of the corner of my eye. Holly, one of our summer hostesses, walks past the kitchen door with a customer in tow. I see the man's face for only a second— but it's enough.

"Isn't that Russell Crowe?" I ask Beth.

"I think you're right," Beth replies.

Beth and I casually saunter out of the kitchen and pretend

we're rearranging napkins. As we perform our little reconnaissance I throw a covert glance toward the back section. Yep— sitting on one of the banquettes is Russell Crowe.

"It's him," I say, walking back into the kitchen.

"Wow," Beth says, star-struck.

"Can you handle it?" I ask. "You know our policy about movie stars."

"Yeah, I know," Beth sighs. "Pretend like they're not famous."

"No problems?"

"No problems."

Beth goes out to take care of Mr. Crowe. I go downstairs to the prep area to look for Armando, our sous-chef.

"Guess who's here?" I say.

"Who?" Armando asks.

"The Gladiator."

"NO FUCKING WAY!" Armando almost shrieks, our earlier animosity forgotten. *Gladiator* is one of his all-time-favorite movies. It's one of mine, too.

"Yes fucking way."

"How cool is that?"

"Get behind the stove, man," I say. "You'll want to add this guy to the list of famous people you've cooked for."

Armando bounds up the stairs. He's really thrilled.

I walk back upstairs. Mr. Crowe's been joined by a guest. Beth's taking good care of them. If she's nervous, she doesn't look it.

The Bistro has always had a fairly ironclad policy regarding celebrities—we don't care. Waiters are not allowed to ask for autographs. We just treat them like any other customer. Don't get me wrong. It's always nice to have famous people patronize your restaurant. It creates a buzz and drives in business. The Bistro has had many famous patrons—ranging from Academy Award– winning actors and directors, famous rock stars, Nobel Prize winners, and crazy-gorgeous supermodels.

But the dangers of becoming a celebrity hangout are the same dangers a restaurant faces if it becomes a Mafia hangout. You end up with rich and powerful people who might start treating the restaurant as their 24/7 preserves for late-night parties and backroom deals. That's bad for business. Celebrities are notoriously unfaithful where restaurants are concerned. It's the noncelebrity customers who pay the light bill. It never pays to alienate the bread-and-butter clientele by fawning over celebrities.

So The Bistro doesn't care, and the celebrities pick up on that vibe. Most of our famous patrons appreciate that we treat them like everyone else. Maybe that's the reason so many well-known people eat at The Bistro. If we made a fuss over them, they'd just go elsewhere, or, worse, start treating us like some L.A. eatery. Screw that. The last thing any restaurant needs is some Jeremy Piven type coming in without a reservation and leaving a DVD of his TV show as a tip.

I head into the kitchen and find Beth gabbing excitedly on her cell phone to a girlfriend.

"He's so handsome," Beth swoons. "He has really hypnotic eyes."

Actually, I think Mr. Crowe looks smaller in person than he does on-screen.

"If he asked me to spend the weekend with him in Mykonos, do you think my boyfriend would mind?" Beth asks the phone innocently.

I shake my head in the affirmative. Beth smiles.

"It's just a thought," she says to her girlfriend. "I've got to run. Later. Bye."

"How you doing?" I ask.

"I'm a little dizzy," Beth replies.

"You'll be fine."

"When I looked into his eyes, I completely forgot the specials."

"I'm sure he's used to that happening."

"Wow," Beth says.

"If Charlize Theron was here, I'd be acting the same way."

"Oh my God," Beth says. "You couldn't handle her at a table."

"Probably not."

Some time passes. Mr. Crowe and his guest finish lunch, pay the bill, and leave.

"Have a nice afternoon," I say as he walks past me.

"You, too, mate," he replies, smiling.

Beth scoops the check off the table. She got a very nice tip.

"I love you, Russell!" she shouts. I'm glad The Bistro's empty.

"Don't start sniffing where he was sitting," I joke.

"I love you, Russell!"

Beth kept it together while the superstar was here, but now that he's gone, she's just decompressing. I did that after I waited on Alan Ruck—the guy from *Spin City* and *Ferris Bueller's Day Off*. I had to fight an insane urge to call him Cameron. *Dude, you killed the car!*

"Wow," I say, "Russell Crowe ate here. We should put up a sign."

But Beth doesn't hear me. She's already talking on her cell phone.

"Mom," she jabbers, "you'll never believe who was just here!"

I leave my star-struck waitress to her conversation. Honestly, I'm kind of star-struck myself. When I get home that night, I write up the entire encounter on my Web site. I title the post "Gladiator."

The next morning my phone rings at the ungodly hour of nine A.M. The caller ID tells me it's Fluvio. I debate whether or not to answer it. When Fluvio calls me at home, it's never a good sign.

"What?" I answer.

"Your computer on?"

"What?"

"Go to your computer."

"Why?"

"Just do it," Fluvio says.

I roll out of bed, slap my laptop out of hibernation mode, and sit down.

"What do you want me to look at?"

"Go to this Web site," Fluvio says, spelling out the URL for me. Within seconds I'm reading an article on some Russell Crowe fansite highlighting the "Gladiator" story on my blog—and giving The Bistro's exact name and address.

"Holy shit!" I exclaim.

"The lady who run the Web site write me and tell me she put it up," Fluvio blabbers. "Now people know where you are!"

I shake my head. How was I supposed to know Russell Crowe has groupies who track his every movement around the globe? I thought that was the paparazzi's job.

"Send me that lady's e-mail address," I say. "I'll ask her nicely to take it down."

"People find out where you work, you have to quit!" Fluvio says. Great. *Now* he cares.

"Relax, Fluvio," I say. "Don't go all Code Red."

"Fix it," Fluvio says.

"I will."

I hang up the phone and look out the window. A spasm of anxiety hits me. My agent's trying to negotiate a book deal for me right now. Part of the appeal of my blog has always been my anonymity. Fuck.

I fire off an e-mail to the administrator of the Web site. To my surprise, the lady quickly writes back and tells me she'll take down the post. I anxiously spend the rest of the day scouring the Internet, looking for some indication that my cover's been blown. No activity. The problem got caught in time.

The next couple of days, however, are a stressfest. My agent calls with updates. I wonder if the prospective writer having a perpetual urge to vomit is usually part of the process. Things at work aren't helping either.

"Why you taking that table?" Saroya asks me on a fairly slow night.

"Because I like to make money?" I reply acidly.

"It's slow," Saroya sniffs. "You're getting paid as a manager. You shouldn't be taking tables."

Part of the problem with the player/manager setup at The

Bistro is that there's a built-in conflict of interest. Fluvio doesn't pay me enough for me to be only a manager. If I'm lucky, my manager pay covers the monthly cost of my health insurance, around $450, and my taxes. Waiting tables constitutes the bulk of my take-home income. When it's slow, I usually hang back and let the other waiters take the tables. But, when the rent's due, no matter how slow it is, I'm on the floor. This drives Saroya nuts. I think she's related to that Wahdi guy from Amici's somehow.

"I've got bills to pay, too," I reply.

"You're greedy," Saroya hisses.

"Gimme a break, please . . ."

"It's not fair!"

I'm not about to be lectured by the chef's girlfriend.

"Tough shit," I say.

Saroya runs off to the kitchen in a huff. I'm sure Armando's about to get an earful. I don't care anymore—and that's a problem.

I'm not the greatest waiter or restaurant manager who ever lived. Far from it. In fact, I can be a real asshole to work with. The staff has some legitimate gripes about my managerial style. Invoking the seigneurial right of headwaiters everywhere, I almost never do side work and I always work the best section in the house. In fact, the waiters snicker that a personalized PROPERTY OF plaque should be embedded in my section's floor. I respond by saying that when I die, my ashes can be interred under it, and then they can walk all over me. Sometimes I think they want to hurry that process along.

Beth especially gets aggravated over what she calls my "customer profiling"—my cherry-picking the good-tipping customers and sending the dregs to the less-senior servers. That's the conflict of interest I was talking about. Do I profile? Of course I do, but only to a degree. First off, my section holds only fourteen customers. The Bistro's a popular restaurant. I can't snag every big tipper who comes along. I'm also not *that* greedy. I have an amount of money I need to make every month. As long as I hit that goal I'm happy. I don't need to suck up every dime. Once I've hit my financial target, I slack off and let the other servers get the rest. I know that sounds mighty white of me, but that's how it works at many a restaurant. The senior server is king.

I know there are other things I do that drive the staff nuts. In addition to my chronic tardiness, I also can be a bit of a bully when it comes to the POS computer. The Bistro has only one computer for placing orders. When things get crazy, a bottleneck forms and everyone gets backed up. Me? I'm famous for cutting in line. My usual MO is to claim a fake manager emergency so I can put my orders in ahead of everyone else. But I've also physically bumped people out of the way, abruptly logged them out of the computer while they were in the middle of placing an order, or hovered close to them, angrily muttering, "Hurry the fuck up" in their ear. Most of the staff learned to deal with my craziness, but some, like Inez, actually pushed back. Good for her. For the tough cases I use deception to cut in line. If I see a server nearing the POS computer when I need to use it, I'll say, "Is that your cell phone ringing?" Once I even pointed to the floor and said, "Eeek, is that a tampon?" While the female server (who earlier had loudly informed everyone that she was having her period) frantically searched the floor around her, I slid in front of her and started inputting my orders. She didn't speak to me for the rest of the night. The lesson here? Keep your bodily functions private.

After putting up with Fluvio's nonsense for six years, I feel like I'm entitled to the special treatments I give myself. When I compare myself to Sammy and the other restaurant managers I've known, I'm a saint. I don't scam tips, extort servers, shake down kitchen staff, or sexually harass the waitresses. I know, I know, not doing something you're not supposed to be doing isn't a sign of virtue. But in the restaurant business it *almost* is.

I'm not the best manager in the world, but I'm not the worst, either. The Bistro has always earned a high Zagat rating for service, so I must be doing something right. In my mind a good restaurant manager is like a good chief of police, always allowing a little larceny to operate in his or her town. Besides acting as a safety valve for the inevitable vices, the chief knows his or her officers can pump the low-level dealers, prostitutes, and bookies they franchise for information on bigger and more dangerous criminals. A restaurant manager is the same way. I overlook the occasional drinking on the job and the pot smoking/low-grade drug dealing going on in the alley. I usually fix checks, cover up mistakes, and smooth things over with the customers when the waiters invariably screw up. Rarely do I have to intervene and drop the hammer on a server. I'm also the one keeping Fluvio off their backs. Without my moderating his rages, the atmosphere of The Bistro would become more toxic than the skies of Venus.

I'm also almost always the last server to leave the restaurant. I deal with the irate and crazy customers, and I'm the one who has to keep his cool in a crisis. After the lady who had that stroke went off to the hospital, Louis had a nervous breakdown and babbled that he was too upset to stay at work. He kept crying about some guy he saw die facedown in his all-you-can-eat platter at Red Lobster. Then again Louis calls in sick if he cuts his finger. I can't imagine him or Saroya handling an emergency. But do the waiters remember that? No. Waiters are always complaining about something. They'll bitch and moan when they're making no money and then they'll complain that they're overworked when they get busy. You can never win.

However, some of their complaints are valid. I've gotten too comfortable in my job, and that comfort had metastasized into a sort of arrogance. The bus girls complain that I'm lazy. I call it energy conservation, but they're right, I don't do anything I don't have to do. Fluvio's shit is getting old, but I know he'll never fire me. If I was Fluvio, I'd fire myself, but his paranoia makes him dread breaking in a new manager. Like Rizzo, I know where all the bodies are buried. And I've gotten away with a lot of shit because I know every dirty, stupid thing he's ever done. With the new restaurant opening up and the personnel shifting this way and that, however, I can begin to feel the ground shifting beneath my feet. New people are coming into the picture, people who could and should replace me. That realization's causing me stress. Like the dynamic between Armando and me, things are starting to change.

The night drags on uneventfully. I grab a few tables here and there. Saroya, for all her crabbing, makes more than I do in tips. Then, five minutes to close, Russell Crowe walks in the door with fifteen people.

"Oh shit," I mutter. "Him again."

"They're going to stay forever," Saroya twitters.

"Great. I'm friggin' exhausted."

"You're stuck here," Saroya says gleefully. "I'm going home to my daughter. Have a nice night."

Saroya hands me her cash and receipts and walks out the door. I head over to Russell Crowe's noisy table.

"Hey there," Mr. Crowe says over the din of his rambunctious entourage.

"Nice to see you again, sir," I say.

"Quiet down, everyone," Mr. Crowe commands, gesturing for silence. "The waiter needs to tell us the specials."

Mr. Crowe's party immediately stops talking and looks at me.

"Thank you, sir," I say.

"You're welcome."

While I've seen Mr. Crowe eat in The Bistro several times, this is the first time I've ever waited on him. I have to admit, for the first time in my life, *I am* really star-struck. Even though I think he looks shorter in person than he looks on-screen, Beth was right about his eyes. There's a powerful quality to them that reaches into you and stirs your insides. No, I don't want to fly off to Mykonos with him, but I can see why he has such a commanding presence on-screen. I somehow manage to get through the specials without making an ass out of myself.

"Excellent recitation," Mr. Crowe says, clapping his hands. "You should be an actor."

The party breaks into applause. I permit myself a slight bow.

"Are you an actor?" Mr. Crowe asks me.

"No, sir," I reply.

"Good. Let's get some bloody wine then."

Mr. Crowe orders several bottles of wine—nothing fancy. After presenting the first bottle, the film star waves off the pretentious wine liturgy.

"Just open them up, mate. Don't be so formal."

"Yes, sir," I say, pouring some wine into his glass.

"So," Mr. Crowe says softly, with a hint of growl in his voice. "You're him, aren't you?"

"Who, sir?" I reply, trying to look innocent. I feel my sphincter twitch. Someone on Mr. Crowe's payroll must have read about my blog on that groupie's Web site and shown him the story I wrote.

"The Waiter."

"I beg your pardon?"

"You're The Waiter," Mr. Crowe says, giving me a look that makes my thousand-yard waiter stare look like a pilot light flickering in a hurricane. "You're the guy who writes that *blog*."

I think about dissembling, but a curious image of Mr. Crowe leaping out of his seat and decapitating me with a Roman broadsword jumps into my head. While that may give The Bistro's waiters the greatest satisfaction, I'm kind of attached to my head.

"Yes, sir," I reply. "I am."

Mr. Crowe smiles. "So where's this Beth girl?" he asks. Oh my God. He read the sniff-the-seat thing.

"She's not working tonight," I say. "She was your server the last time you were here."

"Uh-huh," Mr. Crowe says. "I see."

"But she was thrilled to meet you, sir."

Mr. Crowe stares at me hard. "You're not going to write about me again. Are you?"

"No, sir." (Mentally my fingers are crossed.)

"Good. All right, I'm starved. Let's order."

Mr. Crowe and his table order, eat, tip fabulously, and leave. As his party walks out the door Mr. Crowe shakes my hand.

"Good luck to you, mate."

Millions of people have read my blog. Quite a few of them have tried to track me down. But after three years the only person who ever asked me if I was The Waiter from the Waiter Rant blog was Russell Crowe. Go figure.

"Thank you, sir."

I lock up, turn off the lights, and go home, a curious lightness filling my chest. I resist the urge to write up the story on my blog. I dodged one bullet, best not to tempt fate again.

A couple of days later the book deal is sealed. Russell Crowe was good luck for me.

Maybe he'll play me in the movie.

CHAPTER 20

If It Can Go Wrong, It Will

When news of the book deal spreads, I'm not surprised by the rather lackluster reception my good fortune generates. While some of the staff offers sincere congratulations, Saroya only wants to know how much money I got, and Louis and Armando act like it's no big deal. When I called Fluvio at Bistro Duetto to tell him the good news, his only reaction was an incredulous "Really?" then dead silence. No congratulations were forthcoming. Despite his lack of enthusiasm, I told him that I'd like to ratchet down my schedule so I could spend more time writing. We had discussed this possibility a month ago, but now Fluvio sounded like a man trying to welsh on a bet. After I hung up the phone, a nervous feeling started buzzing in my stomach. I get the sense that I've just crossed some sort of Rubicon with Fluvio and the staff. Some of them used to be delighted to be a part of my blog. Now their attitudes have changed—and not for the better.

I shower and head in to work. It turns out to be a hot and humid Saturday night. According to the heat index, the temperature outside's a sticky 102 degrees. The restaurant's packed with customers. A line of reservation holders, angry they're waiting for a table, stretches out the door. I'm not having a good night.

The customers are cranky, we have yet another new hostess, and Fluvio's at the new restaurant.

"The customers outside want free cocktails," the hostess whines fearfully.

"They can't drink alcohol standing on the sidewalk," I reply. "It's against city ordinances. Tell their waiter to give 'em a free round when they sit down."

"You're gonna be their waiter," the hostess snaps angrily. "You tell them that."

The hostess, a slim blonde of nineteen, is operating at the outermost limits of her maturity. The poor girl's laboring under the delusion that her sex appeal will protect her from the wrath of table-seeking yuppies. The customers couldn't care less how cute she is. Good-looking hostesses are like good-looking girls in L.A., they're such a common sight as to be unremarkable. Surprised at the level of animosity her attractiveness usually protects her from, the hostess buckles under the pressure and seats my section all at once. That may be okay at a Denny's or Sizzler, but not at a fine-dining restaurant. It's impossible for me to give good service when I'm a whirling dervish, cocktailing and specialing fourteen customers simultaneously. Now, ninety minutes later, my first round of customers is getting ready to pay their checks. Since all my tables came in together, they're all going to leave together. That means I'm going to do the dervish routine all over again. I want to wring the hostess's pretty neck, but I need her to answer the phones. I can't give her any constructive criticism, because, no matter how gently I frame it, she'll have a nervous breakdown and run out the door.

Beth comes running up to me. "The printer isn't working again," she pants. "Can you fix it?"

"Sure," I reply. "Give me a sec."

I take a deep breath, remodulate my voice to a customer-friendly frequency, and open the front door.

"Ladies and gentlemen," I say to the people waiting outside. "Thank you for your patience. Your tables will be ready in a few minutes."

"How about a free drink?" a fat man demands, beads of sweat dripping off his chin.

"Your first round of drinks is on me," I say. "City ordinances, however, forbid me from serving alcohol to people on the sidewalk."

"That's bullshit," the fat man growls.

"I'd like to be drinking with you on the sidewalk myself," I say, trying to inject a little levity in the situation, "but I'm afraid the law's the law."

"Whatever," the man snaps, "just get us inside."

My attempt at levity a bust, I head back inside and walk over to the receipt printer. It needs a new ink ribbon. I open the utility cabinet to get one, but, of course, there aren't any. Cursing under my breath, I grab my house keys and run downstairs to the basement office.

I hate going into Fluvio's office. It's a windowless cave smelling of sour sweat and dirty socks. When I pull open the door, my worst fears are confirmed—the office is a hazmat site. Plates encrusted with fossilized bits of food litter Fluvio's desk, while clusters of pint glasses, smudged over with greasy fingerprints, contain the evaporated reductions of several forgotten Diet Cokes. The smell in the office is unreal. Rummaging through the office, I wonder how long I can hold my breath. I can't find any ribbons. Cursing, I grab the phone and call Fluvio at the new restaurant.

"Good evening," the hostess answers. "Bistro Duetto. How can I help you?"

"Get me Fluvio," I gasp, trying not to breathe deeply.

"Who shall I say is calling?"

"This is the manager at the other place."

"He's busy with a customer."

"Get him, please," I say. "I have a problem."

"He told me not to—"

"Get him *now*."

After a minute Fluvio comes on the line. "What the matter?" he barks.

"Where are the printer ribbons?"

"In the utility closet."

"Guess again."

"In my office then."

"I'm in your office," I say. "I can't find any."

"Look under my desk."

I look under Fluvio's desk. No computer ribbons, just a jumbled mass of cables, routers, and power strips.

"No dice, boss."

"They have to be there."

Suddenly, Louis bursts into the office. "Hey, man," he shouts, wild-eyed, "I've gotta run credit cards, and we're out of printer ribbon!"

"Don't have a panic attack, Louis," I say, covering the phone's mouthpiece. "I'm trying to find some."

"Dude, it's fucking crazy up there."

"I know, Louis. Give me a minute."

I take a deep breath and calm myself. "Fluvio," I say gently, "is there any other place you might have put the ribbons?"

"Maybe in the dry-goods area . . ."

"Thanks," I say, hanging up. I've got to get out of the office before the smell makes me throw up.

Sure enough, I find the printer ribbons next to the dried pasta. There's no rhyme or reason where anything goes in this place. I run back upstairs, replace the ribbon, collect all my customers' credit cards, and race back to the POS machine. Since the terminal was down for several minutes, the waiters are now playing catch-up with their checks.

"Fucking great," I mutter.

"Take a number," Beth says.

"I'm gonna go in the weeds," I say. "I can feel it."

"I've been in the weeds all night."

"Your section leaving all at once?" I ask.

"Yep," Beth replies grimly. "You, too?"

"Yeah."

"It's that fucking hostess," Beth hisses angrily. "She doesn't know how to seat people for shit."

"It's her second night," I say.

"That's no excuse," Beth says.

As if on cue, the hostess comes running up to us, looking frantic.

"The customers are complaining it's too hot," she says.

"I'll turn up the AC," I reply.

"It did get hot in here," Beth says.

"I'm roasting up front," the hostess whimpers.

Suddenly I'm aware of the sweat running under my arms and plastering my shirt to my back. It *is* hot in here.

"You're right, Beth," I say. "It shouldn't be this hot."

I walk over to the AC panel. The thermostat reads 89 degrees. I try turning up the air-conditioning, but the digital readout flashes ERROR. I put my hand in front of one of the vents. It's blowing hot air.

The hot sweat running down my back suddenly turns cold. The air-conditioning isn't working on the hottest night of the year. With all the warm bodies crammed inside the restaurant, the temperature is going to go through the roof. We won't even have to cook the food—it'll cook itself.

"Uh-oh," I say. "We're in trouble."

"What's the matter?" Beth asks.

"The AC's down."

"You're kidding me."

"I wish I was."

I race up to the hostess stand, leaf through the directory containing our vendors' phone numbers, and call the AC people.

"Mr. Freeze," a tired voice answers.

"Is this Frank?" I ask.

"Yeah."

"This is The Bistro. Our AC's not working."

"What does the panel say?" Frank asks.

"It's just flashing an error message."

"Is the fan working?"

"Huh?"

"Is the unit blowing out air?"

"Yeah. Warm air."

"Shut the damn thing off, or the motor's gonna burn out," Frank says. "Something's wrong."

"Can you come over and fix it?"

"Now?"

"Frank," I say, "it's Saturday night, and I've got a restaurant full of people."

"Listen," Frank says. "The humidity's stressing the system, and something's gone haywire. To fix it, I'd have to come in with ladders and disturb your customers."

"Yeah, but . . ."

"Besides, I'm on a big industrial job right now," Frank says. "You ain't the only ones with problems."

"So I'm screwed."

"Yep," Frank says. "Tell your boss I'll come by tomorrow to look at it."

"Okay, Frank."

"Bye."

"So is the guy gonna come and fix it?" the hostess asks.

"We're screwed," I groan. "No AC."

"The customers are going to freak," the hostess says, her voice quivering with fear.

"Call Fluvio and tell him what happened."

"He's going to yell at me," the hostess says. "You call him."

"I've got to run checks," I say, forcing patience into my voice. "I need to run my checks so my customers can leave and you can seat the ones waiting outside. *Comprende?*"

The hostess says nothing. Her only reply is to age regress and bite the knuckle of her right hand.

"Keep it together, babe," I say. "You'll be fine."

Suddenly, there's a knock on the window. I look up. The fat man outside points angrily at the thick, expensive watch strapped to his wrist. I hold up one finger, indicating he has to wait another minute. A little voice in the back of my head tells me this guy's gonna freak when he discovers the AC's down.

I go back to the POS machine and run all my credit cards. I deposit the completed checks on their respective tables, wish everyone a good night, and head into the kitchen.

"Armando," I shout above the din, "the AC's broke."

"What?" Armando gasps. "No fucking way!"

"Yes way."

We simultaneously look at the kitchen thermometer. It reads 105 degrees.

"We're all going to die," Armando cries.

"Drink plenty of fluids," I say.

"Did you call the cooling company?"

"They can't get here till tomorrow."

"Of course not," Armando says, shaking his head.

"Just another day in paradise, Armando," I say. "Just another day in paradise."

Armando grunts and gets back to work. The kitchen guys are tough hombres, but I feel sorry for them. The kitchen temp will hit 110 before the night's over.

All the customers in my section get up and leave. The bus people swoop in and clear the tables. Before they can even get fresh silverware on a table the fat guy from outside barges in and plants his ass in a chair.

"I want my free martini," the man says angrily. "And turn up the AC in here."

This guy's gonna be trouble. I decide to get the pain over with early.

"I'm terribly sorry to have to tell you this, sir," I say. "But our air-conditioning is broken."

"What?" the man says, the blue veins in his temples throbbing.

"It went down a few minutes ago," I say. "I called the cooling company. They said the humidity's overtaxed the system."

The fat man's face turns a dusky red. "This is outrageous."

"I'm sorry, sir," I say. "I can't fix it."

"C'mon, Hilary," the man says to his wife. "We're leaving."

Silently, I'm grateful.

"This place is a joke," the man mutters, struggling out of his seat. "And you're incompetent."

I let the man's insult wash over me. To respond would only add another problem to my list. The hostess and I watch silently as the man and his wife storm out into the sweltering night air.

"Can't say that I blame him," I say. "I wouldn't want to eat in this heat."

"Fluvio wants to talk to you," the hostess says, anxiously sticking the phone in my face. "He wants you to tell him what's going on."

"Didn't you explain what's happening?" I ask, pushing the phone away from me.

"He wants to hear it from you."

Fluvio never trusts what anyone tells him. He has to confirm everything he hears with several people. I'm too busy to feed into his insanity tonight.

"Tell him I'm busy," I reply. "Tell him the AC's down and the guy can't fix it till tomorrow."

"But he—"

"Just do it."

The crowds pile in the door, and my section fills up instantly—two six tops, two deuces, and a four. I take care of the two tops first. The six tops are chattering away, so I have time to get to them. I cocktail and special the deuces, head over to the four, ask what they want from the bar, then loop back to the two tops and grab their dinner order. I walk briskly to the POS computer, key in the data, make the four top's alcoholic chemistry experiments, and drop them off. The six tops' heads are swiveling on their necks looking for the waiter. I hit them next. I take all their drink requests—wine and martinis—and take the four's dinner order on the return trip. The bell rings. The deuce's apps are up. The door chimes. It's a reservation. The hostess is gone, probably in the bathroom. I drop off the apps, greet the new arrivals, and seat them. Racing to the wine cellar, I grab two bottles of wine, return to the service bar, make six martinis, deliver the drinks to the first six top, run back, grab the bottles of wine, one red and one white, and pop them open at the other six. I tell the bus girl to bring an ice bucket. The kitchen bell rings furiously. The four's apps are up. The door chimes. More reservations. Where the hell's the hostess? The deuce signals for more bread. The lady at the four top needs another cosmo. Do you take Discover? What are the specials? I'm allergic to rosemary. Does this have to have garlic? Can you make me veal Parmesan? It's hot in here. Can you do something about the AC? The phone rings. I glance at the caller ID. It's Fluvio. I decide to ignore it. He spent thousands of dollars installing video cameras; let him see what's going on for himself.

Suddenly, I feel a tug on my shoulder. It's Beth. She has tears in her eyes.

"What's the matter?"

"The computer's not working."

"Oh shit," I say, my sphincter achieving maximum compression.

"It just went black," Beth says. "I've got a bunch of orders I need to send to the kitchen."

"Okay," I say, taking a deep breath, "lemme try to fix it."

"How am I going to place my orders?" Beth asks.

"Hang on."

I try rebooting the computer. That usually fixes things, but tonight it doesn't. I double-check all the cabling. Everything's hooked up correctly.

"I don't know what's wrong with it," I say. "I have to call the computer guy."

"Oh my God," Beth groans. "I can't believe this is happening."

I signal all the waiters to gather around me.

"Listen, guys," I say. "I've got bad news. The computer's dead. We've got to do things the old-fashioned way."

"The old-fashioned way?" Saroya asks. "What do you mean?"

"You've got to write everything down on a ticket and add up the bill by hand."

"I've never done that before," Saroya says.

"Well, that's how we have to do it tonight."

"This fucking sucks," Louis says, his voice filling with panic. "This fucking sucks."

"You've done tickets before, Louis," I say. "Help Saroya out."

"What about the credit cards?" Louis asks.

Our POS system is responsible for sending orders to the kitchen, tabulating bills, and acting as a credit card terminal. It's a state-of-the-art front-of-the-house system—until it goes wrong.

"We're gonna have to use the old terminal," I say. "The one we used before the POS system."

"That old piece of shit?" Louis shouts. "It only prints the white copy."

"I know," I say. "But it's all we've got."

"The law says we have to give the customers a copy!" Louis shouts. "I'm not doing anything illegal."

Leave it to Louis to get all rigid and legalistic in a crisis.

"Just hit reprint on the terminal," I say, struggling to keep my voice even. "The second printout can be the customer copy."

"This sucks, man," Louis says, his voice taut with anxiety. "This place is a joke. I want to go home."

"Calm down, Louis. This is an emergency."

"Fuck you telling me to calm down," Louis says, storming off. "I can't take this shit anymore. If you don't fix that computer, I'm leaving."

"Louis—"

"You're a joke of a manager," Saroya chimes in. "You're supposed to know how to fix this stuff."

"I'm working on it, Saroya."

The reality is that Fluvio is so paranoid he never showed me anything about the computers. I don't know how to fix them. I could usually get Fluvio to fix it, but he's an hour's drive away.

"You're a clown," Saroya huffs, walking away.

Beth looks at me sadly. "Nice when your coworkers support you, huh?"

I smile at Beth. We both know Saroya and Louis are sunshine waiters, happy and professional when everything's running smoothly, bitchy and vindictive when they're not. The minute things get hairy, they fall into that's-not-my-job mode, and their professionalism goes out the window.

"Stick with me, babe," I say.

"I'll cocktail and special your tables while you call the computer guy."

"Thanks," I say gratefully. "You're a lifesaver."

I fill the old credit card machine with register tape, plug it into the phone line, and test it by charging my personal Amex one penny. Keeping my fingers crossed, I anxiously wait for the terminal to process the transaction. If this doesn't work, I'll have to pull the old embosser out of storage. I haven't used one of those things since the early 1990s. After an interminable wait the old machine starts chattering out paper. I let out a sigh of relief. Finally, a break. I grab the cordless house phone and call the computer guy. I explain the problem, and we run through a checklist of procedures. None of them fix the problem.

"I'll have to come in and take a look," the computer guy says. "Sounds like a cable's severed somewhere."

"Can you come now?" I plead.

"Sure," the computer guy says. "But it'll take a while."

"Where are you coming from?"

"New Jersey."

"Jesus," I say. "Just get here quick. Dinner's on me."

"On my way."

"Oh, Mr. Manager," I hear Louis crowing. "I need a calculator so I can add up these bills."

"What happened to the calculator by the register?" I ask.

Louis smiles at me sweetly. "The battery's dead."

I feel a coil in the back of my head tighten. Stomach acid leaps up my esophagus. For the first time in six years I'm afraid the restaurant's going to crash. A restaurant crash is what happens when a series of events, none of which on its own is serious enough to cause problems, combine to spawn a perfect storm of missteps, fuckups, and malfunctions, initiating a catastrophic system-wide collapse. I saw it happen at Amici's once. The manager had to stop letting new customers into the restaurant until the waiters and the kitchen could recover. The best way to avoid a restaurant crash is to make sure you've done all your prep work and have backups for everything. Losing your AC and computer systems at the same time, however, is a disaster in any restaurateur's book.

"Please go down to Fluvio's office and get the one on his desk," I tersely reply.

"Uh-uh, Mr. Manager," Louis sneers. "That's *your* job."

Summarily executing Louis won't help the situation, so I go down into Fluvio's smelly office to fetch the spare calculator. The minute I walk inside the intercom buzzes.

"Fluvio's on the phone," the hostess says. "I told him about the computer. He wants to talk to you."

There's no avoiding the man this time. I snap up the phone. "It's a mess here, boss."

"I leave you alone and you can't handle things," Fluvio says disgustedly.

"Your AC failed, and the computer systems went down," I say. "What do you expect me to do?"

"I don't have time for this shit," Fluvio growls. "I want to go over the computer problem with you on the phone."

"I've got a section full of customers who just sat down," I say. "They're gonna be pissed—"

"The other waiters can handle it."

"They can't. They're in the weeds, too."

"Listen—"

"Fluvio," I say. "The computer guy's coming. The AC's off till tomorrow. There's nothing more I can do. I set up the old credit card terminal, and we're sending everything to the kitchen by ticket."

"By ticket?" Fluvio exclaims. "I'm gonna lose money."

"I've got to go, Fluvio."

"Explain to me how you're going to keep track of the money."

I can feel my heart racing with anxiety. This is when Fluvio's control issues hurt his business. He'd rather keep me on the phone explaining minute details instead of taking care of the customers who give him money.

"It's a crazy night, Fluvio," I say. "We can go over everything when you get back."

"But—"

"I've got to go, boss," I say, slamming down the receiver. I've hung up on my boss twice in one night.

I run back up to the dining room and get over to my section. Thanks to Beth, two of my tables already have their cocktails. I'm just about to ask the other tables for their drink orders when the hostess pulls on my arm.

"It's Fluvio," she says. "He wants you to talk to him right now."

"I'm busy," I snap.

"He's really angry at you."

"Too bad."

"What am I going to tell him?"

"Tell him if he bugs me again, I'm walking out the door right now."

The hostess stares at me, wide-eyed. "Really?"

"I'm serious," I say. "Tell him to chill the fuck out."

"I'm not going to tell him that."

"Then make something up."

I dive back into my section and get drink orders. All the customers complain about the heat and the slow service. I say "I'm sorry" so many times that my apologies sound like an automated recording. Louis and Saroya run around, sniping behind my back. Fluvio keeps calling for updates. The customers' faces blur into a greedy collage of greasy, quivering lips and fleshy jowls. The heat in the restaurant's driving me mad. My underwear's soaked with sweat and starting to chafe my legs. I'm going to get another rash. The pressure in my head keeps building. That coiled spring I felt earlier is about to snap. I'm heading for a rifle-in-the-clock-tower moment.

"I'm going outside," I tell the hostess.

"You're leaving!" the hostess shrieks. "Now?"

"I need some fresh air," I say. "I'll be back in a sec."

I exit The Bistro, walk around the corner, and disappear into the back alley behind the restaurant. Lined up against the wall are several plastic garbage cans. I take a deep breath, draw back my leg, and drive my foot into the side of one of the cans, smashing it with a loud crunch. I have reached my breaking point.

"MOTHERFUCKER!" I shout.

Experience has taught me that if I don't discharge the negative energy building up inside my body, I'll pay for it later in aches and pains, depression, and sleepless nights. Kicking a garbage can's not exactly a kosher anger-management skill, but it's a hell of a lot better than taking it out on a living, breathing person.

After giving the can a few more swift kicks, I feel the bolus of anger pass out of my psyche like vomit being ejected out of my mouth. A wave of exhaustion hits me.

Dizzy, I lean up against the warm brick wall, fumble a cigarette out of a pack, and light up. I look down at the garbage can. The plastic container's already returning to its original shape— no harm done. Feeling foolish, I take a drag of my cigarette and close my eyes. Suddenly, I hear people murmuring. My eyes snap open, and I look across the street. Two middle-aged women are standing outside a bar smoking. They saw me freak out. I wave weakly at them, embarrassed.

"Tough night?" one of the women shouts.

"The worst," I reply.

"If you're gonna get that mad," the other woman says, "maybe you should find another job."

"You might be right," I reply.

"Take it easy, mister," the first one says, shaking her head.

"Thanks," I reply, feeling like a total asshole. I grind my cigarette under my heel and slink back inside the restaurant.

Eventually everything settles down. Armando keeps the kitchen running despite the heat; the computer guy fixes the POS system; the waiters, including myself, get their shit together; and the customers, feeling sorry for us, end up giving us some very nice tips. Even Fluvio gets over his anxiety. After I close everything up Beth and I stumble out of The Bistro and head to Café American for a well-deserved cocktail.

"Thank God that's over," Beth says, holding out her martini glass.

"Yes, indeed," I reply, clinking my glass against hers. "Thanks for all your help."

"You're welcome."

"I thought we were gonna crash," I say.

"We didn't," Beth says.

"But we could've."

I tell Beth how I freaked out in the alley.

She laughs. "Just don't get angry at me."

"It was Fluvio's craziness that got to me," I say. "I used to be able to handle his bullshit but . . ."

"He gets to everybody," Beth says. "Even the wine reps hate him."

I stare into my drink. "I don't know how much longer I can work here."

"I wouldn't blame you if you left."

"So," I say, shaking myself out of my fugue, "what's going on with you?"

"My boyfriend and I are fighting," Beth says sadly.

"Sorry to hear that."

"We never get to spend any time together."

"Restaurant schedules can be a problem."

"It's not that," Beth says. "I don't think we're in love anymore. It's like we're brother and sister."

"You've been going out since you were how old?"

"Nineteen."

"Five years is a long time."

"I just think it's not going to last."

I want to tell Beth that the odds are good the person you fall for at nineteen is going to be a very different person at twenty-five. Most relationships don't survive this process. Telling her that won't do any good, though.

"I want something better for myself," Beth continues, looking me dead in the eye. "I want to be in love with someone who's crazy about me. I'm worth it."

I suddenly feel my breath catch in my throat. Beth is certainly worth it. I think about telling her that. Then I remember the difference in our ages. There's a moment, but I let it pass. I keep my feelings to myself. Beth and I live in different worlds.

After lingering inside Café American's air-conditioned bar for a second and third round, Beth and I part company. I stumble home after three in the morning and, without taking off my sweat-stained clothes, collapse into bed.

In my dreams a mob of customers, like torch-wielding villagers in a Frankenstein movie, chase me through the streets demanding their money back. Suddenly, I realize I'm not wearing any clothes. I race into the backyards behind my boyhood home, terrified the cops are going to arrest me. A little boy appears in a window and points at me, screaming. I try running away, but a hole in the ground swallows me up. As I fall, I cry out.

I wake up on the floor of my bedroom. The reddish dawn pours through the bedroom curtains and splatters the walls a bloody shade of orange. In the back of my mind the old saying "Red sky at night, sailors' delight; red sky in morning, sailors take warning" runs through my head.

Sitting on my bedroom floor, I realize things have to change and change soon. I remember the women watching me kick the garbage can. I remember my anger, a red blaze of frustration, coloring my vision. There have been too many frustrating nights at The Bistro. I get up off the floor and open the curtains. The sun, swollen and red, is erupting out of the eastern horizon, promising another hot day. Waiter takes warning.

That goddamn AC had better get fixed.

CHAPTER 21

The Demons

t's mid-September. The air-conditioning's still kind of on the fritz, so I'm standing outside The Bistro drinking espresso and enjoying the cool evening twilight. As the day starts crumbling into darkness I watch office girls who had been sleeveless in the noonday heat head off to happy hour with shawls and leather jackets covering their bare shoulders. I feel the briskness in the air with a small pang of mourning. It's as if summer's trying to sneak out of town without anybody noticing. Soon miniskirts will be replaced by long pants, and shapely legs will disappear into unshaven hibernation. I tell myself I should move to a town where short skirts are a 365-day-a-year proposition—someplace like L.A. or Vegas—but I'd miss having seasons too much.

As the sun starts its dive below the horizon the dining crowd starts swarming the sidewalks. I can always tell which demographic is going to what restaurant. The young and hip head for Über Sushi, couples my age eat at Alain's or Café American, and the affluent elderly come to us. You can spot The Bistro's customers coming a mile away. Just look for the quartet of recently retired people—two men strolling side by side while their wives hang ten paces back, stopping in front of every store window. The men look like they're trying to project some sort of financially self-sufficient gravitas, while their spouses subtly compete to see whose children won the parenting lottery.

I sigh to myself. Soon these people will be piling into the restaurant. I take another sip of espresso and try to savor the peace and quiet before the craziness begins. The northerly wind softly rustles the leaves in the trees. I look up. The foliage hasn't started to change, but I know that will happen soon. Autumn is my favorite season.

Then, out of the corner of my eye, I see the new video camera Fluvio installed under the restaurant's wooden sign. Sourness seeps into my thoughts, and my little moment of Zen is wrecked. No longer just content with spying on us inside The Bistro, Fluvio has installed new units to cover the back alley and the front sidewalk. Now he can see the staff whenever they go outside to smoke, talk on their cell, or get a breath of fresh air. I stare into the black eye of the camera. I wonder if Fluvio's watching me now. I'll bet he is. Fluvio's been keeping his distance from me. The last time we talked, I could tell he was keeping something from me, and later I found out from the staff what that something was—Louis has been running around telling everyone that Fluvio's going to make him the new manager. I'm not surprised. Fluvio's offered my job to other waiters when he's been angry with me before, but Louis? The guy who faked a heart attack so he could go home early? That's like finding out someone paid a hit man $39.95 to bump you off. It's insulting.

I'm also hurt. Even though he's a pain in the ass, I've always liked Louis. That makes his going around my back even more painful. If he were up front with me about wanting my job, I'd probably wish him luck. The same goes for Fluvio. He seems to be collapsing deeper and deeper into paranoid anxiety. That explains the new video cameras. Ever since the new restaurant opened, the dynamics among staff members have gotten more acrimonious and bitter. Everyone wants to be the boss. Everyone's stressed and fighting. Everyone's arguing over money and shifts. Louis and Saroya are circling around me like sharks sensing blood in the water. The atmosphere in The Bistro is becoming poisonous.

Thoroughly aggravated, I finish my espresso and head inside. The Bistro's empty of customers now, but looks can be deceiving. In actuality, we're booked to the hilt tonight. Everyone's coming between seven and seven-thirty. All our tables are spoken for. The place is going to be a madhouse.

The front door chimes. A tall mustachioed man in a blazer with patches on the elbows walks in with his wife. They're semi-regular customers. They're assholes.

"Good evening," I say, smiling politely. "Nice to see you again."

The couple doesn't acknowledge me. Instead, they walk over to a four top by the window and sit down. That the table has a reserved sign on it doesn't seem to concern them.

"Are there four in your party?" I ask as I watch the woman push the reserved sign to the side.

"Just two," the man replies brusquely. "Get me a Black on the rocks. My wife'll have a cosmopolitan."

I groan inwardly. I'm not in the mood for what's coming next.

"Did you have a reservation to dine with us this evening?" I ask gingerly.

"No," the woman says, looking surprised. "Do we need one?"

"I hate to say this," I say, "but this table is reserved for a party of four."

"Put them somewhere else," the man snorts.

"I'm afraid I can't, sir."

The man looks incredulously at the empty restaurant. "The place is empty."

"I know, sir. But all our reservations are coming in the next half hour, and I only have one table available for walk-ins."

"Where would you put us?" the woman asks.

"Right there," I say, pointing to a two top on the aisle.

"I don't like that table."

I shrug apologetically. "I'm sorry, madam, but—"

"We'll move to that table," the man declares, pointing to another table with a reserved sign on it.

"I'm sorry, sir, but that table's reserved as well."

"You mean I can't have that table, either?"

"Sir," I reply, "I have those tables set aside for people who have a reservation. I can't give them away."

"Well, we're regulars," the man huffs. "Figure out a way."

This man's arrogance is pissing me off. I've been on the receiving end of entitled bullshit like this so many times I've lost count. I feel my temper start to rise. Usually, I use humor to keep my emotions in check—but tonight I don't feel like making the effort.

"Sir," I say hotly, "if you had a reservation, how would you feel if I gave your table away to somebody else?"

The man looks at me like I'm dog shit on the bottom of his shoe. "C'mon, Dolores," he says, abruptly getting out of his chair. "We're leaving. I don't like this guy's attitude."

"I'm sorry we couldn't accommodate you this evening," I reply, my voice dripping with sarcasm.

"You're a jerk," the man says.

"I sincerely doubt you'd say that to me if we were outside this restaurant."

"What did you say?" the man gasps.

"You heard me."

"I'm going to talk to Fluvio about this."

"Go ahead. Make sure you get the name right."

"I'm never coming back here."

"Good."

The man and his wife storm out.

A sharp pain pokes me from the inside as my digestive juices start cannibalizing the lining of my stomach. I pull a roll of antacid tablets out of my pocket and toss one down my throat.

"Well," I say to myself, "you handled that well." I shake my head. I must be losing my touch.

"What happened with those people?" Beth asks, sidling up to me. "They looked pissed."

"They wanted the front window, and they had no reservation."

"That man looked like he wanted to punch you."

"Can you believe that?" I say bitterly. "Getting that angry over a table?"

"Are you all right?" Beth asks. "You've looked out of it the past couple of weeks."

"I need a vacation, Beth," I reply. "*Away* from people like that."

"Take it easy."

"I'll try."

As Beth walks away I smile ruefully to myself. Deep down in my bones I know what's happening to me—I'm suffering from burnout. Every server eventually faces this situation. Years of toiling in the dysfunctional atmosphere of the restaurant business slowly robs you of any desire to be hospitable. You start looking at the customers, the people who provide your income, as the enemy. Since waiters shouldn't be nasty to the customers, they develop a customer-friendly armor to protect the soft parts of their psyche from emotional assault. You can wear that armor for a while, maybe a long time, but eventually the cracks begin to show. You can't hide forever. The corrosive atmosphere inside The Bistro is rapidly eroding what little armor I have left.

Between Fluvio's nonsense and the normal insanity you find in any restaurant, the spirit of hospitality deserted my soul a long time ago. I feel like I'm doing what I did during my last year in the seminary—faking it, going through the motions. I'll admit, career cluelessness and poverty are some of the major factors that have kept me working as a waiter throughout my thirties. That's my own fault—not Fluvio's or the restaurant business. But after the book deal, when I realized that I didn't need to depend on Fluvio or the customers at The Bistro anymore, a powerful rage emerged. I thought the ego boost would salve my bitterness and make waiting tables fun again. I was wrong. The exact opposite happened. Like a mill worker who wins the lottery and suddenly realizes he *hates* his job, I've been fighting the urge to run around telling everyone to take this job and shove it. *Every day* I feel like walking out the door and never coming back.

The door chimes, interrupting my thoughts. As I expected, the four retirees I saw outside earlier walk through the door and immediately start acting like they're God's gift to the world. There's nothing worse than waiting on people when you're a psychological mess yourself. You become hypersensitive to criticism. So much so that when a customer complains about a dirty fork, you see it as an indictment of your entire existence. Sometimes you want to freak out and disembowel yourself like the waiter in the old *Monty Python* skit. Despite the glow from my recent success, deep down I'm still struggling with feeling like a loser. Trust me, when you're feeling inadequate, there's nothing like waiting on arrogant people to exacerbate that feeling.

"That's enough crybaby bullshit," I tell myself. "You've already unloaded on one customer. Try being professional the rest of the night."

Somehow, as I've done countless nights before, I pull my shit together, stuff my anger and sadness into a secure mental compartment, and smile. My waiter armor will just have to make it through another night. Within half an hour my entire section is seated, cocktailed, specialed, and busy eating their appetizers. There's a tender mercy to waiting tables. You can get so engrossed in what you are doing that you almost forget your troubles. I feel like I'm relaxing inside my brain while my body does all the work. For a few small minutes I find solace in going through the motions of a job I know how to do so well. Of course, my peace doesn't last.

"Louis has got a problem at table nine," Saroya says, tugging on my arm.

"What now?" I reply wearily.

"That lesbian woman's back, and she's drunk."

"Oh, brother."

"You're the manager, aren't you?" Saroya says with a sly smile. "Go fix it."

Aggravated, I head to the back to find Louis.

"What's going on?" I ask.

"You have to tell that lady to leave," Louis snorts. "I ain't gonna."

"Is she drunk?"

"Yeah, and I ain't serving her."

The woman in question is a forty-year-old brunette who used to be one of The Bistro's best customers. When I first started waiting on her, I found her to be standoffish, cold, and exacting—but she gave me a minimal amount of hassle and tipped a solid 20 percent. She'd always come in around five-thirty, order a dirty martini, and read the *New York Times* while she waited for her girlfriend to get off from work. Once her attractive blond girlfriend showed up, they'd order a nice dinner, share a bottle of wine, and cap off the evening with dessert and after-dinner drinks.

As the years went by, however, the brunette woman's martini consumption went from one to two and, eventually, to three. By the time her girlfriend arrived the brunette would be sloppy drunk and unable to enunciate simple words. To make matters worse, she'd polish off a bottle of wine by herself and chug two after-dinner drinks. Eventually she started eating alone. I found out that her girlfriend left her because of her drinking. I later learned that her alcoholism cost her her friends, her job, and even her house. One time the poor woman got so drunk she tried paying her dinner tab with a Bloomingdale's card. After several similar incidents Fluvio decreed we were not allowed to serve her alcohol if she came in smelling like booze. But that was easier said than done. The last time someone tried cutting her off, she got angry and made a small scene.

"So you gonna tell her to leave?" Louis asks. "I don't want to wait on her."

I peek around the corner. The woman's slumped in her chair. The desiccated skin on her face is stretched tight across her cheekbones, highlighting the blotchy patches. The first of many broken capillaries is starting to spider across her nose. The alcohol's now assaulting her health as well.

"All right, Louis," I sigh. "I'll take care of it."

I walk over to the woman's table.

"Hi there," I say softly.

"Hey," the woman replies.

A sickly sweet blast of alcoholic vapor floats out on the woman's breath and up my nose. This lady's been drinking cheap wine all day. Her bloodstream's so saturated with the stuff that it's leeching out of her pores.

"Would you like to hear the specials?" I ask.

"What I'd like is a bottle of Chianti," the woman says, the remnants of her imperious former self making an appearance.

"I'm sorry, madam," I say, modulating my voice to sound as nonjudgmental as possible. "I can't serve you any alcohol."

"Why not?" the woman asks, struggling to focus her eyes.

"You've had a few drinks already."

"So what?"

"I really can't argue with you over this. If you're already intoxicated, I can't serve you."

"I want a drink," the woman blurts, looking like she's collapsing in on herself.

As I look at her and think of what to do next, a snippet from the Scriptures floats into my brain: "Even the little that he has will be taken away." That line is from the Parable of Talents found in the Gospel of Matthew. The parable's a simple story. A master sets out on a long journey. Before he leaves he gives his three servants different amounts of money to invest for him. When the master returns from his travels, he asks the servants what they did with the cash. The first servant reports that he was given five talents, and he had made five talents more. That's better than a high-powered hedge fund, so the master was greatly pleased. The second servant reported that he had received two talents, and he had made two talents more. That was better than the average 401(k), so the master was thrilled, praised the two servants for being good and faithful, and asked them to share in his riches with him. Bonuses for everybody.

The third servant, the guy who received one talent, knew his master was a hard ass, so he buried the money he was given in the ground for safekeeping. He simply returned the original amount. The master freaked and called him a wicked and lazy servant. At minimum the guy should've put the money in a CD to make a little interest. The master commanded that the one talent be taken away from that lazy servant and given to the servant with ten talents. The master then ordered the lazy servant to be thrown outside into the darkness, where there was weeping and gnashing of teeth, saying, "Everyone who has much will be given more, and whoever has a little, even the little that he has will be taken away."

This woman was once a bright, industrious person. Whatever resources she had, whatever talents she possessed, are now buried under a sea of booze. She's literally wasted her talents. Everything's being taken away from her. I don't know why this woman is the way she is, but it's obvious she's in the grip of some awful pain. Instead of confronting her anguish, she's self-medicating with cheap wine.

I can relate to this woman's pain. I've wasted my talents, too. I'm like that fearful servant who just buried the one talent he was given. I know I shouldn't be a waiter anymore. My friends and family, the people who know me and love me, see me doing something else. Don't misunderstand, there's nothing wrong with being a waiter. But if you're a waiter who knows he should really be doing something else, the tension between what you are and who you think you should be can tear your psyche apart. It's like marrying one person but being in love with someone else.

The reason I've been fearful to utilize my talents is because I'm afraid of failure. I'm always waiting for disaster to strike, for the other shoe to drop. That's why I never opened that coffee shop. That's why my relationships have turned sour. It's why I'm still fearful my writing will amount to nothing. That's the real reason I haven't quit The Bistro. I'm afraid I'll fail if I try to do anything else.

My anxiety's been manifesting itself in awful nightmares—angry, wild visions where I howl in rage as the world takes everything away from me. People tell me I'm a fraud, old girlfriends taunt me from the shadows, hard-faced men chase me through the streets, sadists torture my dog, and old people cry as they point at dead babies rotting in the gutter. On the rare occasion I manage to trap one of my tormenters, the dream devolves into a hellish orgy of violence, where I use every weapon at my disposal—including my teeth. These are the dreams of a man who feels his life floating away on the current of time. I am in a place of "darkness and gnashing of teeth."

"I can't serve you alcohol," I say to the woman, pulling myself back into the here and now. "But I'd love it if you ate with us this evening. We have that fettuccine carbonara you always used to order."

The woman slumps in her chair, defeated. "That's okay," she says. "I wasn't really hungry."

"Stay here," I prod. "Drink some water. Get some of your strength back. I'll bring you some coffee."

"That's not necessary," she says, getting up. "I should be going."

"I'm sorry things didn't work out, but please come back again. We miss having you."

"Thank you." As the woman walks past me she grabs my arm. "Thank you for being gentle," she says.

I look into her eyes.

"You're welcome," I say.

"Bye."

I watch the woman walk away, and Louis comes up to me.

"Well, you got her out quietly," he says smugly.

"You couldn't have done it," I snap testily.

Louis just blinks at me.

"And you think you can do my job?" I say mockingly. "Please."

A nervous grin spreads across Louis's face. Like a little boy who's been caught with his hand in the cookie jar—or in a lie.

"I—"

"Forget it, Louis. If you want my job, you're welcome to it."

I walk back to my section by the front window. The entire Bistro clatters and hums with the sounds of happy people eating. Through the expanse of plate glass I watch the drunken woman as she stumbles down the street into the coolness of the night. About a block away from The Bistro she stops and sits on a park bench and puts her head in her hands. I can't be sure, but I think she's crying. I feel my own eyes moisten with tears. This woman's burying her life and talent under booze. I'm burying my talent under fear.

Ever since I was a kid I thought I wasn't good enough. I was always afraid that if I tried to do something, I'd fail, and if I failed, I would be destroyed. My psychological makeup is composed of many factors, but I think that my fear of destruction is partly related to learning I had a twin brother who died at birth. When my parents, gently and with good intentions, told me the news, I cried uncontrollably. I was inconsolable. I would burst into tears just thinking about it months, even years, later. Of course, that ten-year-old boy had no idea what he was feeling—but I do. He was feeling *fear*. As a kid I learned that not even the intimacy of a loving womb could prevent bad things from happening—my brother's fate could have easily been my own. It was a 50/50 proposition who would live and who would die. There was no pity, no second chances, no happy ending. My brother died right next to me. I learned early that the world can be a cruel and unforgiving place. If my brother could be destroyed, so could I. Thus, through some mishmash of survivor guilt and neurosis, I equated failure with annihilation.

So I hid.

I thought God could protect me inside a powerful two-thousand-year-old institution. I was wrong. I tried hiding in a corporate executive fantasy and armoring myself with expensive suits and the pretensions of a wannabe-yuppie lifestyle—but that didn't work either. Eventually I stumbled into the restaurant business and hid there. The Bistro's been like a womb I've been afraid to leave. For all my criticism of Fluvio, I admire him for starting this restaurant. He's a man who's failed many times in his life—and yet he's still plugging away. He's rough around the edges, frustrating, a pain in the ass, fearful, and paranoid as hell, but he's not paralyzed into inactivity. I can learn some lessons from him.

I'm burning out from the fire of my own demons. It's not just the restaurant business or customers—it's me. The man I want to be is fighting the man he's becoming. I want to use my talents before what little I have is taken away. That's what's been causing all my angst. That's why I've started snapping at customers. It may be clichéd, but it's true—the biggest battle is the one you fight inside yourself.

Like a light switch going off in my head, I realize why I've always been attracted to the solitary hero, the man who dwells in loneliness and ambiguity. The man beset by demons who still manages to stand on his own and find beauty in himself and those around him. A man who understands the cruelty of the world but remains unafraid. That is the man I want to be. I want to be like Philip Marlowe—"The best man in his world and a good enough man for any world."

"Down these mean streets a man must go," I say silently to myself, watching the drunken woman cry as the summer night sweeps away the remains of day. "Who is not himself mean, who is neither tarnished nor afraid." It's time to stop burying my talent. It's time to set childhood fears aside. I'm a man. I need to get my shit together. I can't stay at The Bistro forever.

"Waiter," a woman calls out from my section, "I need another drink."

I walk over to her table and take the martini glass from her outstretched hand. I go to the back, make another, and deliver it to her.

"Mmmm," the woman says, sipping her drink. "You make the best cosmopolitans."

"Thank you, madam."

"I always tell my husband you're a great waiter," she says. "Very capable."

"Thank you."

The woman looks at me. She's about fifty, her face shows the life she's led, but her eyes are warm and young.

"But overly capable," the woman says. "I saw how you handled that woman. I was watching. You're more than just a waiter. Aren't you?"

I smile broadly. Customers can be very observant.

"Yes, madam," I reply. "Yes, I am."

CHAPTER 22

Throwing in the Apron

I t's the Saturday night before Halloween. A decomposing hooker wearing fishnet stockings and teetering on a pair of oversize stiletto pumps wobbles past the restaurant's front window. Her boyfriend, dressed up as Jack the Ripper, energetically chases behind her theatrically waving a long rubber knife. Pausing in front of the window, the hooker vigorously waves at the customers, causing the fake intestines hanging out of her short shirt to jiggle nicely. Her breasts jiggle nicely, too. Some of the patrons laugh and wave back. There must be a masquerade party somewhere. The streets are crawling with tipsy creatures and inebriated things that go bump in the night. Not all of the monsters, however, are outside The Bistro.

"So how can I buy that picture?" the drunken middle-aged woman standing in front of me barks. "I haven't got all fucking night."

The artwork adorning The Bistro's walls is for sale. These numbered reproductions of paintings have been languishing unsold for years.

"I'm sorry, madam," I reply apologetically. "I've never sold one of these pictures. I need to call Fluvio to find out what the procedure is. Please allow me a few minutes."

"You don't know how to sell a picture?" the woman fumes. "Take it off the wall, wrap it up, and give it to me."

"I believe you have to deal directly with the artist, madam—"

"I don't care," the woman says, stamping a high-heeled shoe on the floor. "Hurry up and find out."

I don't have time for this lady's crap. This is a restaurant, not an art gallery. Ordinarily the hostess would take care of this situation but, since it's near closing, I thought it was safe to let her go home. Mistake. The second she left a surge of last-minute walk-ins piled through the front door. Thinking the other waiters were busy, I threw all the new arrivals into my empty section. Saroya immediately began crying foul, whining that I was using my authority to steal customers from the other waiters; she even got Beth to start sniping at me. And Louis? He's not even speaking to me. Earlier in the evening I disciplined him for shouting obscenities within earshot of the customers. He's still pissed off that I told him to shut up. I can't blame him. Once when Fluvio and I were fighting, I shouted a litany of obscenities so foul that the entire dining room was stunned into shocked silence. I'm not unaware of my hypocrisy. I just don't give a shit.

Three weeks ago I scaled back my workweek from five days to four. I tried preparing the staff for my eventual reduction in hours, but they laughed it off, thinking it wasn't going to happen. Now that it's a reality, the bad blood between us is reaching the boiling point. Saroya told me point-blank that I shouldn't wait tables anymore because I'm "rich." That'd be nice if it were true—but I'm not in a position to retire to Tahiti anytime soon. My goal's been to keep working and write, but deep down I know my time here is limited. I'm hurt and angry. The worst parts of my personality are starting to run rampant. I've been coming off as arrogant, pompous, rude, and—*gasp!*—entitled. My attitude toward The Bistro's staff is basically "fuck 'em."

The staff hates me. Since all my new customers arrived at once, they've all ordered their desserts at once. This drunken lady's siphoning off the time I need to whip up the fifteen cappuccinos. I'm having a very bad night. I'm not about to go into the weeds over cappuccino. Besides, my inebriated little doyenne's so plastered, she'll be lucky if she can walk bipedal in twenty minutes much less talk about art.

"As soon as I find out about the pictures," I reply evenly, "I'll let you know."

The woman glares angrily at me. At least I think she's angry with me. It's hard to tell. All the plastic surgery and Botox procedures she's endured have frozen her face into an expression of perpetually surprised grimness. Despite her short skirt and StairMastered rear end, if I had to make a choice, I'd take the decomposing hooker.

"Make it snappy," she blurts drunkenly.

"Yes, madam."

As soon as the woman stumbles out of earshot, I call Fluvio at Bistro Duetto. In the background I can hear the other restaurant's packed.

"Why can't I just give the lady the picture off the wall?" I ask.

"NO!" Fluvio shouts. "She has to talk to the artist."

"So what's his number?"

"It's on the card that comes with the painting."

"The card just tells you to ask the server for more information," I reply. "There's no number."

"Isn't the artist number in the computer?"

I quickly scroll through the important phone numbers stored in the reservation computer.

"No dice, boss."

"Go look for it in my office."

"Are you nuts? I'll never find it in that mess."

"Wait! I try and find out," Fluvio says, putting me on hold.

After two minutes of listening to bad Muzak I hang up the phone. I call Bistro Duetto back and tell the hostess to have Fluvio call me when he gets the information. Then I head toward the kitchen to fetch my desserts. As I pass by the drunken woman's table she grabs my arm and pulls me toward her.

"So what's up with the picture?" she asks.

I resist the urge to pull my arm out of the woman's hand. "We're trying to get the artist's phone number," I say.

"Jesus," the woman yells, digging her nail into my arm. "Can you believe this shit?"

"What's so hard about selling a picture?" the woman's husband snaps. Wearing an open-necked blue silk shirt and expensive black-framed glasses designed to project an aura of success, the man looks like he spends every spare minute at the tanning salon or the gym. The effect of his expensive clothes and personally trained physique, however, is somewhat offset by the bad hair plugs stapled in precise intervals across his receding hairline. The couple they're with look like a pair of semi-retired porn stars—staving off old age with gleaming veneers, cartoonishly enhanced bodies, and oversprayed hair. The holes where their eyes should be stare out at me with flat indifference. Something tells me these four all use the same plastic surgeon.

"Sir," I say, "I'm doing the best I can."

"That's not good enough," the man's wife blurts.

"Sorry."

The woman lets go of my arm. No one says anything else, so I take that as my cue to leave. I walk back to the kitchen to start on my cappuccinos. I get only two of them made before there's another demand on my attention.

"Oh, Mr. Manager," Saroya says, tapping me on my shoulder, "Fluvio's on the phone, and that lady at my table's furious about the picture."

"Saroya," I reply, pulling some more cappuccino glasses off the shelf, "I'm really backed up. Could you talk to Fluvio and find out what's going on?"

"No."

"Why not?"

"It's not my job."

"But I'm going in the weeds here."

"Tough," Saroya says, clearly enjoying my discomfort. She's not going to help me. No one is.

"Why are you being such a bitch?" I snap.

Saroya's eyes flare with anger. "Because if you weren't so greedy," she says hotly, "you wouldn't have so many tables, and you wouldn't be in the weeds."

"You're a piece of work, Saroya," I reply. "You steal tables, too."

"Go talk to Fluvio," Saroya says, trying to push me out the door. "I'm not going to do your job."

My temper flares. "You know, Saroya," I say. "Just because you're dating the chef doesn't mean you can tell me what to do."

"What!" Saroya yelps. "You said because I'm *fucking* the chef I can't tell you what to do?"

"That's not what I said . . ." I blurt. There's a difference between the words *dating* and *fucking*.

A glow of triumph washes over Saroya's face. "I'm telling Armando what you said. He'll beat you up."

I shake my head. This is a no-win scenario. I decide to end this conversation.

"I'm finishing bringing my desserts out," I say menacingly. "It's your table. *You* deal with Fluvio. *You* deal with that woman. *You* deal with that godddamn picture."

"Jerk!" Saroya hisses, storming out of the kitchen.

For the next twenty minutes I totally focus on getting desserts to my tables. I'm so angry I ignore everything and everyone. The house phone's ringing off the hook, but I know it's Fluvio, so I don't answer. Fuck him and his disorganized bullshit.

As I'm hustling around I notice Armando talking to the crazy art lady in the middle of the aisle. Saroya must have asked him to intervene. I'm surprised. It's rare for Armando to talk to the customers. Then something happens. Armando, obviously thinking the conversation's over, starts walking away. Startled, the art lady starts snapping her fingers and calling after Armando like he's a little dog. Armando ignores her, so the woman races up and grabs him by the arm. I see an angry look flash over Armando's face. He recovers quickly, pulls the lady's hand off his arm, and politely walks away. Good, I think to myself. It's about time Armando saw how crazy the customers could be.

Armando walks up to me. "Why weren't you able to take care of that lady and talk to my cousin?"

"I'm a busy man," I say. "You saw how many desserts I had to take out."

"You're busy because you took all the tables."

"Don't you start," I grunt.

"I'm not here to do your job," Armando answers calmly. "If you can't handle it—"

"It got crazy at the end," I interject. "There was no hostess so—"

"I don't care," Armando says. We eyeball each other for a few moments. I think about how young lions in the wild push an old lion out of his turf and take over. Suddenly, I feel like the old lion. After a few more seconds of staring Armando quickly walks away. When he disappears into the kitchen, Saroya comes running up to me.

"I told him what you said to me," she says in her smug, singsong voice. "He's really pissed at you."

"Great," I murmur. "Now everyone hates me."

"You deserve it."

"You know he's going to believe you over me."

Saroya sniffs and walks away. The art lady drinks herself into mental retardation and forgets about the picture. The night ends. The staff leaves without saying a word to me. Armando walks out of the restaurant without shaking my hand—the first time he's ever done so. Uh-oh. When kitchen staff turns against you, it's all over. The bus people are eyeballing me strangely, too. I get the same odd feeling I had just before I was fired from the psychiatric clinic. I feel like a dead waiter walking.

When The Bistro's dark and empty, I lock up, go home, and pour myself a large whisky. My brain's in overdrive, so I know I won't be able to sleep. I start reading some Raymond Chandler, but, after a few minutes, I slam the book shut. I'm disgusted with myself. Philip Marlowe would never take the crap I'm taking. Then again, he wouldn't be overthinking things like some whiny introspective little bitch, either. I'm not good for The Bistro, and The Bistro's no longer good for me. It's time for a change. I need to be that man of honor. I need to go. I remember something my seminary rector told me a long time ago. "Never be the corpse at your own wake."

I drain my whisky and turn off the light. I need to sleep on it.

At nine in the morning the phone rings. My head aches dully, and my tongue feels like it's coated with wax. I pick the cordless off the nightstand and squint at the caller ID. It's Fluvio.

I lie in bed and let voice mail take the call. Through half-closed eyes, I watch the tree branch outside my bedroom window rise and fall in the autumn wind, its red and orange leaves dripping like embers from the rigging of a burning ship adrift on a rolling sea. A leaf suddenly gets pasted against the windowpane. It defiantly flaps against the glass until it's peeled away and hurled into oblivion.

I toss myself out of bed, walk into the kitchen, and put on a pot of coffee. While I'm waiting, I toast a bagel, smother it with cream cheese, and throw a few slices of tomato on top. As soon as the coffee stops perking I pour myself a large mug and eat my breakfast standing up in the kitchen. When I finish, I put my dish in the sink, refill my coffee mug, and listen to the message Fluvio left.

"Eh. Call me. I don't like what I hear went on last night. Call me as soon as you get this message. I expect you to watch the restaurant for me. Not cause more problems. Call me. Bye."

I sigh deeply and dial Fluvio's cell phone. He picks up on the first ring.

"So what happened?" he answers. No preamble. No hello.

"It was nuts last night," I say. "What can I tell you?"

"You can't handle it?"

"Fluvio, the lady wanted to buy a picture. I've never sold one of those pictures. I tried talking to you, but you were busy and I had a full section. I asked Saroya to talk to you since it was her customer. She said it wasn't her job and got Armando to talk to her."

"So why you can't handle it?" Fluvio repeats.

"C'mon, Fluvio. These things happen. I was taking care of my customers, there was no hostess "

"I pay you to take care of things while I'm not there. I don't need to be worried you can't handle things."

I want to tell Fluvio he shouldn't be worried since he's already promised my job to Louis.

"Sorry, Fluvio," I say instead. "I wish things had gone differently."

Fluvio says nothing. As I listen to his pressured breathing my breakfast starts boiling in my stomach. I used to be able to tolerate my boss's craziness, but after six years I can't deal with it anymore. Maybe I should tell Fluvio I quit. But for some reason, I can't.

"Anything else, boss?" I ask.

"No," Fluvio replies. "I just don't want to worry anymore."

"I know."

"I talk to you at work."

"Okay."

"Bye."

A few hours later I walk into The Bistro with my dry-cleaned shirt slung over my shoulder. Saroya's eagerly waiting for me.

"You're in trouble," she says, once again in that singsong voice; she's like a little girl tattling on a sibling. "Armando wants to talk to you."

"Oh yeah?" I say, clocking in on the POS system. "What about?"

"About what you said to me last night."

"I'm sure he does. Is he in the kitchen?"

"Yes, but he's—"

I walk away from Saroya and stick my head in the kitchen. Armando's standing next to the stove going over an invoice.

"You need to talk to me?" I ask.

Armando looks up and smiles a terse smile. "Yeah," he says. "Give me a minute."

"I'll be outside."

As I was waiting one of the other servers, Sara, a tall brunette whose husband just got home from Iraq, sidles up to me. "I heard you guys had a tough night last night."

"I've seen worse," I chuckle.

"What happened?"

"Too many chiefs," I reply. "Not enough Indians."

"Oh."

"So you ready?" Armando says, exiting the kitchen.

"Yep."

"Follow me," Armando says, smiling indulgently. "We'll talk in the office."

Part of me bristles at being talked to like a subordinate, but I bite my tongue; I just want to get this over with and clear the air.

We head down to Fluvio's office. Armando slowly lowers himself into Fluvio's chair. I move several articles of stained clothing off a folding chair and sit down.

"Listen, Armando," I start, "about Saroya . . ."

"Forget about that," Armando says, waving his hand dismissively. "I want to talk to you about something else."

"Oh?" I say, surprised.

"I've been talking to my cousin and the staff," Armando says, twisting in Fluvio's swivel chair and looking up at the ceiling. "And we all agree you need to change how you act around here."

"How so?"

"Everyone thinks you're being unfair—that you take all the good tables, that you always get more customers than anyone else."

"The waiters have been griping about that for years," I counter. "What's different now?"

"Listen," Armando says. "People are saying your attitude sucks. They're getting tired of it."

I shift uncomfortably in my seat. The office reeks of grease and sweat. This wasn't the conversation I thought I'd be having. Feeling like I'm being ambushed, I reflexively start defending myself. As I'm talking I begin to wonder why I'm even bothering to explain myself to Armando. He's not my boss. Armando pretends to look interested and nods politely at the appropriate moments, but I can tell he's not listening. He's itching to tell me something. Part of me wonders if Fluvio's somehow recording this conversation. I wouldn't put it past him. Great. Now *I'm* getting paranoid.

"Well, I've talked to my cousin," Armando says when I finish talking. "And he's told me that I'm in charge of The Bistro. If you're not willing to change how you do things, he's authorized me to let you go."

I tamp down a sudden surge of anger. Armando's a nice guy. One day he'll have a successful restaurant of his own, but right now he's just playacting being the boss. He still has much to learn. I'm really furious at Fluvio. After six and a half years of working together he should have had the balls to have this conversation with me himself.

"Wow," I say. For once I'm at a loss for words.

"That's the way it is."

"So what changes do you have in mind?" I half mumble.

As Armando talks I stare at a spot on the floor and pretend to listen. It's no coincidence this conversation's coming three weeks after I reduced my hours at The Bistro. Granted, many of the staff's gripes are legitimate, but the real impetus behind Fluvio's actions is his intolerance of anyone he can't control. That's why he's not here.

I could fight this. I'm not technically being fired. If I wait long enough, Fluvio's craziness and ingratitude will drive the staff back into my corner, and he'll be forced to depend on me again. But how long will that take and at what cost? I'm worn down by Fluvio's nonsense, and I don't have the emotional resources to fend of a mutiny from the staff. I'd win a Pyrrhic victory at best.

Someone once told me, "You're ready to do something when you're ready to do it." A good waiter knows when it's time to throw in his apron. For me, that time has finally come. I needed this last bit of stupidity from Fluvio to snip the last shackles holding me to this place. I don't need The Bistro anymore. It was my haven and crucible for six years. Now I don't need it anymore. I can stand on my own two feet. I'm going to be all right; I'm not afraid. I deserve better than this. I won't fail. I won't be destroyed.

It is time for me to go.

Armando's still talking, but I can't hear him. His words are muzzled by a cottony fog of emotion swirling around me. Happiness, relief, anger, and sadness exchange places in my brain so quickly that they blur into a single unquantifiable sensation. There's nothing to say. I get up from my chair and head toward the door.

"Where you going?" Armando says.

"I'm done here."

"But—"

"Good-bye, Armando."

As I walk through the door Armando calls after me, "I know you can't believe this is happening. But it's happening. Believe it!"

Shaking my head, I climb up the stairs and walk into the dining room. I grab my coat and keys. I feel like an invisible hand is pressing into my back and guiding me toward the front door. In a state of shock I look down at the wooden floorboards gleaming waxily in the afternoon light. I've been here so long that every knot, whorl, and gouge in the wood is as familiar as the landscape of my own face. I must've tread across them enough times to span the Pacific—now I can't believe I'm walking over them for the last time. As I walk past the linen-covered tables I think about the stories each one could tell. Table 3's where that lady had a stroke. Table 9's where the alcoholic lady broke down and cried. Table 15's where that guy proposed to his girlfriend.

Table 17's where I cut my hand opening wine and bled all over the table. Table 18's where the guy had a seizure and poleaxed, unconscious, to the floor. I rolled the drunken guy with the hooker at table 19, and Russell Crowe asked me if I was an actor at table 20. Table 22 was where I took care of the Valentine's Day couple, and table 24's where I once told an obnoxious man to get the hell out. Tables 25's where my favorite customers always ate, and table 26 was where that girl and boy decided on New Year's Eve to try for a baby. I can't believe I'll never work these tables again. I owe them, somehow.

Traffic noises float in off the street. The afternoon sun is hitting the main window, rear projecting the restaurant's stenciled logo against the side wall. As I look at The Bistro's shadowed name in reverse I remember how the sunlight played through the stained-glass windows of my old seminary chapel. I remember the sound of thirty men tenderly singing to the Virgin Mary. I think of Kevin's funeral and the last time I saw him alive. I think about Beth tenderly applying makeup to her dead friend's face. Tears sting my eyes. I feel a tremendous sense of relief, like when a loved one dies after a long illness and you know his suffering is over. Emotions and memories start running through my head like a speeded-up film. I remember a happy Fluvio bringing his son to the restaurant for the first time. I remember kissing my ex-girlfriend in the wine cellar. I remember the brother I lost and the brother I have. I remember my parents when they were young. I remember Amici's. I think about Caesar. I think about Rizzo. I think about karma. I think about sin and redemption. No matter what I think about The Bistro today, in the long run, it was good for me to be here.

As I travel down the aisle the tears in my eyes refract the light shining through the windows into a gauzy haze. By the time I reach the exit they're falling off my face and onto the floor. Placing my hand on the glass door I take a deep breath, whisper goodbye, and walk outside. The autumn air is crisp and pure. The wind's loudly rustling the leaves of the trees. I remember reading that you can hear God's voice whispering in the wind. Maybe that's whose hand I feel on my back. I smile, wipe away my tears, and start walking down the street.

I'm no longer that sad man in the window.

Epilogue: Spring

'm standing outside Café Gerardi's enjoying a beautiful spring afternoon. The neighborhood was in the grip of a violent thunderstorm when I showed up for work this morning. Now the air is calm and quiet. The resurgent sun has evaporated all evidence of the rain. I take a deep breath and enjoy the scent of a freshly laundered world.

I absentmindedly reach for a pack of cigarettes. A few confused seconds pass until I remember that I quit smoking. As I pull my hand out of my pocket I smile ruefully to myself. Quitting The Bistro was the best thing I ever did for my health. Not only did I kick cigarettes, but I started to exercise, lowered my alcohol consumption, began sleeping better, and lost ten pounds. I feel like leaving The Bistro has added ten years to my life. All my friends say I look calmer. They're right.

I turn around and look through Café Gerardi's front window. I have only one customer, a fat, jowly man who comes in every week for a bottle of root beer and a bowl of Zuppa di Pesce. He's one of those sad types who has problems being around other people but craves human company nonetheless. Every restaurant has one customer like him. I've sort of adopted him. It took a month, but now he smiles at me whenever I take his order. You have to savor life's small triumphs. Noting that the man is half-way through his meal, I turn my face back toward the sun to soak up some more vitamin D. I have time.

I've been working at Café Gerardi's for almost two months. It's not the best place I've ever worked at, but it isn't the worst. Since I'm new I get the crappiest shifts, the worst sections, the most problematic customers, and the foulest side work. When I told Beth about my reversal-of-waiter fortune, she laughed her head off and told me it was payback for all the managerial sins I committed at The Bistro. On one level she's right, but I also like being a simple waiter for a change. I don't miss arguing with customers who feel entitled or telling the staff to smoke pot on their own time. Even though I'm making half the money I made at The Bistro, I'm happy. I work only four shifts a week. I have more time for the rest of my life.

When I left The Bistro, I decided to take a little vacation from the restaurant business. I needed a break. I was curious to see how average human beings celebrated the holidays. Let me tell you, it was strange returning to the flow of ordinary time. When I spent Christmas Eve with my family for the first time in seven years, I didn't know what to do with myself. When I was at a New Year's Eve party at a friend's house, it took a concerted effort not to grab a tray and start serving canapés. It took a month before I stopped dreaming about forgotten appetizers and unrefilled sodas.

It was also strange to eat out like a civilian. At first I got aggravated overhearing patrons giving their server a hard time, but eventually I started to relax and see things through the customer's eyes. After dining in more than a few excellent restaurants, I was pleased to discover that The Bistro isn't the entire restaurant world.

Fluvio called me the day after I quit. It was not a good conversation. We didn't speak to each other again until a few weeks ago. I had to call him to straighten out a problem with my health insurance. That's when he told me he lost Bistro Duetto. Something went wrong with the lease, and he had to pull out. He told me he lost a ton of money. Later somebody would tell me that Fluvio's financials were screwed up from day one and that his crash and burn was inevitable. Personally, I think all the bad karma Fluvio accumulated over the years finally came back to bite him on the ass. Before the call ended he told me he still considered me a friend. That pissed me off. If he were my friend, he'd have called me to see how I was doing at least once. Despite my mini–religious experience after I left The Bistro, I struggled with some powerful feelings of anger and loss. I felt like a wife in a battered relationship who leaves her abuser and is suddenly ashamed that she stuck with her guy so long. It wasn't until I left The Bistro that I finally grasped that Fluvio cared about only Fluvio. I told him I was sorry he lost the restaurant and hung up. We never talked again.

The original Bistro is still humming right along, and I keep in contact with some of my old coworkers. Beth left a few months after I did, broke up with her boyfriend, and got a job outside of the restaurant business. Now she's dating a new guy, and she seems very happy. Occasionally we meet up at Café American with Celine, one of the former hostesses, to drink dirty martinis and tell war stories. I've also run into a few of my ex-customers. My old favorites, the Meyers, told me The Bistro wasn't the same without me and they never went back. I was touched to hear that—but I have a sneaking suspicion some of the "friends of the owner" types are ecstatic I left.

Saroya, Armando, and Louis are still working at The Bistro. As the months passed and I got some distance from the restaurant, my anger at them softened. They're just people working within a dysfunctional environment. The people I miss the most are the bus people and the kitchen staff. They're the finest people I ever had the honor to work with.

I passed by the restaurant a few weeks ago. Many of the waiters through the window were new faces. I guess Fluvio's still going through servers at a healthy clip. As I peered through the plate glass a funny sensation tickled my spine. Seeing The Bistro is like passing my boyhood home after my parents sold it. Sure, the building holds many memories—but I don't live there anymore.

When I'm not working at Gerardi's, I spend the rest of my time writing. At first I found it difficult to write every day. After a few months I got so engrossed in the actual process of writing that the six hours I set aside would often slip by like six minutes. I've discovered I get anxious when I skip writing for more than a day. There's something narcotizing about the struggle to put words down on paper. It's addictive.

I keep notepads all over the house to capture ideas before they slip out of my head. Once I woke up and wrote down a snippet of dialogue I heard in a dream because I liked how it sounded. People I meet on the street transform into characters. Articles in the newspapers become plotlines. Sunsets challenge me to describe them. An author friend of mine told me I was experiencing the symptoms of turning into a writer. I think he's right. Writing has been changing me—and for the better.

I look back inside the window. My customer's done eating his soup. I walk back inside, clear the table, and present the man with the bill. The man gives me a nice tip, smiles, and leaves. Gerardi's is now empty, so I grab a newspaper and park myself at a back table. I look at the clock and realize I've got an hour until I can go home.

As I read the paper I contemplate that waiting tables has become much easier since I left The Bistro. The customers don't annoy me the way they used to. Remember the three reasons why people become waiters? Now that I'm a waiter trying to become something *else*, I feel like my life has direction. The chip I was carrying on my shoulder fell off. My sense of hospitality has returned. I no longer feel like a loser. Those horrible dreams about wasted talent have disappeared. For the first time in a long time, I'm at peace with myself. That's why my friends say I look more relaxed. Hey. I haven't crop-dusted a table in months.

The front door chimes. I look up. A tall, beautiful red-haired woman is standing in the doorway. I get up from my seat to greet her. The waiter smile on my face is the real deal.

"Can I still get lunch?" she asks.

"Of course, miss," I say brightly. My eyes flick down to examine her hands. No wedding ring. "Sit anywhere you like."

The woman takes a seat by the window. After bringing her a glass of Sauvignon Blanc, I rattle off the short list of lunch specials. Sadly, the woman picks the worst dish of the bunch.

"I wouldn't get that, miss," I say.

"Why not?" she asks.

"It's just not good."

"I thought you guys were supposed to say everything is good," the woman giggles.

"Only the dishonest ones."

"And you're an honest waiter?"

"Now I am."

"You weren't always?"

"No."

"Ever spit in anyone's food?"

I laugh. "Not yet."

"I waited tables for years," the woman says, lowering her voice to a confidential whisper. "I did it all the time."

"I can certainly sympathize with the motivation."

"What do you do when you're not waiting tables?" the redhead asks.

"I'm a writer."

"Really?" she says, her green eyes evincing increased interest. "Are you writing a book now?"

"Yep."

"Very cool. What's it about?"

"The restaurant business."

There's a long pause. She's staring at me. My goodness, I think she likes me.

"I get off shift in an hour," I say brazenly. "Maybe we can meet for a drink and compare notes. Waiter to waiter?"

"Research for your book?"

"You could say that."

The woman purses her lips thoughtfully. After a long pause she says, "I have a meeting in an hour. I'm afraid I can't."

"Of course, miss," I say, snapping back into server mode.

"But thanks for asking."

"My pleasure."

"So what is good here?" she asks, returning her attention to the menu. I tell her the tuna's excellent. She orders it, eats it, and asks for her check.

"Sorry I couldn't take you up on that drink," she says, stuffing some bills into the check holder. "Maybe a rain check?"

"Of course, miss," I reply, thinking she's politely shining me off.

"My name's Rachel, by the way," the redhead says, extending an elegantly manicured hand.

"I'm Steve," I say, taking it.

"Nice to meet you, Steve," she says. "Good luck with the book."

"Thank you, Rachel."

I escort her to the door, say good-bye, and watch her walk away. Just as she turns the corner and slips out of sight, the relief waiter comes in. I can go home. I head back into the dining room, pick up the billfold off the table, and peek inside. There, tucked next to my 25 percent tip, is a piece of paper with the redhead's phone number scribbled on it.

Sometimes I love this job.

Appendix A

40 Tips on How to Be a Good Customer

1. Make reservations and keep them. On a Friday or Saturday night it's not unusual for 20 percent of a restaurant's reservations not to show up—even if they confirmed earlier in the day. This happens because so many people in this options-obsessed cell phone–enabled world make reservations at two or three establishments and decide which one they'll go to at the very last minute—usually without telling the other restaurant! Not only is that rude, it hurts the restaurant's bottom line, forcing management to overbook. If you've ever wondered why your table's never ready when you show up for your reservation on time, that's usually the reason. Don't blame the restaurant. Blame your fellow customers. With modern computer systems we can track which customers consistently screw us over and blackball them. Don't let that happen to you. Make a decision and stick to it.

2. If you're going to be late for your reservation, please call. We'll hold your table. After half an hour you might not get the special table you requested, but you'll still get in. An hour late? On a busy night turn around and go home. Don't even bother.

3. Never say, "I'm friends with the owner." Restaurant owners don't have any friends. This marks you as a clueless poseur the moment you walk in the door.

4. Sit where you're seated! Whenever the hostesses attempt to seat guests many customers (usually the females) will walk past the proffered seats and hunt around the restaurant for a better table. Please, let the hostess do her job. She's only trying to seat customers evenly so that everyone gets the best service possible without overwhelming one server. And trust me, when your waiter overhears you whining about your table, he or she will know that you're an annoying table snob who thinks you're entitled to undeserved rock-star treatment and that, in all probability, you're a bad tipper to boot. You haven't even met your waiter and you've already got a strike against you.

5. Leave your children at home if at all possible. Don't get me wrong. I love kids. Just not in high-end dining es-tablishments. Smart parents who can't get a sitter will dine at a restaurant early and dash off before their little angels get rambunctious. That's cool. What's not cool is a Ritalin-medicated brat racing around the restaurant and screaming his head off at ten P.M. The odds are good this kid's going to get trampled or have something hot spilled on him. Sometimes grown-ups just want to be with other grown-ups. (We should also charge parents for the space their super-expensive urban assault baby carriages take up.)

6. If you must bring your child and use a high chair, do not make the kid sit on the trafficked side of the table so grandma can make goo goo faces. I know, I'm heartless, but I'd hate to clip your baby's still-soft skull with a tray. Keep sweetums out of the line of fire. Media players on the table to keep your three-year-old occupied? Only if I get to slip in a *Girls Gone Wild* DVD.

7. Be polite. Say please and thank you. Be courteous to the hostess, bus people, coat-check girl, bartender, and waiter. Treat others as you want to be treated. (Yes, people need to be reminded of this.)

8. Never say, "Do you know who I am?" Why? Did *you* forget who you are?

9. Do not snap your fingers to get the waiter's attention. Remember, we have shears that cut through bone in the kitchen.

10. Do not use your cell phone in the restaurant. Yes, you, the always-need-to-be-connected BlackBerry junkie! Didn't anyone tell you it's rude to talk on a cell phone (or to text message) while other people are eating? Unless you're a heart-transplant surgeon on standby, turn it off or put it on vibrate. No one wants to hear your stupid *Godfather* ringtones anyway. And please, don't talk on your phone while the waiter's telling you the specials or getting your order. The classy thing to do when you need to make a call is to go outside. And guys, when you sit down at the table, please avoid the whole throwing-your-cell-phone-on-top-of-the-table maneuver. It reeks of penile and social insecurity. Keep it in your pants, Master of the Universe.

11. Tell your teenage child to put the Game Boy away and sit up straight.

12. Don't use your laptop while eating dinner. Lunch is acceptable because you might be working, but any other time it makes you look sort of creepy. Read a book (preferably this one) or read the paper.

13. Please make your server go through the specials only once. Most restaurant owners think operating a high-class place involves making waiters rattle off twenty specials from memory. It doesn't, but please don't make our lives harder by asking us to detail the specials before the other half of your party arrives. Then we have to go through it all over again. I already get laryngitis once a year as it is!

14. Don't ask the server his or her name so you can shout it across the dining room whenever you need something. I once told an obstreperous patron my name was Sigismund. Now that made for some interesting dinner theater.

15. Order clearly. Say what you want. The waiter is not psychic. Clarify the order with the waiter who, if he's smart, will repeat the order back to you.

16. When ordering wine, don't sniff the cork! This marks you as a total amateur. Why tell some unscrupulous sommelier you're his or hers for the taking? The only thing you need to do is *feel* the cork and make sure it's intact. Is the bottom of the cork moistened with wine? Good. That means it was stored properly. You might want to make sure the name on the cork matches the name on the bottle. Unscrupulous owners have been known to put cheap wine in old wine bottles and recork them. Is there mold on the cork? That's a bad sign. And don't start spinning the wine in the glass like you're trying to separate U-235 in a centrifuge machine. That's so pretentious. What you should do is swirl the wine and see how it coats the side of the glass. The coating that sticks to the side of the glass and runs down in streaks is called "legs." If a wine has legs, that means it contains a high level of alcohol and will taste like a full-bodied wine. When you sniff the wine, you want to check if the wine smells like vinegar, moldy cheese, or feet. If it does, then the wine's bad and you send it back. Don't sweat it; we usually get the money back from the distributor. Remember, the wine liturgy is only to check if the wine's drinkable, not to see if it's to your taste. You should know what you like ahead of time. You don't like the wine even though it's perfectly good? That's your fault.

17. Don't ask for the big glasses when ordering cheap wine, especially by the glass. This pretentious yuppie move drives me nuts. Some wines, usually high-quality ones, need to be served in large glasses that give the wine more surface area to interact with the air and open it up, revealing its true flavors. Status-conscious patrons, even though they're drinking Chianti that could be served in a Dixie cup, want everyone around them to think they're drinking something exclusive and so they ask for the big glasses. I've always remarked how much this maneuver tells you about these customers—large egos with nothing substantial to fill them.

18. If the restaurant serves wine and you bring your own bottle, you will be charged a corking fee. That fee is usually equal to the price of the cheapest bottle of wine the restaurant sells. If you bring your own bottle of wine but purchase a bottle of equal or greater value, some restaurants, but certainly not all, might let you slide on the corking fee. Do not bring in a bottle of wine the restaurant already sells. That's rude. If you have any concerns about bringing your own bottle of wine to a restaurant, avoid trouble. Call the establishment ahead of time.

19. Know your limits where alcohol's concerned.

20. Don't order off the menu. Don't walk into an Italian restaurant and think the chef's going to make you sushi just because he has tuna. Restaurants are set up to make what's on the menu as well as a predetermined list of specials. When you order what's not on the menu, you're forcing the chef into a situation where he's cooking something he doesn't make on a regular basis. In a restaurant kitchen, repetition is the key to consistency. You want your heart surgeon to have done ten thousand bypasses before he cracks open your chest, right? Same thing with a chef—if he makes the same entrée ten thousand times a month, the odds are good that the dish will be a home run every time.

21. Reasonable menu changes are for food allergies. Don't lie and say you have an allergy so the chef will make something special just for you. You know who you are.

22. Spend money. You don't have to break the bank. Splitting entrées is okay, but don't ask for water, lemon, and sugar so

you can make your own lemonade. What's next, grapes so you can press your own wine? Get the fuck outta here.

23. Be well behaved. No hand jobs under the table or sex in the bathroom—unless I'm one of the participants.

24. The secret to being treated like a regular customer? *Be* a regular customer. Everybody likes to have a favorite restaurant where the waiter knows his favorite drink and the owner makes a fuss over him. We all want a special place where we'll always get a good table or a last-minute reservation. The problem is, most patrons think they're entitled to that level of fawning on their first visit to the restaurant. Wrong! If you want to be treated like a regular customer, you have to patronize an establishment at least once or twice a month, minimum. As my former corporate boss was fond of saying, "It's all about relationships."

25. Never aggressively touch the waiters or bus people. Don't grab arms or pull on aprons.

26. Tell all your friends about the restaurant and drive in business. The owner loves that shit. It's free advertising. He'll *almost* treat you like a friend.

27. Don't hit up the owner or waiter for donations. Trust me, the owner *hates* that. There are days when it seems every customer has his or her hand out for a donation—whether it's fund-raisers for orphaned puppies, raffles for acid-reflux disease, telethons for restless-leg syndrome, golf charities, or Kiwanis' silent auctions—no restaurant can give to every charity that comes knocking. Eventually contribution fatigue sets in. What's really tacky is how customers have one meal in a restaurant and think they're entitled to ask the owner for a $100 donation to help send their son's glee club to Paris. Please. Lay off.

28. Cultivate a waiter. If you find a waiter you like, always ask to be seated in his or her section. Tell all your friends about your favorite waiter so they start asking for that server by

name as well. You've just made that waiter look indispens-
able to the owner and increased his or her income as well.
The server will be grateful and take very good care of you.

29. Don't monopolize the waiter's time. Sure, I like talking to
you, but I've got other tables to attend to. Try not to linger.
Be aware the waiter needs to turn the table to make money.
If you want to hang out till closing, that's okay, but increase
the tip to make up for money the server would have made if
he or she had had another seating at that table.

30. Ask for the check. It's impolite for a server just to drop it on
the table. (But we will when it's busy.)

31. Yes, the squiggly sign-the-check pantomime thing is acceptable, even though it irks the hell out of me.

32. Pay the check within five minutes of receiving it. A good
way to signal that the check is ready for payment is to have
the cash or credit card peeking out of the check holder.
For the love of God don't put the bill in your lap, under a
napkin, or, my favorite, lean on it with your elbows. That's
some passive-aggressive shit. It screams that you don't want
to part with your cash. Don't look like a cheap bastard.
Just give me the friggin' check.

33. Don't ask for separate checks at the end of the meal. That's
your problem. You should have told me earlier.

34. If you have no money or forgot your credit card, you will
not be washing dishes to work off your bill. The insurance
company would never allow us to assume the liability. If
you're a regular customer, we'll let you pay us the next day.
If we don't know you? We call the cops and have you arrested for theft of service.

35. Tip at least 15 to 20 percent. If you don't, any regular-
customer status you attain will be negated. Always try to
tip in cash. If you have a favorite waiter, tip at least 20 percent, or even 25 percent. Any higher, however, and the tip
becomes overly lavish. Keep that for special occasions like

Christmas. You don't want to assault the waiter's dignity by trying to purchase his affection. We're not whores. Keep it businesslike and professional.

36. If you pay part of your bill with a gift certificate, make sure you tip on the whole check—not what's left over after the certificate's been redeemed.

37. Tip the coat-check girl. It's a dollar a coat.

38. If you get takeout from a fancy restaurant, a 10 percent tip is considered appropriate.

39. Never, ever come in fifteen minutes before closing time. The cooks are tired and will cook your dinner right away so they can start breaking down the kitchen. While you're chitchatting over salads, your entrées will be languishing under the heat lamp as the dishwasher's spraying industrial-strength, carcinogenic cleaning solvents in their immediate vicinity. Eat at a diner instead.

40. If you can't afford to leave a tip, you can't afford to eat in the restaurant. Stay home.

50 Ways to Tell You're Working in a Bad Restaurant

1. Management hires you the moment you say, "I'm looking for a job."
2. You start working Friday and Saturday nights the first week. (That's because waiters quit with alarming regularity.)
3. Your boss doesn't ask you to fill out a W-2 or ask for ID of any kind.
4. Training consists of a cursory tour of the restaurant and the headwaiter telling you "sink or swim."
5. The restaurant doesn't pay new hires a training wage. Trainees often get used as unpaid slave labor and are told after their "probationary period" that "things aren't working out."
6. There are porn screen savers on the owner's computer.
7. There are porn screen savers on the POS computer.
8. The kitchen guys have names for the mice.
9. The employee bathroom is so gross it would be better just to have a hole in the ground.
10. The toilet paper in the employee bathroom could double for sandpaper.

11. The owner's banging the hostesses. (How déclassé.)

12. There are always either too many waiters on the floor or not enough.

13. Employees threaten each other with physical violence.

14. The manager solicits bribes for good sections on Saturday-night shifts.

15. Owner, GM, or chef screams at employees *all the time*.

16. Owner, GM, or chef makes fun of a staff person's significant others.

17. If a waiter makes a mistake, the kitchen staff would rather go on a power trip and watch the server squirm instead of fixing the problem. Of course, the customer suffers.

18. The chef refuses to make reasonable substitutions.

19. You start drinking more.

20. The restaurant doesn't provide aprons or dupe pads.

21. You have to pay the owner a percentage of the merchant fee on your credit card tips.

22. The manager expects a share of your tips. (*Illegal!*)

23. They take money out of your check for staff meals but don't feed you.

24. There aren't enough teaspoons, so you hoard them in your apron in order to have enough to do dessert service.

25. The manager makes you empty your pockets, looking for aforementioned hoarded teaspoons.

26. There's never any soap or hand sanitizer around.

27. Your work schedule can change without notice.

28. The manager is constantly calling you to work extra shifts and threatening you with dismissal if you don't "help out."

29. You show up for work to find the manager cut you from the floor. No one bothered to call to tell you.

30. Management tells you to work sick. (Good evening, I'm Typhoid Mary, and I'll be your waitress tonight.)

31. If you lose a credit card slip, the owner takes the check amount out of your compensation until the credit card company transmits the funds into his account. You lose the tip.

32. The restaurant makes you pay for breakage.

33. Management makes you pay if a customer skips on the bill. (All too common.)

34. Busboys take uneaten bread out of a table's breadbasket and use it for a new table.

35. You're working a double, and the manager laughs when you ask to take a break.

36. You're asked seven times a day if you're gay or lesbian.

37. The owner tells you that you're part of a restaurant "family" and that going "above and beyond" to "exceed customer expectations" is expected. After a couple of shifts you begin to realize the Manson Family had more on the ball than these guys.

38. The restaurant is dirty.

39. Heavy turnover of waiters, busboys, and dishwashers. The place is a meat grinder, and you are the meat.

40. The salad guy doesn't use gloves.

41. You see the health inspector snoozing in the back.

42. Fire exits are always blocked by extra chairs, tables, or pieces of equipment.

43. The owner's too cheap to give the staff a decent Christmas bonus or party.

44. There's no first-aid kit.

45. The owner's never around when you need him and always around when you don't.

46. The restaurant has a video surveillance system that the owner uses to satisfy his voyeuristic control freakiness.

47. On your first day all the waiters tell you how much the owner, kitchen staff, busboys, and the other servers suck.

48. Waiters surreptitiously drink themselves sober while working Sunday brunch.

49. The hostesses tell the waiters what to do.

50. Waiters tender their resignations by screaming "Fuck this place!" in the middle of the dining room floor on Saturday night.

Appendix C

Items a Waiter Should Carry at All Times (or Have Close By)

CHEAP BALLPOINT PENS. Every waiter should carry at least three; one for signing checks, one for writing down orders, and the other for fellow servers to borrow and never return. Don't bother bringing nice pens to work. The customers will only steal them. Alternative uses are (though not limited to):
- Taking down a cute girl's phone number.
- Emergency tracheotomy tube.
- Weapon. (Think *The Bourne Identity*.)

WINE OPENER. It has a myriad of uses:
- Opens wine bottles.
- Pops open beer bottles.
- Punches holes in olive oil cans.
- Cuts open boxes.
- Cleans under fingernails.

TABLE CRUMBER. Also a multipurpose tool:
- Cleans crumbs off table.
- Tongue depressor in a pinch.
- Scrapes dog shit or gum off your shoe.

PEPPER MILL. (Would you like fresh ground pepper? How I hate saying that.)

GUM. (Keeps your breath minty fresh and covers up the fact you've been drinking on the job.)

NARCOTIC SUBSTANCE OF YOUR CHOICE. Waiters can be a walking pharmacy. I've seen servers with:
- Cigarettes.
- Hip flask of booze.
- Leftover Vicodan from the dentist.
- Prozac. (Should be in the water.)
- Crack.
- Advil, Tylenol, Aleve, Oxycontin.
- Marijuana.
- Chocolate.

LATEX GLOVES. (Now most waiters don't carry this but I do. It's a habit left over from my days working in a psychiatric hospital. You never knew what bodily secretions you'd encounter—you know, vomit, blood, semen, urine, feces, spinal fluid. Well, the same holds true for a restaurant.)

CELL PHONE. I hate them but most waiters have one. Good for:
- Calling home.
- Calling 911.
- Calling a cab.
- Calling your therapist.

- Calling your bookie.
- Calling your drug dealer.
- Using built-in camera to video coworkers doing the wild thing in the linen closet.

DUPE PAD. Some uses are:
- To write down orders.
- For writing down that cute girl's number.
- Doodling unflattering caricatures of customers.

MATCHES. For:
- Lighting birthday candles.
- Lighting cigarettes/cigars.
- Covering up the foul stench in the employee bathroom.
- Burning the place down. (Use dupe pad soaked in Bacardi 151 as a starter.)

GEAR TO BE STORED IN LOCKER:
- Additional narcotizing substances.
- Extra shirt and tie. (In case you get splattered with food or aforementioned bodily substances.)
- Extra socks. (Helps ward off "swamp foot.")
- Talcum powder. (When you're walking all day you might get "the chafe.")
- Preparation H. (Standing all day gives you hemorrhoids.)
- Band-Aids.
- Hand sanitizer. (In case you touch something gross.)
- Tissues.
- Condoms. (You might actually get lucky with that cute girl.)
- Spare pens, table crumbers, and wine openers.
- Copies of all applicable labor laws.
- Resignation letter preprinted and signed. Insert date when needed.
- Firearm where permitted by law.

About the author

2 Meet Steve Dublanica

About the book

3 The Waiter Who Came In from
the Cold

Read on

14 What Your Drink Says About You

Insights,
Interviews
& More . . .

Meet Steve Dublanica

About the author

STEVE DUBLANICA waited his first table at age thirty-one. In 2004, he started his wildly popular blog, www.WaiterRant.net, which won the 2007 Bloggie Award for Best Writing of a Weblog. He is interviewed regularly by major media as the voice of the two million waiters in the United States. Dublanica lives in the New York metropolitan area. ‿

The Waiter Who Came In from the Cold

WAITER RANT is my first book. I'm not an authority on writing or on the business of publishing. In fact, I'm not an authority about anything. But since I just finished an odyssey that began with an embryonic idea for a book and ended with an appearance on *The Oprah Winfrey Show* two and a half years later, I think I have a few postpublication reflections to share. Some of you reading this afterword might want to know what it's like to write a book, or you might want to know what it was like to shed years of carefully cultivated anonymity and enter a media whirlwind. But I have a sneaking suspicion most of you really want to ask, "So what was Oprah like?"

When a friend of mine asked me, "What's it like to write a book?" I replied, "It's like writing the biggest term paper of your life. Only if you fail to hand it in, you won't get an incomplete, you'll get a bunch of lawyers on your ass." I was being facetious, of course. My publisher, Dan Halpern, has always been wonderfully supportive—but I'll admit to staring at an empty computer screen while in the throes of writer's block and nightmare-scenarioing HarperCollins asking for its money back. Now I know why so many writers drink.

I think I got over writer's block and dodged alcoholism by following one simple rule: Don't panic. I realized that if I waited long enough, the million monkeys jabbering inside my brain would eventually string together something I could put down on paper. For me, the trick was making myself sit down in front of that keyboard for several hours each day until the monkeys delivered the goods. That was a bitch. I had a lot of ▶

unstructured time on my hands. There were days when all I wanted to do was lie in unshowered splendor on my couch and enjoy the brain-jellifying effects of daytime television while my underwear started the process of fermentation. Luckily for my roommate, my parents instilled a good work ethic in both their sons—so I usually spent my days clean, sober, and actually working for my paycheck. Usually.

I also learned what *not* to do when writing a book. That was a painful but valuable lesson. First off, I learned not to wait for the spirit to move me to start writing. If I had, I'd still be working on chapter 2. Some authors like to set a daily quota of words to write and, when they meet that goal, knock off for the day. Initially, my goal was to write two thousand words a day. Some days, I'd be done by lunch. On other days, it'd be midnight and I'd have written only three lines. When you factor in the time wasted compulsively clicking on the word-count tab like a rhesus monkey on crack, it becomes obvious that I needed a better system. What worked for me was treating writing like a job and not a religious experience. I would sit down at my desk from nine to noon, knock off for lunch and a nap, and then write from two o'clock until six. That's about seven hours a day. Okay, more like six when you deduct Web-browsing breaks. I must've bought two car payments' worth of music on iTunes while writing *Waiter Rant*. My advice? Disconnect from the Internet unless you need to use it for research. And no, gawking at bikini-clad models on Maxim.com is *not* research.

But writing isn't just about delivering a manuscript to get paid or to avoid litigation. The process of writing is, when you think about it, a lot like being in a relationship. Think about the lovers you've had during your life. When you first fall in love, it's all about lust and having spontaneous sex in every room of the house. Sometimes writing can be like that. You're brimming with ideas and energy, supremely confident in your abilities, and strutting around like some kind of literary sex god. But anyone who's been in a relationship lasting longer than a year will tell you that, while those days spent subsisting on carnality and room service are great, passion eventually cools. Hopefully it develops into a nice low burn with occasional flare-ups—but it can just as easily be reduced to a cold cinder. The "romance" of writing can also wear thin real quick. When I wrote my blog, writing was easy and fun for me. But when I got into the hard slog of writing my book, the realities of my new profession became apparent. It's like when you discover the quirks that you initially found endearing in your partner are annoying the shit out of you. I guess I noticed my new career was carrying around some excess adipose tissue and starting to snore.

In my own humble, one-book-published opinion, I think you have to make time for writing just like you do for a relationship. If you want to do this as a career, you have to work on your relationship with writing. Sure, there'll be days you want to call your muse fat and go out and play with the boys. There'll be days when writing makes you cry with frustration, seethe with anger, or contemplate throwing your computer out the window. But like my married friends who schedule time for sex in their daily planners, I think the secret to writing is making time for it—whether you feel up to it or not. I may have unconsciously followed my friends' example when I started writing at the same time every day. I think that's the secret—spending "quality time" wrestling with words. I'm not going to kid you. There are days when writing's like pulling teeth or watching grass grow. But if you're faithful to it, there are some seeing-god, multi-orgasmic moments too. (I'll avoid the whole book-as-baby analogy. Too weird.)

What *I* found really weird during this whole experience, however, was going from being completely anonymous one day to appearing in front of millions of people on television the next. When I started the blog that begat this book, in 2004, I decided never to reveal my name or the name of the restaurant where I worked. The reason for my anonymity? Simple: I liked eating. If The Bistro's customers found out that I was poking fun at them online, my tip percentage would plunge faster than the Dow Jones. Even when my Web site became famous and the media appointed me the "voice of the American waiter," I'd only do print or radio interviews—never television. I almost never told interviewers my name. After a while, guarding my anonymity became paranoid second nature. I felt like a spy working behind enemy lines, always terrified of discovery and capture.

You can't sell a book while hiding in the shadows, however. Publishing is a team effort, and my insisting on remaining only The Waiter would've been unfair to me and my publisher, and it would've made my publicist's job impossibly hard. As soon as the ink dried on the contract, it became obvious that I was going to jettison my anonymity and step into the light. That scared the shit out of me. Anonymity might've been a pain in the ass, but it also kept me safe. There's a saying among professional gunmen: You're responsible for every bullet that leaves the barrel of your gun. Now I was going to be responsible for every word that left my pen.

But the first printing of my book wouldn't have my name on it. The cover attribution said only "by The Waiter." That was by design. The marketing plan for *Waiter Rant* was to have a big "reveal" and disclose my identity on publication day. Because trade catalogs for ▶

upcoming book seasons are printed several months prior to a book's release date, it would've ruined the surprise if my real name was on the jacket cover. My parents were disappointed, though; they wanted to see their son's name up in lights. My publicist, Rachel Elinsky, however, was hard at work setting up a plan to put it there. As "D-day" approached, Rachel informed me that my "reveal" was going to be held at the Borders bookstore inside the sparkling Time Warner Center on Columbus Circle in Manhattan. Talk about a swanky location! On the day the book came out, there was going to be a big splash about me in the *New York Post*, and I'd be on *The Leonard Lopate Show* on public radio. Most first-time authors would kill for such a venue and that media coverage. Publicity-wise, I knew I was in very good hands.

Despite all that, as the big day approached and I prepared to stop being The Waiter, anxiety started digging its claws into me. What would happen if people lined up *not* to buy my book? What if *Waiter Rant* tanked? I could just hear some of my mean old restaurant customers saying, "I told you he'd fail." My personal goal for my first book was to achieve enough success to be invited to write a second book. That wouldn't happen if I sold less than one thousand copies. My editor, Emily Takoudes, gently told me I was experiencing first-time-author jitters. Maybe she was right—but there's no escaping the cold, hard truth that books can and do fail all the time.

To stave off panic attacks, I tried a bunch of self-soothing cognitive tricks. I reminded myself that Anthony Bourdain had given my book an awesome blurb. Something tells me Tony wouldn't give his imprimatur to book that sucked. I also reminded myself that preorders for my book on Amazon were strong, advance reviews were good, and I was even going to be in *People* magazine. I had publicity most first-time authors can only dream about. Everything was going be okay. Still, I began wondering whether I could use the first-time-author jitters as an excuse to score Xanax from my internist.

On July 29, 2008, D-day finally arrived. That morning, I opened the *New York Post* to find a fiendish picture of myself dressed as a waiter pouring Metamucil into a boiling pot of water. (No customers were harmed in the making of that picture.) As I read the accompanying article, I took a deep breath. There was no turning back now. Later that afternoon, I took a limousine over to WNYC's studios and did my interview with Leonard Lopate. While this was all going on, however, many Web sites were making a full-blown effort to reveal where I had worked as a waiter. I hadn't expected that. My stomach went into overdrive. Part of me worried that abandoning my anonymity would have severe negative consequences. But I didn't have time to let that get to me. I had a reading to go to at seven o'clock.

When I arrived, at six thirty, I got a big shock. Not only was a large group of fans and well-wishers waiting to hear me talk, there were television crews on hand to cover the event as well. That was completely unexpected. But the real kicker came when my publicist pulled me aside.

"You're going to be on the *Today* show this Thursday," Rachel said, barely containing her excitement.

"Holy shit," I replied.

"Congratulations."

Stunned, I realized that I had never been so excited and afraid in all my life. I needed time to collect myself. I slipped out of the bookstore and headed up to an atrium balcony overlooking the entrance to the Time Warner Center.

As I looked at the panorama of glass, concrete, and flesh that is New York City, I somehow willed my nerves to calm down. After several minutes, I took a deep breath and walked back inside the bookstore. The news crews and cameras were waiting. The seating area was full. I walked out to the podium and began discussing my book. I started by thanking everyone who made *Waiter Rant* possible. I thanked my parents and family. I thanked my editor, publisher, agent, and friends. I thanked all the readers, fellow servers, and fans who made the time to come and see me. But when it came time to thank my godfather, a Catholic priest who taught me that God occasionally grants everyone a beautiful glimpse of the "big picture," I felt my composure start slipping away. Teddy died several years ago and was a profound influence on my life. Suddenly I wanted him alive and here with me. Tears stung my eyes.

"Whoa!" I said, reigning in my emotions. "Where did that come from?"

Somehow I collected myself and managed to thank everyone without crying like a baby. Then, grateful for the distraction of my book in my hands, I opened it and started reading a few passages.

As I read about bad tippers sucking in bed and the hell that is a restaurant on Mother's Day, I suddenly understood where that surge of emotion about my godfather was coming from. Everyone in that room was there because of something I wrote. And what I wrote was shaped by everything that had happened to me. All the yearning and loss I had felt, all the rough edges I had chafed people with, and the warmth that brought a few people happiness, had come together in a moment of clarity. I was getting one of those glimpses of the big picture my godfather was always talking about. I was getting a peek. For a brief, ▶

The Waiter Who Came In from the Cold *(continued)*

shining moment, it all made sense. I wonder if my parents got that glimpse when they renewed their wedding vows on their fortieth anniversary. I wonder if my brother got that glimpse when he held his newborn son for the first time. I hope so.

When Thursday morning came, I had to get up at the crack of dawn to take a limousine over to the NBC studios. That wasn't fun—but meeting Matt Lauer and the crew of the *Today* show was a blast. They were such professionals that they put me immediately at ease. People who watched the episode told me I looked like an old television pro. That wasn't my doing. Matt Lauer is a very, very skilled interviewer. He made me forget there were, oh, several million people watching me. A few minutes into the interview, I realized why this guy is paid the big bucks. (And man, is he a snappy dresser.) Of course, Matt was fascinated by the titillating spitting-in-your-food part of waitering. I think he was nervous that some waiter watching the interview might put a goober into his soup if he misbehaved at some restaurant in the future. I assured Matt that most customers enjoy sputum-free entrees.

After the interview, Matt came over and said, "Thanks, Steve. That interview was fun!"

"Thanks for having me!" I replied.

"One thing, though," Matt said, suddenly looking serious.

"What?"

"The cameraman told me that he spat on your seat just before you sat down!" I've heard Matt's a big kidder. Now I know.

Then, as I was in the greenroom collecting my things, one of the *Today* show's producers came up to me.

"It's the waiter who came in from the cold!" she said. "Congratulations!"

"Thank you," I replied.

"How does it feel to no longer be anonymous?"

"Weird," I admitted. "But I'll get used to it."

"Can I give you some advice, Steve?" the producer asked.

"Sure."

"You're going to be doing a lot of interviews in the near future. Don't get spoiled by Matt. He's one of the best interviewers in the world."

"Yeah, he was great."

"But you're going to run into interviewers who aren't as good or well-prepared. Occasionally, you'll be the one doing all the work. Be ready for that."

"I will. Thanks."

That producer's advice was invaluable. While most of the people who subsequently interviewed me for print, radio, and television were seasoned professionals, there were a few duds in the press corps. If you're an author promoting a book in the media and your interviewer is off his or her game, you have to be prepared to step in and politely redirect the conversation back to the subject at hand. Luckily, I had to do that only a few times.

As my crazy week progressed, I flew out to Kansas City, Missouri, to speak at the city library's Order Up! Tales from the Dining Room series. They've got a beautiful library in Kansas City, and I was touched by all the attention Kaite Stover and her staff lavished on me while I was there. They made my first trip as a published author really special. I predict that one day, anybody who's anybody in the literary world will want to speak at the Kansas City Public Library. It was a world-class experience.

While I was in Kansas City, however, I also began dealing with two new stressors in my newborn writing career: reading reviews and fretting over sales figures. First off, let me say a little something about reviews. I've heard it said that some authors never read their reviews. I don't believe that for a minute. It's human nature to want to know what other people think of your work. I read every review of my book—good and bad. Some made me swell with pride. Others made me want to call up the reviewer and chew them out. It's quite simple, really: Good reviews made me happy, and bad reviews pissed me off. I did, however, have an advantage many other writers don't: I wrote a blog for several years. Trust me, blog commenters like to play rough. The comments section of a blog is sort of like criticism boot camp. When you've spent years dealing with profane, pontificating Internet wags who produce nothing but criticize everything, you can handle it when some bitter reviewer snarkily writes, "Don't give up your day job" in an L.A. paper. Luckily for me, my book garnered mostly good reviews, with Jonathan Yardley, who actually won a Pulitzer Prize for criticism, saying, "*Waiter Rant* is as delightful as it is irreverent." (I was really proud of that one.)

So the blog helped me psychologically prepare for published criticism. I had already accepted the fact that there would always be people who wouldn't like what I wrote. Although it's an occasionally aggravating experience, I think every author should always read his or her reviews. Why? Because I also learned from my blog that my commenters' criticisms were sometimes dead-on. That kind of feedback is invaluable to a writer. So, even if you don't like what some reviewer said about your book, pay attention. There may be a lesson in there somewhere. You just need to learn how to separate the wheat from the bitter, hysterical chaff.

The other stress I was contending with was sales. All the good ▶

The Waiter Who Came In from the Cold *(continued)*

reviews were wonderful, but was anyone buying the book? While I was in Kansas City, I pestered my editor and agent with calls, asking how the book was moving. And since we're on this topic, here's another piece of advice for new writers: Don't check your Amazon rankings several times an hour! I have no idea how that crazy system works—and Amazon won't tell you. One hour your sales rank could be 100, and then the next it'll be 34,557. It's worse than watching the stock market. The first week my book was out, I must've checked my Amazon rank ten thousand times. I quickly realized that looking up my stats was turning into a heroinlike addiction, so I decided to go cold turkey. The withdrawal wasn't that bad. After two sweat-filled nights imagining centipedes crawling all over my body, I got over it.

On the day I got back from Kansas City, however, my questions were finally answered. My agent, Farley Chase, called almost as soon as I got off the plane.

"Congratulations, Steve," he said. "Your book made the *New York Times* Bestseller List in its first week."

I was thunderstruck. Never in a million years did I expect that to happen. I was so shocked that I didn't process the news for several hours.

"Enjoy the moment, man," Farley said. "No one will ever be able to take this away from you."

Later that night, my editor, Emily, called to tell me that my book's cover was being redesigned to say "Instant *New York Times* Bestseller." What a thrill. I later learned that this was the first time Emily or Farley had a book make The List. Those two people put a lot of faith in me, so I was very happy *Waiter Rant* came through for them.

Now, of course, I was in hog heaven. Looking back I'm glad this happened to me when I was forty. If this had happened when I was twenty I'd have never been able to get my head through the door. A few days later, however, just when I thought things couldn't get any better, my publicist called.

"You sitting down?" Rachel asked.

"Why?"

"*The Oprah Winfrey Show* called."

I seem to recall saying, "Are you shitting me?" but I could be wrong. I think I had a mini-psychotic break.

Turns out Oprah wanted to do a segment on rudeness, and the producers were wondering if I'd like talk about impolite restaurant patrons on the show. What was I going to say? No? Hectic phone calls and preparations soon followed.

Oprah runs a very efficient, well-organized operation. Every *i* is dotted and every *t* is crossed. And let me tell you, while the *Today* show was great, nothing beats the greenroom at Oprah's studio. They had cookies, fruit, bagels, candies, cake, soda, and bottled water everywhere. Other than needing to pee several times, I was remarkably calm as I waited with Rachel in the greenroom. The makeup lady came in and did my face. Producers flitted in and out with last-minute instructions. Finally, one of the stagehands poked his head in the door and said, "Okay, Steve, we're ready for you."

"Will I be sitting on the couch with Oprah?" I asked. "Or sitting across from her in a chair?"

"I think the couch," the stagehand replied. "Why?"

"I just wanted to know if I could jump up and down on the couch like Tom Cruise."

"Oh," the stagehand said. "That's funny."

"I'm not serious," I added quickly.

"I know."

The stagehand led me into the studio and showed me to my assigned seat. The studio was much smaller and more intimate than I'd thought it would be. My nerves were holding steady until I saw the word OPRAH emblazoned on the studio carpet. That's when I had a small panic attack. I was about to talk to someone more famous than the pope. Maybe I should've hit up my internist for that Xanax. Then I watched as the stage crew removed the couch in the studio and replaced it with two chairs. Come on guys, I thought, I was only kidding.

I was in the middle of hyperventilating when Oprah Winfrey walked into the studio. As the crowd went wild, I thought I was going to pass out in my chair. Then I remembered Tim Meadows's sketch on *Saturday Night Live* when he played Oprah being carried on a bier to the adulation of an adoring crowd shouting, "It's the Oprah! It's the Oprah!" Thanks, Tim. Oddly enough, that visualization calmed me down.

Oprah, of course, was nothing like Tim Meadows's over-the-top impersonation. In fact, she was very nice and had a self-deprecating sense of humor. As she sat down in her chair and exchanged her walk-around shoes for some fancier ones, she made a quip about how made up she was. "I've got more makeup on than Britney Spears," she said, eliciting a big laugh from the crowd. It occurred to me then that Oprah is aware of her celebrity. One of the first things she did when entering the room was to poke fun at herself and put everyone at ease.

Soon I was sitting in a chair across from The Big O talking about waiting tables and rude customers. Just like Matt Lauer, Oprah made me forget that millions of people would be watching me. Talking to ▶

her felt like having a friendly conversation with someone you've just struck up an instant rapport with. It was then that I realized why this woman is one of the most famous people in the world: Oprah is at the top of her game. It was a thrill to be on her show. Then, before I knew it, the interview was over. I was whisked back to my hotel, and I downed a couple of martinis with my publicist, got on my plane, and flew home. Door to door, the entire experience lasted thirty-six hours.

A few weeks after taping *The Oprah Winfrey Show*, the final piece of my annus mirabilis fell into place. Dan Halpern at Ecco asked me to write another book, about tipping throughout the American service economy, titled *At Your Service*. When I started this journey two and half years ago, this is the destination I truly wanted to reach. Being on The List, riding around in limos, chatting with Matt and Oprah, that was all unexpected, amazing, and thrilling icing on the cake—tasty, tasty, multi-orgasmic icing! Now, however, I truly felt in my heart of hearts that I was the waiter who came in from the cold. I knew that I had hung up my apron forever. I knew I had become a writer. I had proved it to myself. I had proved it to the world. (*Waiter Rant* was published in Great Britain and translated into Chinese, Portuguese, Spanish, Italian, and German, so yes, I proved it to a good bit of the world.)

At the end of the classic movie *The Spy Who Came In from the Cold*, the protagonist, played by Richard Burton, gets shot dead within sight of freedom. On some crazy, neurotic level, I was worried about the same thing happening to me as I got closer to my "freedom." Since I've been on the analytic couch for years, however, I recognized my lifelong kookiness in expecting disaster to appear out of nowhere and managed to calm myself down. In the end, I was worried about nothing. Coming in from the cold wasn't anything like my fearful imaginings. The only unsettling thing that happened was that I got a few crank calls and some ugly messages on my Web site that tried to reveal my home address. The police handled that. Otherwise, I had fun. It was nice to get stopped on the street and get asked "Say, aren't you that waiter who spits in the food?" It was also nice meeting the fans and readers who have been so supportive all these years.

The media stuff eventually died down, and now I'm just as unrecognized on the street as I was before. Oddly enough, in many respects, my life remains *unchanged*. I still live in the same old but comfortable apartment with my roommate in New Jersey. I still share custody of Buster with my ex-girlfriend, who's happily married. (Buster's a Japanese Chin, by the way.) I still write for my blog (though not as often as I'd like). Other than upgrading a few material things, I haven't changed my lifestyle. Oh, yeah, I still tip waiters very well.

Now I'm knee-deep into researching tips for my new book, *At Your Service*. As I go around the country interviewing people who derive all or part of their compensation from gratuities, I'm learning things I never knew—or wanted to know. Did you know that if you stiff a car valet one too many times, they have ways to surreptitiously screw up your car's alignment? And don't even think of being cheap with your doorman come Christmas. Some of these guys have surveillance tapes of their tenants boinking in the elevator! Who wants that let loose on the Internet? If you fail to tip, you might be doing so at your peril.

Well, I hope this little afterword answered any questions you might have. If not, feel free to drop me a line at waiterrant@yahoo.net. Now I've got to go. As I write this last paragraph, I'm on a plane and the flight attendant is telling me it's time to shut down my laptop. Within a few minutes, I'll be landing in sunny Las Vegas. I'm spending seven days in Sin City interviewing blackjack dealers, casino hosts, cab drivers, massage therapists, cocktail waitresses, and strippers about tipping. I know, writing a book's hard, hard work. But don't worry about me. I'm a professional. I'll be fine.

Sometimes I love this job. ∽

What Your Drink Says About You

I CONDUCTED an informal poll to see what your favorite drink says about you. The sampling was very small and the margin for error is very large. If you see your favorite drink lampooned, spare me the hate mail. I get enough already.

Vodka Martini
Sophisticated. You're classy, old-school, or a James Bond wannabe. I've been known to drink these.

Cosmopolitan
Prissy, overordered, and passé. Favored by Manolo Blahnik–wearing Candace Bushnell devotees who spend all their money on shoes but live in rathole apartments. Rapidly becoming an old-lady drink.

Sidecar
The last time you got laid was 1932.

Chardonnay
You know what you like. Boring. Predictable. The missionary position of white wine.

Pinot Grigio
You're pretentious or don't know what you like. You follow the herd. The circle jerk of white wine.

Beer
Blue-collar, simple, and an old standby. (I think a girl wearing a T-shirt and jeans while drinking a good ol' Bud is very sexy.)

Chocolate Martini
You're immature or have a sweet tooth. Good for masking the taste of roofies.

Vodka on the Rocks
You want to get drunk as fast as possible.

Malibu Bay Breeze
A gay man's drink (according to Louis).

Sloe Gin Fizz
Same as above.

Gin Neat
Only for mad dogs and Englishmen.

Sour Apple Martini
You have a sense of fun, but overindulgence might cause dancing on tables and bad karaoke singing. (Beth?)

Negroni
Fluvio's favorite drink, so I can't bad-mouth it.

Campari and Soda
You're a gourmand. This is a good aperitif. A bitter drink for bitter people.

Manhattan
An old-fogy drink. Stuffy. Where did I put the bitters?

Sweet Vermouth on the Rocks
You're so old that if you're not already in the grave, you soon will be.

Pinot Noir
You've seen *Sideways*. 'Nuff said.

Sex on the Beach
You've been to Club Hedonism, haven't you?

Sex Up Against the Wall
You own shares in Club Hedonism, don't you?

Galliano
You're a waterbed-, lava-lamp-, and reel-to-reel-having, gold-chain-wearing, wall-to-wall-shag-carpet-loving, swinging '70s disco fool.

Gimlet
You're old-fashioned and like to drink. Usually the province of classy cerebral babes.

Rob Roy
You're an alcoholic.

Margarita
You're fun, good in bed, and naughty, with a sense of style. Unless you don't have it with salt. Then you're a wimp.

What Your Drink Says About You *(continued)*

Shirley Temple
What? Are you five years old? On the wagon? Get the fuck outta here.

Bloody Mary
You need an excuse to start drinking before lunch.

Gin and Tonic
You're kinda boring, but this is an excellent drink when it's hot outside.

Mint Julep
You're a hospitable Southern guy/gal. This is good stuff. Rarely ordered.

Tequila
You're not afraid of spending a little time in jail.

Champagne
You're reserved, classy, or a stripper.

Vodka and Red Bull
Party person, young, possible cokehead.

Southern Comfort
Where'd we put those Lynyrd Skynyrd eight-tracks? I know I saw 'em around here somewhere. . . .

Mojito
You're not afraid to try new things, have low frustration tolerance, and are prone to wild rages.

Rum and Coke
You've been arrested for assault once or twice.

Whisky Sour
Have another one, Grandma.

Alabama Slammer
You've read the "Have a Cocktail" placemat at the diner once too often.

Whiskey, Single-Malt Scotch, or Bourbon
You're a sexual athlete. Women want you and men want to be like you. You have class, talent, wit, and brains. Of course, this is what I drink.

Don't miss the next book by your favorite author. Sign up now for AuthorTracker by visiting www.AuthorTracker.com.